ACCOUNTING
for
MANAGEMENT

ACCOUNTING
for
MANAGEMENT

Eric L. Kohler

PRENTICE-HALL, INC., Englewood Cliffs, New Jersey

Library of Congress Catalog Card No.: 65-13571

PRENTICE-HALL INTERNATIONAL, INC., *London*
PRENTICE-HALL OF AUSTRALIA, PTY., LTD., *Sydney*
PRENTICE-HALL OF CANADA, LTD., *Toronto*
PRENTICE-HALL OF INDIA (PRIVATE) LTD., *New Delhi*
PRENTICE-HALL OF JAPAN, INC., *Tokyo*

Printed in the United States of America [00242-C]

Preface

The object of this book is to set forth the principal features of the accounting art with which management ought to have more than a passing acquaintance. These features the author has had occasion to present from time to time to management personnel without burdening them with the dreary tasks of model bookkeeping and problem solving. Accounting today has attained a conceptual level: a modest intellectual discipline that leads not only to an understanding of financial statements—their construction, interpretation, and limitations—but also to the addition of scope and depth to the practice of management.

With this in mind, the author is speaking in this book to executives of any grade who must deal with and be dependent on accounting and accountants; to investors, investment analysts, and others who hope to extract information from accounting statements and reports; and to students of management and accounting who need an initial exposure to the subject. Some familiarity with business customs is assumed. But this need not extend beyond the forms

v

of business and the general methods by which business is carried on. At the university level this would mean a brief survey course in business structure and operation.

In the first chapter the reader is exposed to the accountant's general background and some of his vocabulary. A good deal of what is often referred to as accounting techniques, and even principles, may be ascribed to word uses a practical grasp of which can reduce many an alleged technique or principle to a definition. A reader who has had dealings in the business world will undoubtedly be familiar with many, perhaps most of the hundred-odd italicized terms in Chapter 1 and with an even greater number spread through Chapters 2, 3, and 4; as a consequence, he will find himself well on the road to an appreciation of the accountant's preconceptions and preoccupations.

Accounting is probably best known to the public as a medium for transaction recording and external reporting. Of at least equal importance, however, are its internal uses as providing a wide variety of control devices for management planning, ranging from organizational structure to operating specifications; moreover, without the smoothly operating linkages provided by a scheme of accounting carefully conceived and executed, no large-scale business could be carried on under a single management. Various aspects of accounting applications are suggested in these pages; but the author's emphasis throughout is on the relation of accounting to these possibilities, rather than on the legion of forms and methodologies by which they are realized.

The reader is asked to follow through in detail the few illustrations the book provides, with the aim of understanding the source and meaning of each item. Accounting statements are interpreted principally in terms of the details they contain.

The author wishes to thank William W. Cooper, Willard J. Graham, Maurice E. Peloubet for reviewing the manuscript and offering constructive suggestions.

Eric L. Kohler

Contents

CHAPTER ONE

Environment

Readers of a basic technical book such as this can be plagued by a too-immediate exposure to words and phrases which to them, in their innocence, have only everyday associations: but to which the author—unaware of the impediments he has interposed—attaches a special significance. In this chapter we will consider a number of terms, on the surface deceptively commonplace but of particular importance to an understanding of the environment in which accounting functions; we thus in some measure bridge the initial gap between author and reader. We will also say something about number, *the medium through which accounting traditionally speaks: its basic usage and involvement in* transactions.

1

Accounting, in its unique way, reflects much of the passing scene of human activity; its roots extend into the past and its superstructure reaches into the daily lives and the futures of all of us. The subject matter of this chapter should, for the most part, strike a familiar note; and by a careful reading of these first pages the reader should find himself a little nearer to the themes of succeeding chapters.

The economics of accounting

An obvious but nonetheless notable characteristic of our society is that most *material things* (food, clothing, housing, other necessities, and luxuries) associated with human subsistence, well-being, and satisfactions generally are available in limited quantities (i.e. are *scarce*[1]) and must somehow be obtained by us from others who have them. Out of the relationships created by this neverceasing give-and-take have emerged *economics* and *accounting:* the former concerned with the understanding, criticism, and improvement of these relationships and their effects on the social structure; the latter, with their quantification, transcription, and interpretation as they relate to individual members of society. The *economy* or *economic world* is that complex of human effort dealing with scarcities which in varying degrees involves all of mankind; it is often characterized as "good" or "poor" in a community or in a

---

[1] *Scarce* has two meanings: the first implying *rare;* the second, *anything less than free.* It is in the latter sense that the term is used here.

nation depending on the relative ability of individuals to obtain the material things they desire. *Economic activity*[2] is the participation of individuals and groups of individuals in obtaining, transporting, and disposing of scarce material things.

Familiar terms in the commercial world

Material things are *goods* or *services.* Goods are physical or *tangible* objects that can be seen and touched (a *good* or *commodity* is one such thing), as houses, machines, tables, and books; services, or *intangibles,* are illustrated by the work of a factory employee, the mental effort put forth by a teacher or an office worker, and the functioning of a manager as a supervisor.[3] Services also include the benefits arising from the assumption by others of one's risks (e.g. fire and other forms of insurance), the use of another's property (*rent*) or money (*interest*), and many types of benefits obtainable by individuals and groups from others. These are known as *economic* goods and services.[4] There are also *free* goods and services (e.g. the air we breathe and the courtesies people display toward one another); notwithstanding their importance as necessary constituents of daily life, they are not "scarce"; and being "open to all comers" they fall outside the subject matter of both the economist and the accountant.[5] Scarcity and the problems of human

[2] As employed in this chapter, "economic" does not mean "money-saving" or "low-cost" but has reference to the economy. It may be of interest to note that "economy" in the original Greek meant "household management" (*oikos* [house] + *nomein* [manage]), and that the association of the word with low cost has always been a natural accompaniment of the prudent management of one's household affairs. From this we may fairly conclude that the present close association of accounting and management is by no means a modern development.

[3] An intangible often recognized in certain types of commercial transactions, and referred to again in later chapters of this book, is *goodwill:* a generic term covering such diverse factors as customer satisfaction, nearness to market, absence of competition, and excellence of management.

[4] The phrase "goods *and* services" covers the whole range of the subject-matter of economic activity.

[5] Economists dealing with the problems of national income include a few intangibles not otherwise recognized (e.g. "implicit" interest of banks) and from time to time discuss the possibility of including other items (e.g. family housekeeping); accountants, on the other hand, have remained wholly unconcerned with such matters.

relationships it creates give rise to the activities of economists and accountants.

The needs and desires of people (*consumers*) for material things are termed *wants;* collectively, present and prospective wants are known as *demand,* and the satisfaction of wants as *consumption.* In the possession of others (*suppliers*), but in limited quantities, are the material things (the *supply*) that people desire, and the processes of creating a supply and making it available to consumers are called *production* and *distribution.* Wherever a demand for a specific good or service arises, a supply in some form is likely to appear, the supplier, following age-old tradition, being motivated by the prospect of a *gain* or *profit.*

Suppliers, engaged in satisfying wants, are said to be *in business.* *Business,* however, has a number of meanings. It may refer to the collective effort put forth by all suppliers in making goods and services available to consumers: e.g., when one says, "Business [volume, profits, trends, etc.] has improved (or declined) this year"; to the nature of the work carried on by a single supplier: "Our business [activity] is selling merchandise"; or to the organization maintained by a supplier: "Our business [establishment or enterprise] has been carried on for many years." [6] Current usage permits either the addition or omission of the words in brackets; without them, "business" is a noun; by adding any one of the bracketed words "business" becomes an adjective. A business [establishment], depending on the form of its ownership, may be a *proprietorship* (owned by one individual), a *partnership* (owned jointly by two or more individuals), or a *corporation* (owned by any number of individuals).[7] Several other forms of business ownership are possible; but these three forms are the only ones most people encounter.

Through the *exchange* of goods and services[8] supply is channeled into demand and consumption follows. Exchanges are facilitated

---

[6] The word "business" is frequently used by accountants and others as signifying *any* form of operating unit within the economic world, whether or not motivated by the prospect of gain. Economists tend to employ *firm* in referring to a particular business enterprise, whatever its form of organization; however, in law and accounting, "firm," without a qualifying adjective, more often denotes a partnership or other noncorporate structure. See also footnote 9.

[7] In recent annual reports American Telephone and Telegraph boasted of 2,250,000 "owners," General Motors of 1,068,000.

[8] In this sense, an office or factory employee "exchanges" his skills for a salary or wage, and money or a promise to pay for an automobile or groceries.

by *markets, monetary systems,* and *price mechanisms.* The exchange of goods and services, the main economic activity of most businesses, always involves the "giving" of something to another person[9] and the "taking" of something from him in return; the "something" may, in either case, consist of or include money. In a narrower sense, as in income-tax laws, "exchange" means the transfer of goods or services for goods or services other than money, as in the expression "sale or exchange." [10]

Both *trade* and *commerce* signify the economic activity—the exchanging of goods and services—carried on by business concerns. "Trade" at times may refer to (a) exchanges conducted by businesses within limited areas ("the local trade"), (b) *retailing* as distinguished from *manufacturing,* (c) a particular class of business ("the clothing trade," "the retail trade"), or (d) business relationships as between persons in two or more countries ("foreign" or "international" trade). "Commerce," although generally interchangeable with "trade," often denotes exchanges between business concerns of different countries. But a *commercial enterprise* is any business organization as distinguished from a *nonprofit enterprise* such as a city government or a public school.

Markets, the points of contact where sellers hope to encounter buyers, exist in such varied forms as retail stores, the advertising columns of newspapers and other periodicals, catalogs issued by mail-order houses, and calls by salesmen. The initiative for and expense of establishing and maintaining a market usually comes from the seller, since it is he, and not the buyer, who profits immediately from transfers of goods and services. Some markets (e.g. a stock exchange) are maintained by both buyers and sellers.

A *monetary system,* coupled with numerous price mechanisms, facilitates exchanges of goods and services by providing a valuation unit for buyers and sellers. Monetary systems, in modern times maintained by government fiat, embrace: (a) the establishment of

[9] *Person* in law and accounting may mean not only a human being (a *natural* person) but also any business or other organization (an *artificial* person).

[10] A transfer of goods or services for money or with the understanding that money will be paid in the future is, of course, a *sale* by the transferor (seller) and a *purchase* by the transferee (buyer). As employed here, "supplier," "transferor," and "seller" are very nearly synonymous; likewise "consumer," "transferee," and "buyer." They differ only in emphasis. A supplier might be a potential transferor or seller; a consumer, a potential transferee or buyer.

a basic *monetary unit* (in the U.S., the "gold" dollar[11]) and supplementary multiples or fractions of the basic unit; (b) the creation and supply of *money* in the form of *cash*, i.e. currency (*paper money*) and coin (*hard money*); and (c) the legalization of *credit*, i.e. orders for money (*checks*, and the various forms of *promises to pay* money in the future which serve in lieu of money).[12] Every monetary system has a dual purpose. It furnishes a single, easily understood scale in terms of which, taking the form of *prices*, sellers and buyers can express their relative willingness to supply or acquire any particular economic good or service. And of even greater importance, a monetary system makes possible the sale of a commodity or service without involving a *barter* or swap (i.e. the concurrent acquisition of another good or service other than cash or a promise to pay cash).[13] In fact, the highly specialized productive or distributive activity of the ordinary seller could not be maintained if he were compelled to engage in barters and in the disposition of the assorted goods and services that barters

[11] Since 1934 the statutory value of an ounce of pure gold in the United States has been pegged by the Congress at $35 per ounce (13 5/7 troy grains = .88867088 grams per dollar); many other countries now maintain their monetary standards in terms of the dollar. Gold is recognized everywhere as being the only "near" fixed-price commodity.

[12] For our purposes here we are regarding credit as a sector of a monetary system. When a consumer buys now and agrees to pay a month or even years later, the credit extended him by the seller serves both parties in lieu of cash. If both buyer and seller patronize the same bank and the buyer ultimately pays for his purchase by check, a three-sided credit operation has occurred and no cash changes hands. More involved multilateral credit operations become necessary as the distance between buyer and seller increases. Credit, which expands with good times and shrinks in hard times, is the elastic part of a monetary system, and the quantity of credit "in circulation" is an important factor during periods of inflation and depression.

[13] Cash, being merely a *medium of exchange*, is sometimes denied classification by economists as either a good or a service. Accountants, however, and the business world generally, take a different position: to them, cash—such as a checking account in a bank, or an agreement to receive cash in the future in return for some present benefit—is a material thing *to the person possessing it*, and it is convertible into goods or services at his pleasure. It may also serve him as a store of value during periods of declining prices. This distinction is an important one, for traditionally the economist concerns himself with a community of persons, a nation, or the world as a unit, where money, offset by the fiat of the country that has authorized and issued it, is an intracountry convenience for promoting exchanges. The accountant, dealing with the same subject matter, expresses the outlook of the individual person to whom money is always a treasured possession.

would entail. The receipt or eventual receipt of cash for the goods and services he sells enables him to buy the raw materials for more goods and services of the same kind, thus permitting him to restrict his activities to his chosen limited field of specialization.

Each principal country of the world has its own monetary system. International trade is made difficult, even where governments step in and not only fix the ratio at which their respective monetary units may be exchanged but also accept payments from their nationals who purchase (*import*) from abroad, and make payments to their nationals who sell (*export*) abroad. Where imports exceed exports, the country becomes a *debtor nation* with claims owing to other countries; where exports are in excess, the country becomes a *creditor nation* with obligations owing from other countries.[14] Large excesses often result in shipments of gold by a debtor nation to creditor nations: also loans, or bilateral or multilateral credit agreements may be arranged between countries: an important function of the International Monetary Fund (IMF), the Bank for International Settlements (BIS), and the European Fund (EF).[15]

Price mechanisms attach to goods or services that are the objects of exchange. A *price* is the amount that a buyer pays (*actual* price), is invited to pay (*asked* price), or offers to pay (*bid* price). Most price mechanisms are established by and continue to be subject to the interaction of many market forces. Some are the result of agreements between sellers who control the bulk of or all production or distribution. Others are instituted, regulated, or maintained by government, such as "supported" farm prices and the rates charged consumers by public utilities,[16] and by interna-

[14] An excess of imports is often described as resulting in an *unfavorable* balance of trade because of the likelihood that gold may have to be exported to pay off the balance; with an excess of exports, in a *favorable* balance of trade, the prospective importation of gold presumably gives added strength to the economy. But today's emphasis is on a *balanced* economy the skilled management of which, through intergovernmental arrangements, minimizes gold movements and encourages (and often subsidizes) additional commodity movements to make up the difference.

[15] The last-named was the successor in 1961 to the European Payments Union (EPU) which was organized in 1950 with a U.S. credit of $350,000,000.

[16] Further aspects of *price* of interest to accountants may be found in the author's *Dictionary* under such headings as *administered price, fair-trade price, free price, list price, nonprice competition, normal price, price leadership,* and *pricing policy.*

tional government-approved agreements or cartels, such as sugar, coffee, and crude oil.

The emergence of an accounting language

It may already be apparent to the reader that in the development of our subject it would be impossible to proceed very far without making active use of the words that have come to be associated with accounting and linking these words to everyday language. A technical term in the form of a single word or phrase is a language shortcut or *symbol* that stands for one or more concepts—sometimes a whole chain of concepts. Through its use one avoids the many words that would otherwise be necessary to identify already-developed, undisputed subject matter. Some technical terms have acquired precise meanings; others have uncertain meanings because underlying notions are in the process of change and have not crystalized or are too new to have become generally accepted, or because in some instances single terms have been made to apply to more than one concept or related group of concepts. Words newly concocted from Greek and Latin roots, particularly in the business world, are no longer common; instead, old words may gradually acquire new technical meanings or may be associated with other words in sequences (phrases) that have the effect of creating new terms.[17] In certain fields, as chemistry, a high degree of precision is given to the uses of both old and new terms by world-wide agreements that not only delimit their meanings but fix their spellings and applications. No such discipline exists in economics or accounting.[18]

[17] In the author's *Dictionary*, 732 single words and 1,911 phrases (consisting of two or more words) are defined, many of the latter having arisen from the attempt more clearly to pin down a concept by including an extra word or two by way of explanation. The result has not usually been completely successful; two or more words, linked together as a single term and often not directly related to a concept, may, indeed, add only to the uncertainty of the term. In recent years there has been some tendency to cloak old ideas in new terms, especially by accountants who, in reactivating an aberrant concept, have justified their position by language suggesting a new and progressive outlook.

[18] In his *Dictionary* the author was confronted with the need for standards that might govern more precise uses of the accountant's language. He felt compelled, however, to reproduce existing usages, although in many instances attempting to point out generally preferred applications.

The reader must be cautioned against the common assumption that within any word lies an "unfolded" significance arcane even to the technician. No word can have any more than a currently associated or assigned meaning, regardless of its roots or past usage. If a writer wishes to express in the form of a term a new, expanded, or otherwise-modified concept, he is obligated in the interest of clarity to define or employ the terms in such a manner that the words of his definition offer no obstacles to a mutual understanding between himself and his reader.[19] But of course he must take care that these words do not extend beyond the present stage of knowledge of the reader he is aiming to impress.[20]

In this book the author is addressing those approaching the subject of accounting for the first time; it has been designed to fit the experience of what he conceives to be the intelligent reader. But unlike other accounting texts, it omits detailed descriptions of business practices that lead to, result from, go hand-in-hand with, or are otherwise inextricably bound up with accounting practices. The author once estimated that the subject matter of the average accounting text is 75% business practice and 25% accounting.[21] Whatever the proportion, this study of accounting should serve at least two purposes: it not only will introduce the reader at an early stage to the processes of accounting but will also present the more common practices and customs of business in the light in which they are viewed by the accountant.

---

[19] A frequent pitfall for unwary economists and accountants continues to be "income." Some have assumed, and ask others to assume, that certain elements should (or even *must*) be regarded as inherent parts of an income concept without at the same time being either willing or able to disclose the motivation, such as simple self-interest or individual social outlook, behind the assumption other than an allegation of the public interest; or they may try to rest their case on an adjective ("sound" and "fair" are favorites). But it is always to be remembered that in the field of accounting, as elsewhere, the bond between a word and a concept can only be a common agreement among those who use the word.

[20] Accounting terms used by authors of articles that one may find in technical journals, such as the AAA *Accounting Review* and the AICPA *Journal of Accountancy,* are undefined because readers are presumed to be accountants (or at least persons with a grounding in the subject). If the authors were in the position of addressing beginning students or the general public, their articles would have to be studded with definitions, descriptions, and explanations of usages considered unnecessary for more sophisticated readers.

[21] The assumption is made throughout this book that the reader is familiar with the everyday ways with which business is carried on.

Accounting, conforming to and reflecting organizational practices, and often described as the *language of business,* is recognized
today as the language of management as well. We will, therefore,
have frequent occasion to refer to current management concepts
and their close relationship with and influence on the accounting
process.

Some accounting elements

We will now take a preliminary look at several definitions and
concepts for the purpose of laying down the broad basis on which
accounting rests. It is important to the understanding of later chapters that these terms be employed and interpreted in the senses
indicated here so that reanalysis and reiteration may be minimized.

Implicit in any scheme of accounting is the *entity:* any organization regarded as having an existence separate from its owners and
operators. A corporation, for example, is often described as a legal
entity or as an *artificial person:* a term that may also be applied,
however, to the smallest unincorporated, individually owned retail
shop. This separateness, universally recognized for example in relationships with suppliers and customers, although not given full
recognition in law,[22] is fundamental to business operations, management, and accounting. For accounting purposes the entity idea
is also extended to any independently functioning activity. Thus
a separate management and separate scheme of accounting may be
present in a branch office or factory.

The most basic of all the elements of accounting is the *transaction.* A transaction is an exchange between entities or other business
action expressed in money terms. The work of any active enterprise
may be viewed as consisting of a never-ending stream of transactions. In subsequent chapters we will observe that the money
amounts appearing on the financial statements of an enterprise—
often called the endproducts of accounting—are simply transaction
summations. Transactions are *classified* and accumulated by type;
thus, exchanges with customers are invariably brought together and
in the aggregate are known as "sales."

[22] The owner of a proprietorship, and the owners of most forms of partnership, must make good on any or all of its debts; no such liability attaches to
the stockholder of a corporation.

External transactions, arising from sales, purchases, acquisitions of services of employees, and other exchanges, are distinguished from *internal* transactions which involve reclassifications of external transactions within an entity and the expression of anticipated or only partially consummated external transactions. Both classes are discussed at length in the next chapter. For the present we need to bear in mind that without transactions there would be no accounting.

A third element implicit in the concept of accounting is the lapse of time known as an *accounting period:* a year,[23] a month, four weeks, a week, or any other time unit determined by management need or trade custom, and often by income-tax laws. Methods of accounting are always dependent on and are shaped by the periods of reckoning adopted by the organization.

At this point we would do well to pause for a moment and attempt a first identification of accounting with its primary objective: *the recording and reporting of transactions.* (The whole field of accounting is often defined as the process of transaction recording and reporting.) Accounting *principles* deal with the recording and reporting practices of a typical business enterprise or other organization, as dictated by established *conventions* or by widely accepted professional fiat; they have universal application. Accounting *policies* are principles expanded and adapted to the needs of a particular organization; often involving choices from among alternative principles, they originate as top-management-level decisions established as general guides for the organization's compilers, reporters, and disposers of transactions. Accounting *practices* (called an accounting *system* when referring to an individual enterprise) are concerned with the methods, procedures, and records that give tangible, workable meanings and effect to approved policies; very broadly, an accounting system links men, clerical effort, and recording machinery with transactions: a basic essential to the smooth functioning of any organization. In a particular business enterprise these terms and concepts may not have found deliberate expression; however, an experienced observer from the outside will always discover their existence in one form or another, ranging from a careful, up-to-date exposition in an accounting *manual* to a series

---

[23] E.g., a *fiscal year:* a 12-month period ending on the last day (sometimes a specified week-day) of any calendar month.

of assumptions long forgotten from which an accounting routine has been developed over an extended period of time. An important function of today's professional *public accountant*,[24] within the limitations of his employment, is to improve on imperfectly conceived and ill-fitting principles, policies, and practices.

Revenue, cost, and profit

Revenue (or *gross income*) is the amount, in terms of price, of one or more transactions involving the *sale* of goods or the *performance* (for others) of services. *Revenues* (or *sales*) are the *total* of such transactions, usually those falling within a specified accounting period.

An *expenditure* is a transaction involving the present or future outlay of cash or other property in exchange for any acquired good or service; it is *incurred* [25] (i.e. occurs) at the time the good or service is received. A *cost* is a term applied not only to the required outlay but often to the thing acquired when an expenditure is made; if the good or service has already been consumed, or is to be consumed within the current accounting period, a cost is referred to as an *expense*. *Current expenses* and *operating costs* mean the same thing when they relate to a given period of time within which an enterprise is functioning. Where the good or service benefits or is to be utilized in future periods (e.g. office furniture) it is said that an *asset* has been acquired, or that a *capital expenditure* has been made, or that an expense has been *prepaid*.

Profit is the excess of revenues during a given accounting period over expenses associated (for any of various reasons we will subsequently examine) with that revenue. In its plural form it may relate to the increase in the wealth of an entity during a particular period of time and thus be "net" after considering expenses associated with the period (although not necessarily with any item of revenue). *Income* is often used interchangeably with "profit"; how-

---

[24] Further references will be made to the public-accountant's functions in later chapters.

[25] "Incur" always implies a point of time at which a transaction enters the accounting process. This point, as will be seen, is partly conventional, partly legal. For example, if supplies are purchased, that point is the moment of delivery to the buyer, although the order may have been placed at an earlier date and payment may not be required until a later date.

ever, some accountants prefer to limit its use to compensation received by an individual for his services (a salary or wage), or to interest, dividends, rents, and minor items received by an individual or a business concern. "Gross profit," "net profit," and "net income" have narrower meanings with which we will be concerned at a later point.

Revenue and cost transactions do not always *fit* into accounting periods. Thus, only one-fifth of the premium paid on January 1 on a five-year fire-insurance policy will benefit the accounting period (calendar year) that follows. This we can describe as resulting in the incurral of a species of capital expenditure (or prepaid expense) as at January 1 equal to the whole premium, the expiration of one-fifth of the premium cost during the year (an expense), and a "leftover" (prepayment) of four-fifths of the cost at the end of the year which will be carried (as an asset) into the expenses of succeeding years.

Number

As the subject matter of this book emerges, we will be equating it with figures, mostly dollars. The mathematics of accounting is extremely simple, involving no more than addition and subtraction once the details of a transaction have been determined. The routine collection, classification, and recording of transactions, each expressed in dollars—the process we call *bookkeeping*—results in a series of transaction totals, or *balances* as most accountants call them, each total representing a named transaction type. Most of these totals are *net* amounts; by this we mean that both additions and subtractions—positive and negative elements—have entered into their determination.

An example will make this clear. Let us assume that at the beginning of a certain month the balance in one's checking account in a bank is $1,000. During the month two deposits of $250 each are made in the account and four checks of $100 each are drawn against it. At the end of the month what is left in the account— the balance—is, of course, $1,100. There has been a total of six transactions, two having an additive or plus effect on the balance at the beginning of the month and four a subtractive or minus effect. The balance remaining is the result of combining all these elements. Now it happens that from the point of view of the depositor the opening balance and the additions are called *debits;* and the subtractions, *credits;* the remainder is a *debit balance.* If we had drawn checks totaling $2,000 (instead of $400) against this account (for the sake of our illustration assume that the bank had permitted us to do this), a *credit balance* of $500 would have resulted: which means that we would have owed that sum to the bank. Many people not versed in accounting use these terms in referring to their bank accounts.

We must note at the same time what appears at first glance to be a contradiction—or at best a confusing situation: one's debits in his bank account are credits from the point of view of the bank, and one's credits are bank debits. Or, let us say that *B* owes $100 to *A*; if we look at *A*'s side of this relationship, *B* is *A*'s *debtor.* And to *B*, *A* is his *creditor.* Thus, if a bank performs a service for us (supplying a batch of blank checks is an example), the bank will issue a *debit slip* or memorandum on which the service charge appears. This slip will be mailed to us at once or returned with our canceled checks at the end of the month, and the balance in the account will have been reduced in the amount of the indicated charge. We should remember, therefore, that a debtor's debits are his creditor's credits; and from this we may reasonably infer that a debtor's credits are his creditor's debits.

In subsequent chapters we will be considering the *classification* of transactions in some detail. By classification we mean the particular groupings or types of transaction items under different heads. As we will be using the term, this involves an advance determination—before any transaction has taken place—of what these different groups are to be; and then, when the transaction occurs, the designation of the group into which the transaction falls.

At this point, to add to our general background of figure relationships, let us assume that the transactions of a certain organization are to be classified or grouped under six heads which, in lieu of more descriptive titles, we will call *A, B, C, D, E,* and *F.* Now it happens that in building up accounting records, every transaction, regardless of its character, is recorded twice—once as a *debit* and once as a *credit.* Why this is so we need not examine at the moment, but we can at this time profitably observe the arithmetic consequences of this centuries-old accounting practice. If we assume further that under each of our six classifications we are providing for both debit and credit elements (i.e. additions and deductions), let us now give effect to, say, 10 transactions:

Debit	Credit	Debit	Credit	Debit	Credit
A		C		E	
(1) 250	(3) 100	(3) 40	(7) 40	(6) 100	(10) 10
(2) 250	(4) 100	(5) 100		(9) 70	(7) 10
	(5) 100	(8) 20			
	(6) 100				

B		D		F	
(7) 30	(1) 250	(4) 100	(8) 20	(3) 60	
	(2) 250	(7) 20	(9) 70	(10) 10	

Classification A looks like the month's changes in our bank account; the other classifications we will not attempt to identify since we are limiting ourselves here merely to the arithmetic involvement. A scanning of our six classifications leads to the following observations:

1) For each transaction the debit element(s) equal the credit element(s). The debit of transaction (3) has for some reason been divided beween classifications C and F. Transaction (7) involves two debits (30 and 20) and two credits (40 and 10).

2) Only the first two transactions are debited and credited to the same classifications; the other eight transactions are distributed in a variety of ways over the six classifications. These variations are characteristic of what happens in the accounting process wherever it is found.

3) The *balances* in the six classifications we can determine in this instance by simple inspection to be as follows:

A	100
B	−470
C	120
D	30
E	150
F	70
Total	0

The one credit balance (470) exactly *offsets* the five debit balances: the obvious consequence of assigning positive and negative elements of equal amounts to each of the ten transactions.

4) No one classification or classification balance as it has thus been built up can be said to be directly related to any other classification or classification balance. For example, the counterparts of the four items making up classification E are to be found in classifications A, B, D, and F, but these four classifications contain items from other sources; hence the counterpart of the balance in E, 150, can be regarded as residing in nothing less than all of the other five classifications. Occasionally as a practical matter the transaction totals of certain classifications *can* be matched against those of other classifications, or the debits of one classification may be matched against the credits of another, as, for example, the debits of A match the credits of B; but with the great admixture of many thousands of transactions this would not be a normal expectation. The conventional intermingling of transactions is a condition to be reckoned with at a later stage when we will be attempting to judge the significance of a particular classification balance or of complexes of classification balances in their relation to each other.

5) Notwithstanding what we have just said, we will discover in a later chapter that by subdividing any one classification we may preserve the cross-identification of similar transaction groups where for some practical reason this appears to be desirable. Thus, suppose that, in lieu of A, we had established two classifications: A-1 for debits and A-2 for credits; and, in lieu of B, classifications B-1 and B-2. We would then have the following balances:

A-1	500
A-2	−400
B-1	30
B-2	−500
C	120
D	30
E	150
F	70
Total	0

By following this unconventional bookkeeping process and expanding the number of classifications, we have preserved the identity of the transaction types that make up classifications A-1 (a debit balance) and B-2 (a credit balance).

6) Because in ordinary situations the balance of any one classi-

fication cannot be verified against any other one classification, a first requirement in establishing the accounting process is recording accuracy. There are three important elements of accuracy in accounting which we may profitably consider at this juncture:

a) Accuracy in determining the transaction *amount*. Since even in small organizations the transactions of a single month may number many thousands, most transactions are not again reviewed for their correctness once they have been "spread" on the accounting records. We would expect to find, as a normal and essential part of any accounting process, a carefully laid-out procedure for establishing the accuracy of transaction amounts.

b) Accuracy in determining the transaction *classification*. Classification shares an equal importance with transaction amounts, and the safeguards to insure the correct designation for each transtion are generally combined with those covering transaction amounts.

c) Accuracy of *entry*. A transaction may have been accurately determined as to amount and classification, but if a clerical error is made in the entry on the records of one transaction out of, say, several thousands of transactions, the error, if it is classificational, may never be discovered, or may be difficult to discover if a wrong amount is entered. Thus if the debit half of our transaction 10 is erroneously added to classification D instead of classification F, the error may remain undetected; but if the amount is entered as 100 rather than 10, the total of the six classifications will be 90, rather than zero as it should be. Various devices exist for locating this second type of error.

We have now considered the major characteristics of the arithmetic of accounting. A given organization may distribute its transactions over hundreds of different classifications, but always the totals of their balances must equate to zero—or as many accountants express it, the total of debit balances must offset (i.e. equal) the total of credit balances.

Accounting, however, is much more than a device for keeping track of transactions. In any but the smallest organizations, the authorities within the entity for planning, initiating, and incurring transactions involve activities, often numerous and complex, that precede any entry in the records. Classifications must be carefully devised and maintained, and not infrequently they must be changed to meet new conditions. Again, classification totals must be gathered together into statements that serve many purposes: features we will be concerned with shortly.

Summary

We have now been exposed to more than one hundred terms that will be found to be important elements in the structure of accounting. Most of these will require very little change in one's notions of their everyday meanings. Many of their applications will have to be considerably amplified in later chapters. But their importance here lies in their ability to provide a framework on which additional accounting concepts may now be erected.

We have also observed the arithmetic features of the dollar-recording process: the build-up of transaction classifications and the complex of relationships between classification balances.

Let us repeat that the roots of our subject may be observed in the phenomena of the commercial life about us. We will note, as we proceed, that accounting not only supplies order and precision to these phenomena, but provides standards for their interpretation and a vehicle for communicating their significance to both insiders and outsiders.

CHAPTER TWO

The Transaction:
Its Origin and Disposition

Transactions are the raw material of accounting and management. Some transactions, e.g. sales, are sought for; others, such as operating costs, are deliberately sustained in the effort to secure and process sales but are minimized whenever possible; others, such as taxes, are frequently characterized as being endured. Whatever their origins, whatever their effects, however contrasting their purposes and forms may be, transactions are indigenous to all human enterprise. Here we examine their general attributes, their basic relation to management, and some aspects of their classification and accumulation in accounting records.

19

Bookkeeping and accounting are often put into a contrasting functional relationship by describing the former as a transaction-recording, compilatory activity, and the latter as the determinant of transaction classification and bookkeeping patterns, and the basis of reporting and interpreting the results of the transaction-recording routines. For our purposes in this chapter we will regard both as accounting, and our attention will be focused on the inside of an organization where these two functions are responsibilities of the *controller* or top accountant. An advantage of this combination will be apparent as we examine the various aspects of the transaction; in fact, it is quite common to assume that the attention now given to what was once regarded as the lowly status of the transaction has made impracticable, if not impossible, the continuance of the vague distinctions between these two terms.

In this book we are concerned with function rather than form, and we will be dealing principally with the purposes served by the recording process, the management controls governing them, and the varieties of information that transaction summaries may be expected to yield.

The nature of accounting records

Accounting records, or *books of account,* comprise the whole of the detail relating to transactions: the tangible evidence supporting an accounting system. A purchase of supplies, for example, is likely to require such supporting papers as a purchase order, a receiving report, a seller's invoice, approvals within the buyer's organization after tests of quality and quantity received and comparisons with grade and quantity ordered, proofs (in the case of commodities) of entry on stock (inventory) cards, and so on, all of which are component elements of the accounting process. In every organization an important feature of the accounting system is the establishment and maintenance of procedures designed to accommodate the transaction and thereby to ensure accuracy, promptness, and the receipt of money's worth. Accounting records also include *daybooks, journals, ledgers,* inventory compilations, cost sheets, communications with debtors and creditors, voucher files, and various other data supporting or otherwise associated with transactions.

The daybook has played an important part in the development of accounting. In some countries the daybook, required by law, bears an official stamp and is the evidence of a form of license to do business. Entries therein constitute a kind of official record of business activity having a legal standing. In an earlier period in this country the daybook was a chronological, narrative record of each day's events, often including literate comments on the weather, personal reflections, and other varieties of information not recognized today as having significance in the transaction-recording process. Purchases and sales were described in the order of their occurrence along with payments to employees, receipts from customers, remittances to creditors, and so on. At a later date, with many transactions and other events intervening, considerable skill might be required in locating a particular happening, unless some sort of index or recapitulation had been made. Once suited to a slow pace of doing business, the daybook is now virtually obsolete in this country. The *blotter* of stockbrokers—a listing of security movements in and out—is sometimes cited as a survival; but this record, with its entries limited to particular transactions, has a quite different purpose.

Journals

Journals, originally supplementing, but ultimately replacing daybooks,[1] are known as *books of original entry.* More formal than

---

[1] The two words, daybook and journal, come from the same root, *dies,* day. *Diurnal,* the early version of journal, survives as a connecting link, but is no longer associated with accountkeeping.

the daybook, the journal is limited to transactions involving money or money's worth; money columns are provided, and uniform procedures are employed within an organization for recording transactions. There are many types and forms of journals, and today even in a small enterprise one may find several journals simultaneously maintained, each serving as an original record for some specialized, recurrent type of transaction. Thus, within a single enterprise, there can be a *cash-receipts journal*, a *cash-disbursements journal*, a *check register*, a *sales journal*, a *purchases journal*, a *voucher register*, and so on—with a *general journal* serving as the repository of transactions having no place in any of the specialized journals. Every transaction has its place, and its conventional method of entry, in some one journal.

Journals were once bound books; some still are, especially the general journal which, even in a large organization, may contain only a few entries in a single year. Journals may also be a collection of *journal vouchers*.[2] Other journals, following no common pattern, are loose-leaf and of various sizes and shapes, and are subject to varied procedures. The sales journal of a certain department store, for example, contains two entries for a single day, these being a total of charge-sales slips and a total of cash-register readings. In other types of enterprises we may find no formal sales journal; instead, a carefully preserved monthly or other periodic recapitulation, possibly on a single sheet, or copies of customers' invoices serving to supply the need for daily, monthly, or yearly transaction totals which are then recorded in a general journal. Here the conventions[3] of accounting provide no set requirements for methods of compilation; convenience, simplicity, divisions of authority or labor, habits of long standing, and other on-the-spot, environmental factors may be the determinants. But it is axiomatic that whatever the forms and procedures may be, speed of recognition and record-

---

[2] A *voucher* is a document, usually with attachments, that establishes the authority (for example, signatures) and contains supporting evidence (such as a creditor's invoice) for a single transaction or a group of closely related transactions.

[3] A *convention* (mentioned in the preceding chapter) is a commonly approved choice from available, acceptable possibilities; there are many conventions in accounting, such as the essential features of the voucher and journal forms in general use.

ing, precision,[4] and a "good audit trail"[5] must invariably be "built in" as component parts of journal-keeping methods.

Journalization, then, is the formal induction of the transaction into the accounting records. Because transactions are entered in a journal as they occur, a journal is often described as a chronological record, contrasting with a ledger where, as we shall see, transactions are classified by type or purpose.

Where mechanical bookkeeping devices are in use, a journal entry and a ledger posting (which we are about to describe) are often accomplished in a single operation: the one a carbon copy of the other.

Ledgers and accounts

Journals or their counterparts are made up of transaction entries in chronological sequence, as we have noted. By employing additional money columns on the same form, or by utilizing an equivalent in the form of supplemental *worksheets,*[6] breakdowns can be added to the information concurrently made available as transactions are recorded. But journals, or cumulative totals of journal entries and of journal columns, do not supply information in sufficiently classified and readily accessible, compact form. *Books of final entry,* or *ledgers,* are necessary. Amounts of individual transactions, or of transaction summations, posted [7] to a ledger, become additions to groups of continuous, cumulative totals by months or even years—classified or subdivided in whatever way desired. A ledger can be thought of as serving as a *subject index.*[8]

[4] Here in the sense of the presence of a high degree of accuracy.

[5] "Audit trail" is a term used by accountants to designate the presence of a number or other symbol accompanying a transaction which permits tracing the transaction back to its journal source and to a supporting voucher or other original data. See footnote 7.

[6] A worksheet is in this case simply a multicolumnar form having as its purpose the breakdown of a group of more or less related items into subclasses. A multicolumnar journal is itself a form of worksheet.

[7] Money amounts of vouchers or transactions are said to be *entered* in a journal; journal totals or amounts of individually journalized transactions are thereafter *posted* to a ledger. As we have already observed, the posting operation carries with it some identification with the journal source, such as page number, known as the *folio reference,* or *F.* The folio reference is an important part of the audit trail.

[8] Another way of contrasting the journal and the ledger is to regard the

The illustration below is not presented as an example of a form of recordkeeping one would look for in practice; rather, the object is to help the reader visualize the meaning and application of the terms we have been using here.

Extract from a sales journal depicting sales of four different products, with chronological entries and horizontal (here four-way) spread covering a given period of time (here one month)

Date	Amount of sale	Products sold			
		A	B	C	D
Oct. 1	1,000	100		900	
10	800		800		
31	250		150		100
Totals	2,050	100	950	900	100

The three journal entries, appearing on a single journal page (or supporting worksheet), would in practice be considerably embellished by references to source documents, quantities, customers' names, and perhaps other essential information.

A listing of one or four resulting ledger classifications to which postings of totals are made at the end of each time period

Name of account	Account total
Sales	2,050
or	
Sales of A	100
Sales of B	950
Sales of C	900
Sales of D	100

Here we have alternative postings and ledger classifications: a single total in a single classification covering the sales period represented in the journal, and a listing of four classifications into which the breakdown of the month's sales has been carried. The choice of method calls for conformity to management needs to which the accounting process is readily adjusted.

Each ledger group of classified (or similar) transactions is called

---

journal as a continuous vertical record because of its chronological "build-down," and the ledger as a device permitting the horizontal spread of journal entries over many pages, each page representing a different classification.

an *account* (a term we have thus far avoided because of our emphasis on "classification"), and the one (and usually only one) principal ledger of an organization, containing mostly periodic summations posted from journals, is called a *general ledger*. Special-purpose ledgers subsidiary to the general ledger are in common use; like journals, there are many forms serving many purposes, and their installation and particular application are dependent on organizational needs, mechanical requirements, the accountant's preferences, and other factors already mentioned. Where there are several journals and several ledgers, more people can work on the records at the same time, thus making possible the divisions of bookkeeping labor, and a larger degree of specialization on the part of the persons responsible for each record. A *customers ledger*[9] may be expected to contain a separate page or account for each customer to whom credit has been extended. The reader has doubtless become familiar with one or more forms of customer accounts by observing monthly statements (including bank accounts) sent to him on which such details as opening balance, itemized current purchases (withdrawals), payments on account (deposits), and balance now owing (or owned) are featured. The copy sent to the customer may be the original, carbon copy or *exact duplicate*[10] of an actual account maintained by his creditor, or it may be a summary abstract or a list of items still "open," i.e. unpaid. Invoice and statement forms are also varied; sometimes they are fairly uniform in certain types of businesses. But accounting conventions demand no stylized size, form, or even content.[11]

Further comments on the classification and meaning of general-ledger accounts will be deferred to the next chapter.

The transaction: additional considerations

Now that we have had a preliminary look at the accounting process whereby transactions, individually or in group totals, are

[9] This term is sometimes written with a possessive sign following "customers." But the customers of a business do not own its ledgers!

[10] An exact duplication (also called a second original) is turned out automatically by some bookkeeping machines.

[11] In some types of businesses, no monthly statements are sent out to customers, reliance being had on remittances from customers on original invoices.

carried through journals into ledger accounts, we must retrace our steps and examine attributes of the transaction which are more or less directly related to this brief look, and which take on added significance now that we have some idea of how transactions are disposed of. First we must examine the meaning of a transaction as it is related to the organizational setting:

> A transaction arises from the recognition within an organization of an event or condition, following as the consequence of (1) the acceptance of responsibility for its initiation, propriety, execution, and correctness, (2) the incidence of the completed event or observed condition, (3) the ascertainment of the money amount involved, (4) the administrative review of supporting data that supply evidence of component elements, (5) the determination of its effect on specific accounts, and (6) its formal absorption in the records.[12]

The meaning of the items making up this description of "transaction" may be explained as follows:

1) The full acceptance of a transaction is here made to turn on the peculiar meaning of *recognition*, a word often employed in a specialized sense by accountants. It has an organizational significance: that is, not until all six conditions embodied in the quoted description have been complied with may the transaction be said to have been added to the accounting record. Before all of these steps have been completed, the transaction remains in an embryonic state.

But there is a further, important implication in the use of this term as expressed in the first of these numbered conditions: that, when applied to a transaction, "recognition" refers to its activation within the organization as the result of some form of decision[13] or series of decisions by individuals. No matter how small, commonplace, oft-repeated, or routine a transaction may be, it is never spontaneously generated; and regardless of its character some one or more persons[14] must have been associated with its origin and propriety, and with its flow through the organization. This idea is further expanded in (3) below.

---

[12] Based on the definition in the author's *Dictionary*.

[13] *Decision* as employed in management circles today includes *action to give effect to*, as well as the determination to act; required here is action on each of the indicated transaction elements.

[14] Management practices today call for the approval of every transaction by at least two persons.

2) Behind the recognition of a transaction is the occurrence of an *event* or the existence of a *condition,* the former originating from without the organization, the latter resulting from an internal adjustment of one or more completed and already recorded transactions, or from the anticipation of an event to come that, for one reason or another, will not be fully consummated until some future date. An "event" is illustrated by the delivery to an organization of merchandise it has ordered, or by the installation on the premises of purchased equipment that will aid in future operations. Deliveries of goods to customers and of payroll checks to employees are further examples of what we mean by "events." Other types of events are found in the levying of a tax, a windstorm that has damaged property, the receipt of a dividend. A "condition" is found to exist, in the case of the five-year prepayment of a fire-insurance premium which we have already referred to, at the end of the first year: this condition being that one-fifth of the premium has expired; as a result, we will have to reclassify (i.e. transfer), by means of an internal transaction, that portion of the premium from its classification as an asset to a new classification as an expense. An analogous situation exists where a machine has been acquired for factory use and has been classified as an asset: each year, looking forward to its eventual disposal as scrap, we will have to initiate a transaction in which we "expense" a portion of its cost. We are reserving for future discussion the various methods employed in determining the amount of the expensing transaction; here it is sufficient for us to know that it supplies us with an example of what we mean by "condition." [15]

An event or condition is, then, the necessary initial ingredient of a transaction, the phenomenon on the occurrence or existence of which all accounting is dependent. And to keep one of our central points in mind: financial statements, the more immediate sources of which we have already referred to, are reflections of events and conditions that lie behind the accumulations of transactions out of which the statements have been compounded.

3) The phrase *acceptance of responsibility* contributes to the concept of the transaction a reflection of the ultimate charging to

[15] Whether any given transaction gives expression to an event or condition (or both) is of little importance to us here; but the term "event and condition" is an all-embracing one used by accountants in referring to any source or cause that leads to the recognition of a transaction.

representatives of management both the authority and necessity for approving a transaction in each of its several stages. An important part of management's job is to identify clearly each of these stages and to make sure that the management pattern embraces it. In the purchase of materials, for example, these stages often involve several persons and go back as far as planning; thence to budgeting, requisitioning, purchasing, delivery, inspection, disposal, and payment. *Acceptance* by authorized persons is of course essential at each stage.

4) For every transaction there is thus a moment of *incidence* (in the sense of "impact" or "occurrence"): a point in time when the transaction is to be accounted for in a particular organization, in accordance with some current *custom*[16] governing similar transactions. Thus a contractor, working on a project that will require several years for its completion, may wish in any one year to record a profit on that portion of the work which he has already performed and for which he may have been paid in whole or in part. Customs of the trade and those of professional accountants have devised standards that provide methods of determining the timing and amount of the profit that the contractor may recognize. A wholly different kind of situation, but one involving transaction timing, may be found in the existence of transactions at the end of an accounting period that are complete except for their recording. Here a standard of *materiality*[17] applies; for the present we may say that the timing of the recording of items that are of a minor character or amount is looked upon with indifference by many accountants—the recording might be made in the current period or deferred to the next. But a "must" for an immediate recording would attach to any material item.[18]

---

[16] A custom may be described as a convention which through *general acceptance* is more often favored than not, "general acceptance" embracing long-followed habits and preferences such as those advocated in textbooks. Less formal than an imposed "principle" to which we have briefly referred in the preceding chapter, a custom is at the same time more dynamic; but it is likely to change slowly because causes of change develop slowly and because individuals hesitate to adopt measures that have not been fully accepted by the majority.

[17] This word is of considerable importance to accountants, although basically this importance has not extended the ordinary meaning of the word. We will refer to this word in more specific terms in a later chapter.

[18] These remarks, however, must be taken with caution. Minor items are

5) The phrases *ascertainment of the money amount . . . administrative review . . . determination of its effects on specific accounts* indicate functions (not always simultaneously performed, as we will observe at a later point) of the "voucher audit"—an activity immediately following the incidence of a transaction, designed to assure the precise amount, the fullness of objective evidence supporting the emergence of the transaction, and the prospective disposition in the accounts of the transaction amount.[19]

6) *Entry in the records* usually follows the preceding steps without delay; some exceptions we have already noted.

The generalizations we have now completed concerning the transaction will be illustrated by specific examples as we proceed. For the present we need only reflect that the processing of the transaction is of vital importance in management planning and operation, and that the transaction, small or large, in its several stages is related to persons who have assumed processing responsibilities for its origin, consummation, and entry in the records.

Transactions and accounting periods

We have already observed that revenues and expenses are accounted for within relatively limited periods of time: days, weeks, months, or years, and that the "fit" of transactions into these periods is sometimes imperfect. The shorter the period, the more misfits there are likely to be. The payment for a service may take place before the service is rendered, such as that covered by the fire-insurance premium we have previously mentioned, or a machine which is to contribute to future production; or after the service is rendered, as in the case of labor. An important part of a controller's responsibilities is to identify costs with particular periods. He does this on several different bases, depending on the character of the item. For the present we will consider illustrations of the principal classes of such items, and in later chapters the conventions and standards upon which allocations[20] as between periods are based.

---

not safely overlooked if they are numerous or if during another period similar items might assume a much greater importance.

[19] Designating, as on a voucher, the account to be affected, and the amount and legend to be posted, is often referred to as a *coding* operation.

[20] The division of costs as between periods benefited is wherever possible based on the relative amounts of services yielded during such periods; but if

None of the illustrations is likely to present to the reader any wholly
unfamiliar situation; the effort at the moment is to anticipate, in
terms we have introduced thus far, the subject matter of succeeding
chapters.

Current transactions or portions thereof that relate to future
accounting periods can be regarded as "residuals" and "anticipa-
tions"; or, in the language of the accountant, prepayments (including capital expenditures) and *accruals* (including payables).
Here are characteristic, often-recurring examples, as viewed at the
end of an accounting period:

1) *Prepayments:*

Land, buildings, machinery, furniture (capital assets) bought and
paid for in one period and yielding services in future periods as well
as the present; except for land, the services from which continue indefinitely, these items are amortized [21] over the periods of their usefulness.

Raw materials, purchased for processing (and thereafter as finished
goods) and merchandise purchased for resale; in either case, appearing as assets are the amounts remaining unsold at the end of
the period.

Supplies, such as office stationery: the portion not consumed during
the period of acquisition.

Insurance premiums: that portion representing protection against
possible fire or other loss in future periods.

2) *Accruals—assets:*

Interest receivable, whether or not due,[22] on a note given by a customer in settlement of his account; interest may be called for, say,
semiannually, but the interest is conceived as accruing ratably over
each of the six months preceding, and thus "assignable" to those
months.

---

these amounts cannot be accurately measured, a time basis (as in the case of
the insurance premium) is usually followed.

[21] To *amortize* is gradually to reduce a money amount to a predetermined
minimum figure or to zero. By "expensing" each year one-tenth of the cost of a
desk, for example, the whole cost is being amortized or *depreciated* over a ten-
year period. Amortization may also apply to the liquidation of a debt which
becomes due in periodic installments, thus ultimately diminishing to zero.

[22] *Due* means now receivable; *accrued* means the portion of an amount ultimately to become due that relates to periods already ended. Thus, *A* owes *B*
a debt on which he pays interest each December 31; on June 30, one-half of
that year's interest has accrued to *B*; on December 31, the year's interest has
fully accrued and is also due.

3) *Payables:*

Unpaid purchases: goods received and put into stock and even sold, but payment to the supplier may not be required until several days or weeks later: for example, at the end of a discount period.

Salaries and wages for a monthly payroll may not be payable until the month following.

Taxes, such as income taxes, may not be payable until the following year, although pertaining to (and chargeable against) the income of the current year.

4) *Accruals—liabilities—other varieties of negative assets:*

Interest payable—a negative version of interest receivable—on a note owing by the organization to some outsider, such as a bank.

Salaries, wages, and taxes, the amount of which, yet to be paid, pertains to a period now ended.[23]

These illustrations could be multiplied, but it is perhaps sufficient for the present to regard them as typical of the leading types of transactions that must be adjusted or anticipated periodically to fit in with the process of dovetailing revenues and ordinary operating costs. The reader will likely be able to think of further examples of the imperfect fit of transactions within any given time period, taken from his own experience.

In the next two chapters we will deal with accounting concepts surrounding transaction compilations and adjustments, and with some of the accounting conventions that underlie statements based on accounts.

Summary

Transactions arise from the events and conditions encountered. A number of attributes attach to the transaction as it enters the accounting process: there has been a determination of when it occurred; its propriety is a responsibility resting with persons; it has been evaluated in terms of money; its documentation and its cor-

---

[23] A salary or other expense payable (i.e. unpaid) is to be distinguished from a salary accrued; the distinction corresponds to the one we have drawn between interest due (i.e. immediately receivable) and interest accrued (to become receivable [i.e. "maturing"] at a later point in time). A salary is payable at the end of a payroll period but accrues (on a *pro rata* basis) during the period.

rectness generally have been reviewed; and the accounts it is to modify have been identified.

Money amounts of transactions are entered in journals, and are thence posted to accounts in ledgers. These records make possible the processes of classification and summation that pave the way for financial statements. Any typical item in a financial statement is composed of many individual transactions.

Allocations of certain types of transactions or transaction totals are made as between time periods, in order to make possible an equitable relationship between expenses and revenues. Thus, wherever a material expenditure benefits two or more periods, the expense for any one period is in general determined by the benefits received during that period as compared with estimated total benefits, present and future.

CHAPTER THREE

The Accounting Pattern

Accounting, wherever found, follows the same basic pattern, notwithstanding wide procedural differences when it is applied to particular situations. The elements making up this pattern are considered here: the dualism inherent in the recording and reporting process which we have already referred to as debit and credit, classifications that preshape the record, journal entries that initiate the record, and the financial statements that constitute the endproduct. A simple illustration shows this pattern in action.

We have thus far mentioned but not fully related several types of accounts. Our object now will be to show the relationship of these types to each other and to the accounting system as a whole. To do this, we must first consider the meaning of *double-entry bookkeeping* and give further attention to the words *debit* and *credit*. These three terms point to the methodology universally followed in recording the transactions of both large and small organizations.

The traditional functions of bookkeeping, which we have already described as an inseparable branch of accounting, are concerned with the acceptance, classification, and recording of transactions; moreover, the bookkeeping process involves a system that embraces two equal, opposing, contrasting, initially interdependent elements, neither of which can be conceived as existing without the other or as having an importance greater or less than that of the other. We call these elements debit and credit. Since the final stage of the processing of every transaction requires its full expression in the books of account, we unfailingly record at the same time the transaction's debit and credit elements.[1]

Debits and credits: assets & equities

The explanation of debit and credit may be found in the underlying nature of every accounting unit:[2] that it is a person (as we

[1] Hence the term *double entry*.

[2] An *accounting unit* or *accounting entity* is an organization or organizational

have previously defined the term) conceived as being independent of its owners to whom it must account.[3] We must, we repeat, be prepared to look at every accounting unit, just as we look at a corporation, as an artificial person. We create such a person every time we install a self-contained system of accounts. Even an individual who keeps a double-entry record of his personal assets and expenses creates an artificial person by so doing.

Let us assume that A, an individual, is the sole owner of three unincorporated business activities: a bank, a flour mill, and a hardware store, each operating under separate management, and with no employees in common. A single bookkeeping system combining the affairs of the three organizations would obviously result in the utmost confusion; hence each has its own books of account in which the owner's investment and the various possessions of the unit have been duly recorded. The owner, of course, would invariably regard each unit as an "independent" organization. He has in each a separate investment: an investment he considers as being *owed* [4] to him by the unit. The relationship thus established has created an obligation on the part of an artificial person not only to account to its owner for the cash or other assets it has received from him but also at the same time and in the same amount to keep track of the obligation it has taken on to account to its owner for his contribution to it.[5] The reason for this is that if the artificial person is to perform some kind of business operation, a good deal of the cash will immediately be exchanged for such business assets as merchandise, fix-

---

subdivision for which a full accounting system is maintained. A retail branch of a large organization, for example, that keeps its own books of account is such a unit. This is basically the same concept of "entity" we considered in Chapter 1.

[3] "Account": here in its nontechnical sense as expressing, for example, a reporting by an agent to his principal.

[4] In early English *owe* meant *own*, the latter in its modern sense. Gradually "owe" began to be employed as a symbol attaching to the thing owned and implying an obligation, both pecuniary and custodial, to the *owner*. The development of the need for establishing a concept of separateness between the thing owned and the owner appears to have paralleled the development of debit and credit: "debit" indicating something owned; "credit," something owed.

[5] Notice that we are saying that the organization, as though it were a natural person, has an obligation to its owner: a figure of speech that can be applied to any accounting unit. This usage is not confined to accountants, however.

tures, and other assets, while the original obligation to the owner must continue to be accounted for as a lump sum which we call *owners' equity, investment, invested capital, capital paid in,* or simply *capital.* It is this relationship that has given rise to the bookkeeping dualism: assets on the one hand, or debits, and owners' equities on the other, or credits.

We have thus established the separateness of artificial persons from their owners. Equally important to the bookkeeping concept are the long-established commercial relationships between artificial persons and outsiders. Not only does an owner contribute property to an artificial person of his own creation, but others, suppliers of goods and services, also contribute[6] property to it and, in doing so, look for payment from the artificial person at some agreed or understood future date. The existence of our *credit system,* whereby a buyer acquires goods or services which he may put to immediate use or even dispose of before he pays for them, makes it necessary for us to recognize a second form of equity which accountants often call *creditor equities.* Again we have assets, or debits, on the one hand, and creditors' equities, or credits, on the other. Our artificial person must account to its creditors also: this is done by paying them off as their bills fall due. The owner's equity could be similarly satisfied; but if this took place there might be no assets remaining and the artificial person would cease to exist. Owners' equity is a permanent contribution; creditor equities, a temporary contribution.

A third form of contribution of property to an artificial person engaged in commercial pursuits comes from customers who buy the goods or services it sells. If, over a period of time, selling prices have exceeded both the cost of the items sold and all operating expenses, the resulting *profit* represents a contribution from customers that we often call *net income* or *earnings.* This, too, like other contributions, is an equity and by custom it belongs to the owner,[7] although it is usually accounted for separately; accumulations of profit increase with continued profit and decrease with losses or with profit withdrawals by the owner, the balance being called *retained earnings* or *earned surplus.*

[6] "Contribute" is used here in the sense of "convey" or "transfer."

[7] The bulk of the profits of a cooperative organization is usually returned to its customers in proportion to the sales made to them, rather than to their ownership equities.

The equities of creditors we call *liabilities;* owner's equity (investment and retained earnings) we often call *net worth.* When we add them together, we have a total of contributions that by virtue of the transactions as we have described them equals cash and the other assets that have been contributed or acquired. But, because of commercial practices which have been honored for many centuries, we cannot in most situations say that any one asset or a part of any one asset pertains to any one item or group of items among liabilities or net worth. The identification or tie of a contribution with the asset it has brought into an organization is lost the moment the contribution transaction has been completed. All we can say is that the total of assets equals the total of liabilities[8] and net worth. Amounts owing to present creditors may even be paid out of earnings from future sales of goods or services.[9]

And so the *first* element—of each transaction that represents a contributed asset or service—is a thing of substance that is thereafter identified with the artificial person apart from either the owner or seller. The *second* element is an expression of the interest or *equity* of the owner or seller up to the time of the transaction. *After* the transaction takes place, the equity remains, but only as a claim against all of the assets of the artificial person.[10]

To a seller, a promise to pay—an equity in his customer—is a valid asset that takes the place of the goods or services he has sold: an asset that in turn is replaced by cash when the customer pays off his debt.

If all these transfers, in and out, were cash transactions, the bookkeeping required would be greatly simplified: there would merely

[8] "Liabilities," as the term is often used by accountants, may include net worth (liabilities to owners) as well as creditor equities (liabilities to outsiders).

[9] The situation has its origins in the law of debtor and creditor: where, following an ordinary sale, the creditor's claim against the debtor is not identified with the asset sold, but extends to all of the debtor's assets. In the usual form of installment sale, however, the creditor, by specific agreement with the buyer, may repossess the asset sold if installment payments are defaulted.

[10] If the artificial person does not have a standing at law comparable to that of a corporation (in some states certain noncorporate forms of organization may have a limited-liability status resembling that of a corporation), the legal claim attaches, of course, to the owners of the artificial person. An accounting entity, although a well-recognized commercial concept, may not always be a legal one.

be an exchange of an asset or service for cash or of cash for an asset or service. But the credit[11] system on which the operation of our economy is dependent today pervades all commercial activity; and in every artificial person we find a complex of assets for which there exists an offsetting complex of equities.

Debits and credits: things acquired and their sources

We have said that owners, creditors, and customers are contributors of property to the artificial person that accounting helps to create, that having been transferred, an item of property is no longer identified with any one contributor, but that the relative interests of the contributors are preserved in the form of capital, liabilities, and earnings; also, that capital and earnings together are termed net worth. To explain these relations in other terms, we may say that accounting, at the moment a transaction is recognized, requires the recording of both the thing acquired (the asset or expense), a debit; and its source (a liability, an item of net worth, or an item eventually to be merged with net worth), a credit; thus,

Debits	*Credits*
Assets	Liabilities
Expenses	Net worth—
	Owners' contributions
	Sales
	Other income

Accounting, wherever found, can always be explained in these terms. In governmental and institutional accounting, as compared with the accounting for business organizations (with which we are mainly concerned in this book), only the first two items under net worth would differ: for these two items we would probably have some such designation as "donors' contributions" or "legislative appropriations."

Illustration of the pattern

With this concept of assets and equities in mind, we are ready to examine a simple situation that will serve to illustrate again the

---

[11] Not to be confused with the "credit" of debt-and-credit!

practical significance of these two terms: Let us say that *A* and *B* decide to open a joint bank account for the purpose of making a number of investments; *A* has contributed $10,000 to the undertaking, and *B*, $5,000. Profits, losses, and expenses are to be shared in proportion to these contributions. Accordingly, a bank deposit of $15,000 is made in the name of the venture. At this point the one asset is this item of cash, and the equities of the venturers in the asset are $10,000 and $5,000, respectively.

A half-dozen subsequent transactions then take place during the period of the venture's existence, as follows:

a) Contributions of the two venturers $15,000
b) Shares of *M* Company purchased by check at a cost of 4,400
c) Shares of *N* Company purchased by check at a cost of 5,000
d) A fourth of the *M* Company shares sold (and proceeds deposited in the bank) for 2,150
e) Clerical costs, paid by check, amounting to 60
f) A fifth of the *N* Company shares sold for 850
(However, only $750 is deposited, the broker having erred in his remittance in the amount of $100; this will be collected from him later)
g) Privilege tax on the joint operation, incurred but not yet due, amounting to 120

When this point has been reached, the venture is terminated and the remaining cash is distributed, *A* agreeing to take over the remaining *M* shares and pay the tax when it becomes due, *B* to take over the remaining *N* shares and collect and retain the amount owing from the broker. How is the cash distributed? Simple, you say; it's elementary arithmetic:

A: 10,000 + 2/3 (2,150 − 1,100) − 2/3 (1,000 − 850) − 2/3 (60 + 120) − 3,300 + 120 = 7,300

B: 5,000 + 1/3 (2,150 − 1,100) − 1/3 (1,000 − 850) − 1/3 (60 + 120) − 4,000 − 100 = 1,140

But to make sure there is actually $8,440 in the bank at this juncture, we will have to indulge in a little cash arithmetic:

$$15,000 − 4,400 − 5,000 + 2,150 + 750 − 60 = 8,440$$

An accountant, not knowing how long the arrangement between *A* and *B* was to continue, would have installed an accounting system which would have included at least a general journal and a general ledger, and at the conclusion of the venture, just before the settlement is effected (transaction *g*), he would probably have represented the then state of affairs in ten ledger accounts as follows:[12]

A and B

Abstract of Ledger—January 31, 19-2

Account Number	Name of Account	Debits	Credits		Balances
1	Cash in bank	$17,900	$ 9,460		$ 8,440
2	Due from broker	100	—		100
	Investments in:				
3	M	4,400	1,100	or the ac-	3,300
4	N	5,000	1,000	countant	4,000
5	Tax unpaid	—	120	might have	−120
	Contributions from:			prepared a	
6	A	—	10,000	listing of the	−10,000
7	B	—	5,000	accounts as	−5,000
8	Sales of investments	—	3,000	on the right	−3,000
9	Cost of investments sold	2,100	—		2,100
10	Expense	180	—		180
	Totals	$29,680	$29,680		0

Since we have already summarized the transactions as they concern *A* and *B*, the sources of the figures in the ledger summary will not be difficult to trace; but better to understand the significance of "debit" and "credit," let us see how the seven transactions have affected the ten accounts:

Account Number	Transactions Debit	Credit
1	a, d, f	b, c, e
2	f	—
3	b	d
4	c	f
5	—	g
6	—	a
7	—	a
8	—	d, f
9	d, f	—
10	e, g	—

Up to this point the transactions have been of the external variety. To wind up *A*'s and *B*'s joint affairs, we need now to give expression

[12] Accountants would call the "debit" and "credit" listings, as well as the "balances" listing, a *trial balance* in which total debits and total credits (or a single column of debit and credit balances) are displayed.

to three more transactions: the first an internal transaction (h) eliminating accounts 8, 9, and 10 (the revenue and expense accounts) and transferring the net amount (i.e. $720, the net profit equal to the excess of 8 over the sum of 9 and 10) to A's and B's accounts—which will raise A's account to $10,000 + 480, or $10,480, and B's to $5,000 + 240, or $5,240. After this has been done, our accountant might prepare a somewhat different form of statement for A and B to see:

A and B

Second Ledger Abstract—January 31, 19-2

Cash in bank	$ 8,440	Tax unpaid	$ 120
Due from broker	100	A's investment	10,480
Investment in stocks	7,300	B's investment	5,240
Total assets	$15,840	Total equities	$15,840

Here we have a *balance sheet:* assets on the one side and equities on the other. Owners' equities include their respective shares ($\frac{2}{3}$ and $\frac{1}{3}$) of the net operating profit.

The final two (external) transactions (i and j) will record the distributions to A and B: A receiving a check for $7,300, the investment in M (at cost), $3,300, and the obligation to pay the tax, $120, when due; B receiving a check for $1,140, the investment in N (at cost), $4,000, and the right to collect $100 from the broker.[13] When these two distributions have been made and the transactions reflecting them have been carried into the ledger, the balance of each ledger account will have been reduced to zero.

The bookkeeping dualism

The reader has now been carried through the basic operation of the bookkeeping process. Several new terms have been introduced but not fully explained, and the effect of certain procedures has been shown without an adequate analysis of the reasons for them.

[13] If the agreement between A and B had provided that the final distribution of assets was to be based on current market values and the market price of the M shares had been $3,500 and of the N shares, $3,950, a separate (internal) transaction would have been required to record the net gain in market value. A's share of the remaining cash would have been reduced $100, and B's share would have been increased by a like amount.

But the basic process has been indicated, and this we must now review to make certain that the principal features of the process have been clearly understood. By means of the simple situation described —without resort to formal methods of accounting—the reader will be able to pause at any point and look to the "real" situation behind these procedural formalities. Of course, in the practical world, no set of conditions would be as simple as the one presented here, and the need for a better-patterned, more formal set of records—suitable for handling transactions, say, by the hundreds—would be apparent.

We opened the chapter by mentioning "double entry," and we have observed from the first ledger summary that there have been entries of the money amount of each of the seven transactions in at least two accounts, one entry designated as a debit, the other as a credit.[14] *Four* fundamental types of *debits and credits* and *two* fundamental types of *accounts* have emerged:

Type	*Transaction*
1) Acquisitions of *assets* (debit)—cash; investments purchased; receivable acquired	a, b, c, d, f
2) Reductions of *assets* (credit)—cash; investments sold	b, c, d, e, f, i, j
3) Creation of *equities* (credit)—contribution by venturers; liability for tax; profit from sale of *M* investment	a, d, g, h
4) Reduction of *equities* (debit)—expenses incurred; loss from sale of *N* investment	e, f, g, h, i, j

The debits and credits, and the accounts of all organizations can be fitted into these categories. As to the varieties of transactions, any combination of any of the four types of debits and credits with any of the same or other types is possible—and we may expect, therefore, that altogether there would be sixteen of them (4^2). Only a few of these varieties are illustrated here. Others will appear from time to time as we progress in our study of the many situations with which accounting must deal.

Equities of owners, as we have said, are increased with each profit made and decreased with each expense or loss incurred: a truism we

---

[14] The origins of these two words, *debitum,* that which is owed (to us), and *creditum,* that which is loaned (to us), are only slightly helpful to our understanding of their present application; their equivalents in German (*soll* and *haben*) and French (*doit* and *avoir*) are even less so.

can readily apply to ourselves without resort to bookkeeping procedures. Thus, if we buy a car for $2,000 cash, we can say, in the language we have been using, that our asset is the car, valued at its cost, and our equity the same amount. If we sell it for $2,200 the car is replaced by cash, and our equity (now in cash) has been increased from $2,000 to $2,200. In keeping the accounts of an organization we make only periodic adjustments of the owner-equity accounts, in the meantime maintaining accounts for sales and other items of income and expenses—all of which, when taken together, will give us the required adjustment, as did transaction (*h*), above.

Journal entries

The first seven external transactions in our illustration together with the one internal and two external transactions winding up *A*'s and *B*'s joint affairs may be *journalized*, that is, put in *journal-entry* form. We will follow a mode of expression universally recognized by accountants in displaying—for example, to management—the effect of transactions on accounts.[15] Other forms may be used in recording transactions in journals; in practice, there are many patterns of journals, the single exception being the general journal where the form reproduced below may be regarded as typical:

(*a*)

January 2, 19-2

Cash in First National Bank	15,000	
A's account		10,000
B's account		5,000
Contributions of *A* and *B* to joint		
venture, deposited this day		

The principal features attaching to this conventional form of journal entry are these: *date* of the entry—if the transaction date differs it should be cited in the explanation; names of *accounts affected*, with indentations for each account name and amount to be credited; the *amounts* that are to be carried to the two or more accounts in-

---

[15] The form we use here is the same as that appearing in bookkeeping and accounting textbooks, in accounting manuals, and often in books of account; it is frequently required in solutions of problems appearing in examinations given to prospective members of the accounting profession.

volved appearing opposite each account name; *explanation,* indented as shown, describing and justifying the transaction as completely as possible—referring, where necessary, to underlying files or other sources. Journal entry (*a*) is called a *compound* journal entry, involving, as it does, more than two accounts.

(b and c)

January 6, 19-2

Investments	9,400	
Cash in First National Bank		9,400
Purchase of *M* and *N* stocks from (details		
of seller, price, and other information		
would be shown here or reference made to		
a supporting voucher or file)		

(d)

January 16, 19-2

Cash in First National Bank	2,150	
Cost of shares sold (1/4 of 4,400)	1,100	
Sales of investments		2,150
Investments (*M*)		1,100
Sale of *M* shares, yielding profit of 1,050		
(further details, similar to preceding entry)		

Transaction *d* is another compound entry. Two entries, instead of one, could if desired have been made of this: the first recording the sales and receipt of cash; the second, recording the cost of the sale, which could have been deferred until the end of the month, jointly with other similar transactions. The profit does not appear as such in a separate account; rather, the two accounts, sales of shares and costs of shares sold, give us that information when they have been merged. There are no rules or customs to be followed here in disposing of (or *clearing*) these two accounts; convenience and simplicity are usually the principal determining factors.

(e)

January 23, 19-2

Expense	60	
Cash in First National Bank		60
Clerical help paid		

If the operation were to be a prolonged one, several different expense accounts would probably be created, one for each class of expense; under the same circumstances, but one investments account could have been provided in the general ledger (again for convenience) with a supporting record for the items making up the total.

(f)

January 24, 19-2

Cash in First National Bank	850	
Cost of shares sold (1/5 of 5,000)	1,000	
Sales of investments		850
Investments (N)		1,000
Sale of N shares, yielding loss of 150		

The fact that a loss from the second sale of investments has been sustained does not change the form of the journal entry.

(g)

January 25, 19-2

Expense	120	
Tax unpaid		120
Tax assessed against the venture		
by city of Z		

Here we have for the first time the creation of an equity in the form of a *liability*, which may also be described as a postponed but ultimately-to-be-made disbursement. We may presume that the tax pertains to the current period or—if extending beyond—is small enough to be absorbed at once.[16]

---

[16] We have already commented briefly on this practice. It is not uncommon, even in large enterprises, to regard minor costs as current expense although they may actually benefit future periods. In a subsequent chapter we will further consider the question of *significance* and *materiality* that may be raised concerning any adjustment. In an organization, for example, in which annual profits exceed six figures, the precise timing of small costs as in (g) would be a matter of indifference; we shall see that *consistency*, however, in their disposal is much more important. An alternative to immediate expensing would be this: suppose the tax is a license to do business covering the current calendar year; ten dollars could have been regarded as a January expense and $110 as a prepaid benefit to be included among the assets and carried into February; a similar action in February would result in carrying forward $100 into March, and so on; each month's expense would be debited with and hence increased by $10, and the prepayment (asset) account would be credited with and decreased by a like amount until (in December) it would have been exhausted.

A little more figuring will reveal that the journal entries as shown above have built the ledger accounts up to the amounts appearing in the schedule at the top of page 40, this schedule being the summation of totals from the ten accounts we have created. Since we are to have no further operations, accounts 8, 9, and 10 can be *closed*. Revenue and expense accounts, which are subdivisions of the owner's equity account, are often called *nominal* [17] accounts, as contrasted with *real* or "carryover" accounts, here seven in number. Real accounts are perennials; they remain alive and carry over from one period to another; nominal accounts are the annuals among accounts; they are closed (i.e. terminated and eliminated) at the end of some predetermined time period—here one month, but in most instances, especially in the case of business concerns, at the end of each 12-month period. The nature of the closing will be apparent from an inspection of the following journal entry:

(h)

January 31, 19-2

Sales	3,000	
Cost of investments sold		2,100
Expenses		180
A's account		480
B's account		240
Nominal accounts closed; profit of 720 distributed, by agreement, 2/3 to A, and 1/3 to B		

Two entries could have been made just as well: the first consisting of the first three items with a new account ("net profit," perhaps) to receive a credit of $720, the amount necessary to balance the entry; the second would eliminate the new account and credit A's and B's accounts with the amounts as shown. The new account would then constitute a permanent record of the profit as determined for the month of January.

A's account now reflects his equity in the assets [18] as $5,600, and

---

[17] In a subsequent chapter, we will also apply the word "nominal" to subdivisions of cash and other asset and liability accounts.

[18] More correctly *net* assets, as there is a liability of $120 to be subtracted from the assets in considering the amounts to be distributed. The term *net assets* means assets less liabilities which at various future dates are to be paid for out of the assets (whether or not the liabilities constitute a legal claim against them). "Net assets" is generally identical with *net worth,* a term

B's, $3,300. As they withdraw the assets and take over the liability, entries (*i*) and (*j*) are made:

(i)

January 31, 19-2

A's account	10,480	
Tax payable	120	
Investment in M		3,300
Cash		7,300

(j)

January 31, 19-2

B's account	5,240	
Due from broker		100
Investment in N		4,000
Cash		1,140
Distribution of assets to A and B, and assumption by A of liability for tax		

All accounts, now with zero balances, are closed.

Classification

We are now ready to reexamine our comments on the classification of accounts and to extend them to a number of subclasses.

Basically, as we have already pointed out, there are but two kinds of accounts: assets and equities. Every account we have described thus far and, in fact, all accounts to be found in this book and elsewhere, belong to one or the other of these two categories. And assets ≡ equities because we never express a transaction without completely balanced elements. This is in harmony with the fundamental notion of debit and credit and with the concept that any given system of accounts involves an organization or entity having an existence apart from the assets on the one hand and the equity holders on the other.

Again, let us repeat: the accounting process recognizes the commercial concept that when an ordinary commodity changes hands, the seller must look to the organization (or to the individual if the

we have already used earlier in this chapter as meaning the equity of owners in the organization's assets.

sale has been made to a proprietorship) for payment; legally, the seller becomes a general creditor, and if he remains unpaid, he has no direct claim on the commodity (conditional and installment sales excepted) after it has left his hands, or on the proceeds derived from its sale by the buyer. Because of this concept of carrying on business, fortified not only by custom but, in the United States, by state laws governing debtor and creditor, the seller becomes the holder of an equity in the buyer, his claim being on the assets as a whole. Accounting classifications call for the recording of his equity along with equities of other creditors and of the organization's owners.[19]

A feature of the accounting process which must be noted here is the recording of causes of changes in owners' equities by setting up a variety of temporary (nominal) accounts. Periodically, as we have seen, these accounts (revenues and expenses) are closed out and their net amount (balance) is added to (if a profit has been earned) or deducted from (if the organization's operations have resulted in a loss) the owners' equity—which is to say that nominal accounts have no effect on creditors' equities.

These basic concepts should be kept in mind while examining the following typical classification of the accounts of a small retail establishment:

Continuing (Real) Accounts

Assets	*Equities*
Current assets:	Current liabilities:
1) Cash	11) Bank loans
2) Receivables	12) Unpaid bills
3) Accrued interest receivable	13) Accrued interest
4) Inventories	14) Accrued taxes
5) Prepaid expense	Long-term liabilities:
Fixed assets:	15) Mortgage bonds
6) Land	Net worth (owner's equity):
7) Buildings	16) Contributions of owner
8) Machinery	17) Retained earnings
9) Equipment	
Intangible assets:	
10) Goodwill	

---

[19] There are, of course, various classes of equities recognized by law: secured, partly secured, preferred, unsecured, and, finally, proprietors—terms relating to the order of payment in case of liquidation. In a going business, these rankings are given no recognition in the classification of accounts.

Temporary (Nominal) Operating Accounts

Expenses	*Income*
Cost of sales:	Revenues:
21) Merchandise sold	18) Sales
Operating expense:	19) Interest earned
22) Sales salaries	20) Rents
23) Executive salaries	
24) Store expenses	
Interest expense:	
25) Interest on mortgage bonds	

We have here two general classes of accounts—real and nominal —and 25 accounts grouped in ten subclasses. Our purpose here is to acquire a very general idea of the meaning of these ten subclasses. In Chapter 5 we will consider a number of the individual accounts in greater detail.

1) *Current assets* are so called because of their constant employment and their changing amounts as the result of day-to-day operations. Another characteristic is the continuous conversion of one current asset into another: inventories are sold and with a profit added become receivables; receivables are collected and become cash; cash is reinvested in inventories; and the cycle begins again. Prepaid expense, of which an insurance premium is an example, appears in the category of current assets because of its participation as a necessary ingredient of current operations. As to the sequence of the items making up current assets, it will be noted that they are arranged in the order of their liquidity.

2) *Current liabilities* we have already described as having their origins in transactions that have created assets or expenses, and they will disappear from the accounts when current assets have been applied to their liquidation. If the credit system were not a part of our economy, and purchases of merchandise and the incurring of expense had to be accompanied by cash payments, current-liability accounts would not exist. The two items of accruals may be looked upon as prepaid expenses in reverse: costs, not yet paid for, that pertain to benefits already received.

The excess of current assets over current liabilities is known as *working capital,* and the total of current assets divided by the total of current liabilities, the *working-capital ratio*. These terms will be recalled in a subsequent chapter.

3) *Fixed assets* other than land are only relatively "fixed"; they too participate in the operating cycle by contributing services that make operations possible; their costs are gradually transferred to operating expenses over their useful lives.

4) *Long-term liabilities,* such as mortgage notes, are creditor equities that make acquisitions of fixed assets possible without immediate outlays of cash from working-capital sources; and, like current liabilities, assets must ultimately be expended in their liquidation.

5) *Goodwill* is the only form of intangible asset we need refer to at this time; it is, for example, that portion of the purchase price of B's business that A, a prospective buyer, is willing to pay for as "excess earning power" over and above what he acquires in the way of current and fixed assets. Thus if B's business stands to earn for A a comfortable net income of $10,000 a year, A, although willing to pay B $100,000, and acquiring current and fixed assets worth $80,000 in the deal, would be paying $20,000 for goodwill. There are, of course, many ways by which earning power is computed. But, as we shall see later, goodwill, like fixed assets, has usually a limited life and over a relatively short period after acquisition is gradually expensed.

6) *Owners' equity* which we call here "net worth" is, as we have already seen, made up of the contribution (investment) of the owner(s) to the organization, and the profits (net income) yielded by operations that have been permitted to remain in the business (retained earnings). By a somewhat more extended stretch of our imagination, these too may be called liabilities since, to extinguish them, assets would have to be withdrawn from the enterprise. On a smaller scale, this is exactly what happens where the owners decide to extract profits from the enterprise (in the case of a corporation, it would be the payment of a dividend): cash is credited and retained income is debited, the effect being a simultaneous reduction of both assets and equities.

The net-worth accounts of a corporation have a similar appearance. The collective contributions of owners (stockholders) are termed "capital stock" and the evidence of the contributions takes the form of "share" certificates issued to the stockholders. In published balance sheets of corporations the title "capital stock" is usually followed by the number of shares issued and the money amount of the contributions that the original stockholders have paid in to the corporation.[20] Retained earnings (also known as earned surplus) is a remainder account: the excess of profits the corporation has reported less payments (dividends) that have been distributed to the stockholder-owners. Further details concerning corporate net worth appear in Chapter 8.

7) *Operating* (*or nominal*) *accounts* consist of items of revenue and expense the general nature of which we have already discussed.

Although pertaining to a small retail establishment, most of these real and nominal accounts will be found as a minimum in any commercial organization. Account titles will vary: instead of one "receivables" account there may be several, and there may be breakdowns of other items as well. A classification of accounts is always tailored to the individual organization's characteristics and to management's needs; and these will be found to differ quite widely even as between members of the same industry.

Summary

Our review of the accounting process followed in a very small operation has demonstrated the direction taken by transactions generally as they are inscribed in books of account. Journalization is succeeded by ledger postings in such a manner as to maintain a constant equality between the organization's assets and the equities of creditors and owners in these assets. Revenue and expense accounts—which are temporary owners'-equity accounts—are kept open usually for the period of a year, then eliminated, and the net balance remaining (a credit if a profit and a debit if a loss) is carried to an owner's-equity account. For all business organizations there is this common pattern of accounting, and the content of the remaining chapters will be found to coordinate closely with the outline we have presented here.

---

[20] A new stockholder—one who has acquired shares from an "original" stockholder—has made no contribution to the corporation, and, regardless of the price he pays, the transaction has no effect on the corporate accounts.

CHAPTER FOUR

Adjustments

The likelihood of external revenue-and-expense transactions fitting into accounting periods varies directly as the length of the period, as we have already observed: the shorter the period, the more imperfect the fit. Periodic adjustments in the form of allocations and accruals are necessary if accounting records are to reflect operating results and financial condition. Internal transactions are required for spreading revenues and expenses over time periods conventionally associated with them. An illustration is provided wherein a number of items in given financial statements are traced back to original book figures by examining the recorded adjustments that preceded the preparation of the statements.

We have already considered certain types of expenditure made for the purpose of acquiring goods and services that yield benefits to the purchaser over different time periods. A machine, bought today, may through use yield services for many years; merchandise purchased in a past period may not yet be converted, through sales, into cash or promises of cash; and so on. Our object now will be to describe several common varieties of period adjustments, including the types mentioned in the preceding chapter, by looking back from endproduct (end-of-the-year balance sheet) to source. This will also enable us to review some of the concepts and terms we have discussed in the first three chapters.

An example of financial statements after adjustment

A is the proprietor of a retail enterprise in which he invested $50,000 in 19-2. Its sales for the past calendar year (19-6) exceeded a quarter of a million dollars; these resulted in earnings of something more than a tenth of that amount. A's general ledger at the beginning of 19-6 contained the items making up the balance sheet issued as at that date. During the year only cash receipts and cash disbursements were posted to the general ledger. Shortly after the end of the year an outside accountant was called in to prepare financial statements; at the conclusion of his work he left a series of adjusting entries to be "spread" on the records by the bookkeeper. When these entries had been journalized and posted to the general ledger, the latter was in agreement with the accountant's year-end financial statements which, rounded off, appear on the next page.

53

A, a proprietorship
Income Statements—Years ended December 31, 19-5 and 19-6

	19-5	19-6
Sales	$249,000	$256,000
Operating costs:		
Merchandise sold	$131,900	$141,550
Clerk hire	52,000	52,300
Rent	24,000	24,000
Fixtures writedown (depreciation)	5,800	6,600
Bad debts	2,490	2,560
Fire insurance	730	680
Other insurance	510	520
Interest (less interest incomes of $150 and $160)	500	390
Total expense	$217,930	$228,600
Net income	$ 31,070	$ 27,400

A, a proprietorship
Balance Sheets—December 31, 19-5 and 19-6

Assets	12-31-19-5		12-31-19-6	
Cash		$ 15,400		$ 19,100
Customers unpaid accounts	$ 12,000		$ 22,000	
Less estimated uncollectibles	1,300	10,700	1,500	20,500
Customer 4% note		4,000		3,500
Merchandise inventory, at cost		42,300		48,000
Unexpired insurance		1,200		1,300
Fixtures, at cost	$ 66,000		$ 66,000	
Less portion expensed	23,100	42,900	29,700	36,300
Total assets		$116,500		$128,700

Liabilities				
5% loan from *B*, including accrued interest		$ 12,300		$ 10,250
Accounts payable (merchandise)		24,640		31,180
Salaries unpaid		1,910		2,330
Rent payable		2,000		2,000
A's account:				
Original investment in 19-2	$ 50,000		$ 50,000	
Accumulated earnings	77,450		104,850	
Accumulated withdrawals	−51,800	75,650	−71,910	82,940
Total liabilities		$116,500		$128,700

Cost of merchandise sold

1) Purchases of merchandise first appear in A's records when merchandise bills are paid. For each such payment throughout the year, we may assume that a single account entitled Merchandise Purchases[1] has been debited (net of all discounts) and Cash credited. At the end of the year the accountant found it necessary to add to the purchases account unpaid bills of $31,180 for merchandise already received and not paid for, with a corresponding credit to Accounts Payable. And since merchandise bills paid during the year included a number of deliveries completed but not paid for in the preceding year, the Purchases total was reduced by the corresponding liability ($24,640) at the end of the preceding year. This reversal of last year's accrual was accomplished by debiting the payables account which had remained unchanged since the beginning of the year, and crediting Merchandise Purchases. An alternative of these two transactions would have been to telescope them into a single transaction, debiting Merchandise Purchases and crediting Accounts Payable for the difference ($6,540). Merchandise Purchases, adjusted for the opening and closing amounts of unpaid merchandise invoices, now stands with a total representing merchandise *received* (but not necessarily sold) during the year.

2) This was not enough. Another adjustment is called for if we are to determine the cost of merchandise *sold* during the year. For small retail establishments recording the cost of individual sales as they are made would require a much too elaborate process of recordkeeping. The customary alternative is an annual merchandise inventory: the counting, listing, pricing, extending, and totaling of all individual salable items on hand at the end of each year.[2] This was done in the case of A, and the balance sheets show $42,300 and $48,000 as the amounts of these inventories at the end of 19-5 and 19-6. Two adjustments were made transferring the beginning inventory ($42,300) to Merchandise Purchases, and transferring from

---

[1] Capital letters are employed here to signify the names of ledger accounts where the word "account" has been omitted. This practice is not followed in the case of titles appearing in financial statements; these are regarded as descriptive and not necessarily coinciding with ledger names.

[2] Estimated inventories are also possible, especially for interim statements.

Merchandise Purchases the year-end inventory ($48,000) to the inventory account. Here again, the alternative of these two internal transactions could have been but one: a debit to the inventory account for the difference ($5,700), with a credit to Merchandise Purchases of an equal amount. The balance in Merchandise Purchases[3] is now the *cost of sales* for the current year, and this amount we find reported in A's 19-6 income statement.

Let us now determine by a backward look what we might expect A's books to have shown as cash paid out during 19-6 for merchandise purchased in 19-6 and 19-5. We must bear in mind that the general commercial practice of paying for goods or services may involve a delay of several days or weeks between the time the commodity or service is received and the time[4] the recipient pays for it; also that the purchaser must "stock up" on merchandise or, in the case of a manufacturer, on raw materials, parts, and supplies—that is, he must carry as "inventory" quantities of his purchases for widely varying periods of time before they can be processed or sold.[5]

Making use of the figures we have been discussing, we can make the following "backward" analysis:

[3] This balance could have been transferred to a *cost-of-sales* account, but in this instance nothing would have been gained by so doing. The merchandise-purchases account has become a cost-of-sales account; but since everyone understands its significance, we do not need to relabel it.

[4] A *cash discount* of one or two per cent (sometimes more) is often offered by the supplier as an inducement to his customer for payment within a specified discount period of days. The proffered percentage deduction and the length of the discount period vary considerably, although we will find them fairly uniform for a particular class of commodity; competition between suppliers is always a factor. Some purchasers (who qualify as "good" customers) ignore the discount period allowed by their suppliers and deduct the discount anyway. This may happen where a purchaser has arbitrary "payment dates"—for example, the tenth of each month.

[5] Minimizing the quantities and hence the investment in an inventory containing thousands of different kinds of commodities is a major management problem in both small and large enterprises—a problem to the solution of which mathematicians and machines have in recent years been applying themselves. A 60-day (or even larger) supply of some items will be necessary where suppliers are located at distant points, or where, to benefit from competitive prices, time must be allowed for securing bids from a number of possible suppliers, or where the items must first be manufactured by the supplier. In constrast, only a few days' supply may be required for small or fixed-price items that are available locally.

Cost of merchandise sold during 19-6,		
as reported above		$141,550
Reversal of inventory adjustments:		
End-of-year inventory	$ 48,000	
Beginning inventory	−42,300	5,700
Merchandise received (paid and unpaid)		
during 19-6		$147,250
Reversal of payables adjustments:		
End-of-year merchandise payables	$−31,180	
Beginning merchandise payables	24,640	−6,540
Cash paid out for merchandise (= purchases		
of 19-5 and 19-6 paid for during 19-6)		$140,710

The figure we have now arrived at in this way can seldom be obtained (admitting that there is any reason for doing so) from financial statements because the balance-sheet item of current payables is usually a conglomerate of numerous types of costs incurred but not yet paid for; in practice, if cash paid out against purchases is a figure regularly required, the form of journal in which cash or purchases are first recorded can be adapted to provide a running total for the month, year, or other period as desired, or, even better, the split-account procedure, which we will examine in the next chapter and illustrate at full length in Chapter 14, can be followed. Our reason here for the "backward look" is to enable us realistically to interpret the principal items commonly found in financial statements, with the aim of forming a first-hand acquaintance with the transactions of which they are composed.

A *perpetual inventory* is one that is kept current at all times by recording prices and quantities of items received into stock, and by "pricing out" on the same basis quantities as they are put into production, or finished stock or merchandise as it is sold. In a manufacturing operation this often involves many thousands of inventory types, a storekeeper with a number of assistants, the keeping of "minimum-maximum" records that reflect quantities on hand, and any of a varied assortment of electronic devices now available to speed the process of recordkeeping and reordering. But even here periodic physical counts must be made because of spoilage, pilferage, inaccurate counting during the year of additions and withdrawals, and other types of errors which at times neither men nor machines can avoid.

Other adjustments

3) Salaries of clerks were paid on the first and sixteenth days of each month for services rendered during preceding 2-week periods. This practice required adding (debiting) to the salaries account the two-week payroll ($2,330) for the last half of December, at the same time crediting Salaries Unpaid (instead of Cash). The corresponding accrual ($1,910) at the beginning of the year was transferred (credited) to the expense account. Following the lead of the preceding paragraphs, the reader may readily verify the figure of payrolls actually paid during the year ($51,880).

Payroll deductions which accompany all salary and wage payments today are not illustrated here in the interest of keeping our specimen accounts on a simple basis. If in the second December payroll-tax deductions of $100 had been made, the full $2,330 would have been debited to Salaries, but the liability credit would have been split between Taxes Payable ($100) and Salaries Unpaid ($2,230).

4) The same procedure is applicable to rent: here, although monthly rentals are normally paid in advance, it appears that the rent paid each month relates to the month preceding. No adjustment was required since the accrual at the beginning of the year is also the required accrual at year's end.

5) Fixtures, all of which had been purchased at the outset of the business, were being expensed (*depreciated*) at the rate of one-tenth each year. At the end of 19-6, four and one-half years of writedowns had been accumulated. The year's writedown was effected by charging (debiting) the expense account and adding (crediting) $6,600 to Fixtures Expensed (or Accumulated Depreciation) which has had the effect of raising the accumulation from $23,100 to $29,700. We have already applied the word "depreciation" to this expensing operation; we will have a great deal more to say on this subject in Chapter 6.

6) All sales we may assume were credit sales. In every sizable group of receivables, experience tells us that at least a few will be uncollectible. We cannot positively identify the particular accounts that will not be collected; if we could, we would eliminate them immediately. Hence we must rely on a percentage factor or on some

other estimate dictated by experience. Bad-debt estimates were made and recorded here in amounts equal to 1% of each year's sales. An *allowance* account[6] had been provided in A's records for receiving the credit accompanying the charge to expense. In providing for bad debts, the effort is to regard the amount as an expense of the period in which the need for the provision is recognized; since the estimate may, for one thing, be based on economic conditions arising during the period of the estimate, the provision may not coincide with the period in which the sale is recorded or with the period in which the bad debt can be identified.

For the year 19-6 a provision of $2,560 equal to 1% of sales was debited to expense and credited to the offset account. This raised the total amount from $1,300 brought over from the preceding year to $3,860. Inspection of the account balance indicates that during the year uncollectibles of $2,360 must have been identified and eliminated,[7] leaving a balance of $1,500 to be carried forward into 19-7.

7) Let us assume that we have been told that the unexpired-insurance figure carried over from the preceding year represented a premium balance of $1,200 on a five-year policy dating from the beginning of 19-5 and that at the beginning of 19-6 additional fire insurance covering a three-year period had been taken out, the premium being $600, along with a one-year policy with a premium of $180 which had been charged to Other Insurance. Arithmetic gives us 300 + 200 + 180 or $680 as this year's fire-insurance expense. Short-term premiums accounted for the other types of insurance carried. Unexpired Insurance thus becomes 1,200 + 600 − 300 − 200 = 1,300.

8) Interest income, credited to interest expense during the year,[8] was $160, or 4% of the customer's note held at the beginning of the year. This and the balance of the note at the end of the year leads to the inference that $1,000 and the $160 had been collected by A by the end of December.

---

[6] Also known as an *offset, adjunct, valuation, reserve,* or *absorption* account. This varied series of names obviously reflects attempts to provide a descriptive title. It is also possible to record the credit in the receivables account itself; but since the particular items eventually to be recognized as bad debts cannot yet be identified, confusion would arise from having the balance in the receivables account stated at a figure less than the total of the "open" items.

[7] By debiting the amounts to the offset account and crediting Receivables.

[8] It would have been better, perhaps, to provide a separate account for

9) From the amount of interest expense, $550, and the balance-sheet information on the 5% loan payable,[9] we can deduce the following: the note to *B*, with a $12,000 unpaid balance at the beginning of the year, was paid in part ($2,000 at the middle of year) along with a year's accrued interest of $600; at the end of the year a half-year's interest has accrued on the balance of $10,000. We now have the three ingredients of interest expense for 19-6: 600 − 300 + 250.

A series of adjustments has thus been incorporated in *A*'s financial statements; they are typical of those made in business organizations of this size at both month-ends (a preliminary for monthly statements) and year-ends. Often the month-end merchandise inventory is estimated, especially where there are many varieties and prices involved; the cost and time required for taking interim (intrayear) physical inventories would usually be prohibitive. Perpetual inventories are rare in smaller retail businesses.

Summary of adjustments

Another way of looking at periodic adjustments is to bear in mind that a more exacting booking of accruals would call for day-by-day entries of wages, rents, interest, depreciation, and other overlapping items; obviously, impractical procedures would be involved, and no comparable benefit would be yielded thereby. Only at the end of accounting periods—when financial statements are prepared—are adjustments necessary so that the books of account may provide a backing for the statements; if at odd times interim statements or the amounts of certain accruals are called for—which occasionally happens—estimates of the actual adjustments required can usually be provided without difficulty.

We may now summarize the adjustments made on *A*'s records at the end of 19-6:

---

interest income, but the amount here is relatively small and the entries few; hence the practice would not be objected to by most accountants, as long as the amount is disclosed, as here, in financial statements.

[9] Here again, the combination of two types of transactions in a single item does not reflect the more precise practice; yet both the booking of these items and their presentation in the financial statements can be condoned because of the small accrual involved. An outsider, looking at the comparative statements would readily observe in both the portion of the total (2½%) represented by the included interest.

Purpose of adjustment	Accounts debited	Accounts credited
1) Transfer of amount owing on merchandise purchases at January 1	Accounts payable	Merchandise purchases
2) Recording unpaid merchandise received but not paid for at December 31	Merchandise purchases	Accounts payable
3) Transfer of January 1 inventory which has either been sold or is on hand at end of year	Merchandise purchases	Merchandise inventory
4) Setup of inventory at December 31	Merchandise inventory	Merchandise purchases
5) Unpaid salaries at January 1	Salaries unpaid	Clerk hire
6) Unpaid salaries at December 31	Clerk hire	Salaries unpaid
Rent unpaid: no adjustment since the amounts at beginning and end are the same; cash paid out during year is the exact equivalent of rent expense for year		
7) One-tenth of fixtures expensed	Fixtures writedown (depreciation expense)	Accumulated depreciation
8) Bad-debt provision estimated at 1% of sales	Bad debts	Allowance for bad debts
9) Fire (and other) insurance	Insurance expense	Unexpired insurance
Interest received on customer's note to December 31, 19-6; no adjustment required since cash received coincides with interest earned during year		
10) Half-year accrual of interest expense on 5% loan	Interest expense	Loan payable

In larger organizations, adjustments (1) and (2) would be unnecessary where the recording of unpaid bills follows their approval for payment; in such cases the asset or expense is debited and Accounts Payable is credited, regardless of the time of payment; when the bills are paid, Accounts Payable is debited and Cash is credited. Some accountants would regard the immediate recording of approved expense bills as indispensable to the concept of accurate accounting: they might even question the propriety of calling these two items *adjustments*. But if we broaden our definition to include any and all end-of-period modifications of the accounts, criticism will not likely arise, especially if simplicity in record-keeping is achieved and if at least once each year systematic and complete adjustments bring the books into agreement with financial statements that reflect financial condition and operating results.

Timing the adjustments

In every organization the character of the *end-of-period adjustments* is anticipated at the time its accounting system is in the planning stage. Sources of information would be specified, responsibilities of designated persons for preparing basic data for adjustments would be indicated, and deadlines for the completion of the data would be established. The last-named feature is of particular importance. Adjustments must be timed; the figure for depreciation expense, for example, can as a rule be computed and entered on the records in mid-period. Other items, especially those involving estimates, can likewise be determined and recorded substantially before the end of the accounting period. And, under any well-integrated plan of accounting, there should be no *preclosing* for external transactions; sales and costs should include all transactions through the final day of the accounting period. Speed as well as accuracy is of the essence in preparing financial statements. Adjustments, under adequate planning, should never become stumbling blocks. We will give further emphasis to these points in a later chapter.

Adjusting the cash basis

In furthering our study of adjustments—and of the accounting process generally—we can, for the moment, look at the *accrual basis* of accounting as an adjusted *cash basis*. Understanding statements built up exclusively from cash receipts and disbursements requires no knowledge of accounting; with a preconceived, agreed classification of transactions we could proceed to identify each cash receipt and each cash disbursement with a particular class, and accumulate class totals. In preparing a budget it is necessary to project the amount of cash required for financing proposed operations. And because cash is the ultimate resolution of all external transactions, and because one must always have enough funds on hand when the time comes to pay his bills, analyses of past as well as projected cash income and outgo can be helpful management guides.[10]

To demonstrate the interrelated character of the two bases, let us, then, take the point of view of the accountant called in to prepare *A*'s financial statements and work from *A*'s balance sheet at the beginning of 19-6 and from a 10-item breakdown of *A*'s cash receipts and disbursements for that year. We find that the accountant in this instance has prepared only six adjustments. Since nearly all the figures making up the adjustments are the results of arithmetic computations we have already made, along with a few new facts, the accountant's worksheet and a digest of the explanations he has provided will tell us his story. If the reader will carefully follow through these explanations, he will have learned, through this simple illustration, the essential differences between the cash and accrual bases of accounting in most kinds of organizations.

The form of the worksheet on page 64 betrays the typical accountant. The main heading identifies the organization, the purpose, and the period of time it covers. Horizontal subheads relate to broad classes of transactions, and the vertical headings to accounts or other detail being analyzed—or, in this case, reconstructed. Credit items are preceded by minus signs to distinguish them from debit items when both appear in the same column,[11] but where this results in too much crowding, two columns (here illustrated by money columns 4 and 5) may replace the one. Note that the end-product of this worksheet is money column 6 each item of which is a crossfooting of the other columns; note, too, that the footing of each vertical column is given. Those who prepare worksheets of this type always foot them in these two directions in order to insure clerical accuracy.

Cross-relations between real and nominal accounts are of special interest. We did not know originally, from the information supplied in the preceding illustration, to which account merchandise purchases had been originally charged. It could have been the

---

[10] Statements of "cash flow" are illustrated in Chapter 14.

[11] Accounts with credit balances appearing in the same vertical column with accounts having debit balances can be earmarked in a variety of other ways: by printing them in red, by enclosing them in brackets, by following or preceding them with an asterisk, and, where the statement is printed, by using italics. At the expense of a wider form, separate debit and credit columns could also have been provided for "opening balances" and "adjusted accounts."

A, a proprietorship

Transformation of cash basis to accrual basis—Year 19-6

Account	Cash transactions during 19-6 Disbursements	Receipts	Opening balances	Adjustments to effect accrual basis Debit	Credit	Adjusted accounts
Cash	−240,600	−244,300	15,400			19,100
Receivables			12,000	a) 10,000		22,000
Allowance—bad debts			−1,300		a) 200	−1,500
Customer note			4,000		a) 500	3,500
Inventory	140,710		42,300		b) 135,010	48,000
Unexpired insurance			1,200	c) 100		1,300
Fixtures			66,000			66,000
Accrued depreciation			−23,100		d) 6,600	−29,700
5% loan	2,000		−12,300	e) 50		−10,250
Accounts payable			−24,640		b) 6,540	−31,180
Salaries unpaid			−1,910		f) 420	−2,330
Rent accrued			−2,000			−2,000
A's investment			−50,000			−50,000
Prior profits			−77,450			−77,450
Withdrawals	20,110		51,800			71,910
Sales		244,140			a) 11,860	−256,000
Cost of sales				b) 141,550		141,550
Clerk hire	51,880			f) 420		52,300
Rent	24,000					24,000
Depreciation				d) 6,600		6,600
Bad debts				a) 2,560		2,560
Fire insurance	600			c) 80		680
Other insurance	700				c) 180	520
Interest expense	600				e) 50	550
Interest earned		160				−160
Totals	0	0	0	161,360	161,360	0

Explanations of adjustments:

a) Cashbook totals of receipts from customers were $244,140; of this total $10,800 applied to sales made in prior years, including a payment of $500 on the note from a customer. Customers balances of $510 held over from 19-5 proved uncollectible as did $1,850 from 19-6 sales. Remaining uncollected at the end of the year were 19-6 sales to customers amounting to $20,810. The amount for 19-6 bad-debt expense was based, as in previous years, on 1% of the year's sales. From this information we can convert to an accrual basis as follows:

    Current sales = 244,140 − 10,800 + 1,850 + 20,810 = 256,000
    Customers' accounts = 12,000 − 10,300 − 510 + 20,810 = 22,000
    Allowance (reserve) for bad debts = 1,300 + 2,560 − 510 − 1,850 = 1,500

b) Payments on purchases, $140,710, included the liquidation of the preceding year's unpaid bills of $24,640 but, of course, did not include the corresponding unpaid purchases at the end of 19-6 amounting to $31,180. Since the inventory at that time amounted to $48,000,

    Cost of sales = 140,710 − 24,640 + 31,180 + 42,300 − 48,000 = 141,550

c) Unexpired insurance premiums of $1,200 remaining from the preceding year were augmented by a three-year premium of $600 and a one-year premium of $180 at the beginning of the year. Hence,

Fire insurance expense = 1/4 of 1,200, + 1/3 of 600, + 180 = 680
Unexpired premiums = 1,200 − 300 + 600 − 200 = 1,300

d) Since there had been no change in fixed assets during 19-6, annual depreciation of 10%, or $6,600, involving no cash, is charged to expense.

e) Interest paid, amounting to $600, includes the accrual of $300 at the end of the preceding year, but excludes the accrual of $250 at the end of the current year; therefore,

Interest expense = 600 − 300 + 250 = 550

f) Similar to the preceding item, salaries paid must be adjusted for the two year-end accruals including $2,330 at the end of 19-6:

Salaries (clerk hire) paid = 51,880 − 1,910 + 2,330 = 52,300

inventory account (as it turned out to be), a merchandise-purchases account (which we had assumed), or a merchandise-sold (cost of sales) account. Any of the three would be acceptable, provided a consistent practice had been followed. If perpetual inventories are maintained, purchases would always be charged to the inventory account, as in the illustration, and issues therefrom (sales at cost) would be credited to that account, in which case the ending inventory would be the account balance. Here, as in most smaller enterprises, merchandise sold or cost of sales is the residual figure: purchases adjusted both by beginning and ending physical inventories and by unpaid merchandise bills covering items included in the physical inventory count or among goods already sold.

Summary

We have now had a closer look at the accounting structure: in this instance, that of a simple retail concern which has followed straightforward bookkeeping procedures. The accounting process illustrated involves the combination of external and internal transactions, the latter consisting mostly of accruals and other adjustments at the beginning and end of the accounting period. We have also observed how a summary of cash receipts and disbursements can be converted by adjustments into an accrual basis of accounting. Larger organizations require more numerous and more intricate adjustments, but they bear close generic relationships to those we have illustrated here. Finally, planning for adjustments speeds their preparation and entry in the records, thus contributing to the prompt issuance of financial statements.

CHAPTER FIVE

The General Ledger

Most important of all accounting records is the general ledger. It features all accounting systems, whether the organization be a business enterprise, a nonprofit institution, or a governmental subdivision. Every step in the accounting process contributes and is subsidiary to it. It is the final repository of every transaction and, in turn, the source and immediate backing of the figures that appear in financial statements. Current practice requires that annual financial statements be in agreement with the general ledger. Its form is flexible. It may contain mostly control accounts. At this stage it is of importance that we envisage the effects of any given transaction on general-ledger accounts.

General ledgers have already been referred to and their function briefly described. Our purpose now is to amplify what we have already covered, examine a representative general-ledger trial balance, and trace characteristic relationships between accounts in order that we may better understand the source of financial statements and how they are built up from transactions.

The general-ledger perspective

The general ledger may be viewed from several approaches:

1) It ordinarily contains relatively few accounts, most or all of which are summary accounts supported by subordinate (subsidiary) ledgers. If a single receivables-from-customers account is found in a general ledger, it can almost certainly be assumed to be a *control account:*[1] i.e. an account the balance of which equals the total of a group of accounts maintained in another record under the names of individual customers. Inventory, fixed assets, and payables are other control accounts commonly found in a general ledger.

2) As the "top" financial record, the general ledger serves as the intermediary between journals and financial statements, both

[1] A control or summary account contains all the debits and all the credits that are posted to the *detail accounts* in the *subsidiary ledger* that supports it, the only difference being that the control account is likely to receive these debits and credits in the form of periodic totals of books of original entry, whereas the subsidiary ledger receives the same debits and credits in detail throughout the period.

internal and external, just as a journal serves as a waypoint between individual transactions and the general ledger. The debit and credit of every transaction, even the smallest, find their way through these two stages to the ultimate output of the accounting process—financial statements.

3) Because of its importance in the hierarchy of accounting records, the general ledger is usually kept by or under the immediate supervision of the controller. Totals of external transactions are posted to general-ledger accounts, as a rule each accounting period, as are internal transactions such as income and expense accruals, and prepaid-expense amortizations. These actions are followed by an *abstract* or *trial balance* from which financial statements are prepared. The "adjusted-accounts" column on page 64 may be presumed to be a listing of balances of general-ledger accounts.

4) The nominal income and expense accounts in a general ledger are eliminated (or "closed out") only at the end of a fiscal year. In the elimination process, revenue items are debited and expense items credited in amounts equal to their totals for the period. If the revenues have exceeded the expenses, a *net profit* has been earned; if the reverse is true, a *net loss* has been sustained. The net profit is credited or the net loss is debited to a retained-earnings account, as previously described. The whole "closing" operation can be accomplished by a journal entry similar to the one that might be employed in the illustration appearing in the preceding chapter:

December 31, 19-6

Sales	256,000	
Merchandise sold		141,550
Clerk hire		52,300
Rent		24,000
Depreciation		6,600
Bad debts		2,560
Insurance		1,200
Interest		390
Accumulated earnings		27,400
Income and expense accounts for year		
closed out to Accumulated Earnings		

Only one of the nine accounts affected by this entry now remains open: the accumulated-earnings or earned-surplus account.

5) The general-ledger pages on which the real accounts appear

may be renewed each year (with remaining balances as the first postings thereto) or continued in use until they are filled, at which time they are removed to a *transfer* ledger. If renewed annually, the old sheets may be closed by a formal journal entry crediting the assets and debiting the equity accounts.[2] The nominal-account pages of the ledger also find their way into the transfer ledger, usually *in toto* after the annual closing.

Like other accounting records, the form of the general ledger and the methods followed in maintaining and renewing it vary widely. Because of the small number of items carried to it and because of the importance of each item, it is often hand-posted where other records are kept on machines. There are no standards except that the mechanics adopted must assure the accuracy of postings, and a good "audit trail" must always be laid as the postings take place. Often, explanations are at the same time written into the general ledger indicating the nature of less routine postings. This practice may he helpful where accounts are subject to frequent analysis. A code may be devised for explanations in order to minimize the posting burden. Every public accountant in examining his client's records hopes to find general-ledger postings accompanied by intelligible explanations; the detail of tracing postings may be simplified thereby, and, where the nonroutine components of the accounts are numerous, sampling methods for testing postings may be more readily employed.

To illustrate the infinite variability of the general ledger and the practices surrounding it, the author can cite a somewhat extreme example from his own experience where as controller he was free to choose both form and method. The general ledger he devised contained approximately 1,500 accounts of the following categories:

Asset	40
Liability (equity)	30
Revenue	30
Expense	1400

[2] An annual closing entry balancing each real account—reducing its balance to zero—was once a "must" for every general ledger. So formal and circumspect was this entry that its publication as a "balance" sheet became a general practice: equities on the left and assets on the right. Today, however, the inherited term "balance sheet" is employed in America without reference to this custom—but British balance sheets still follow the original pattern.

The obvious question, "Why not an expense ledger?" can be answered by pointing out that all the accounts were kept on two bookkeeping machines and that the mechanical methods followed were such as to insure speed in posting as well as accurate monthly balancing. Each account was maintained in duplicate—the original being kept as a permanent general ledger, the duplicate serving as a medium for internal reporting; the accounts were renewed in their entirety each month, prior balances being picked up as the last posting of the month following, in order to provide a monthly transaction total just prior to that final posting.[3]

General ledger illustrated

Next we will examine analytically the trial balance of the general ledger of another imaginary retail business which has just completed its third full year of existence. The situation depicted by this trial balance resembles in many respects the one we have already examined in the preceding chapter; it differs in that here we will trace to source-transactions from the total debits and total credits of the general-ledger accounts. The firm's general ledger contains fourteen accounts, the year-end balances of which are shown in the first column below. Let us assume that an examination of the general ledger has enabled us to present the breakdowns appearing in columns 2, 3, and 4. The breakdown is obtained by merely extracting from each ledger account the opening balance, and then the total of the other debits and the total of the credits. The respective totals of columns 1 and 2 are zero; the total of column 3 might be expected to equal that of column 4; these items the reader may test for himself. The "year's postings" are transaction totals, regardless of source, for the 12-month period that began January 1 and ended December 31. And, of course, the items in columns 2, 3, and 4 crossfoot to column 1.

Let us now follow through on an analysis that an accountant might be expected to deduce from these accounts.

Sales: Sales of 135,700 may well consist of both charge and cash sales, the former a debit to Receivables, the latter a debit to Cash.

---

[3] Other features of this system and many others that we will find in use today included the preparation of a journal (or *backing sheet*) as a byproduct of the general-ledger posting operation, and the preparation of financial-statement items by automatically reproduced trial-balance subtotals.

	1	2	3	4
			Breakdown of accounts	
	Balances in accounts on	Balance on	Year's postings	
Account in general ledger	December 31	January 1	Debits	Credits
Cash	36,000	21,500	124,100	109,600
Receivables	29,800	16,800	125,500	112,500
Inventories	38,300	27,700	97,500	86,900
Fixtures	34,000	36,000	—	2,000
Depreciation accumulated	−5,100	−3,600	300	1,800
Payables	−29,800	−12,200	105,200	122,800
Investment	−80,000	−80,000	—	—
Accumulated profits	−6,200	−6,200	—	—
Sales	−135,700	—	—	135,700
Cost of sales	86,900	—	86,900	—
Salaries	24,700	—	24,700	—
Depreciation	1,900	—	1,900	—
Bad debts	200	—	200	—
Other expense	5,000	—	5,000	—

Since the Receivables debit stands at 125,500, we may presume for the moment that the balance of 10,200 was debited to Cash.

Purchases: The addition of 97,500 to Inventories is very likely to be the year's purchases of merchandise, the opposing credit being the Payables account, or, if purchases had been paid for on receipt, Cash. We will defer this separation for the time being.

Receivables: Receivables account has been credited with 112,500; this amount we might assume represents the cash received "on account" from customers, were it not for the fact that we have in the trial balance the item of bad debts, 200, the opposing credit of which could only be in Receivables. Hence, we may conclude that the cash paid in by the credit customers amounted to 112,300. Combining this with the presumed cash sales of 10,200, we find we have cash receipts of 1,600 not yet identified.

Fixtures and Depreciation: The Accumulated-Depreciation account has been debited with 300 and credited with 1,800. Since the business has completed its third year, the item of 1,800 looks like a third full-year's provision of depreciation at 5% on fixtures of 36,000. But depreciation expense is 100 greater than this provision, the Fixtures account has been decreased by 2,000, the allowance account has been debited in the amount of 300, and we are still looking for the as-yet unexplained cash receipt of 1,600. The very plausible deduction that may now be made is that fixtures having an original cost of 2,000 were sold at the end of the (third) year for 1,600; and since only 300 had been accumulated on this item over the three-year period, a "loss" of 100 is indicated. This item of 100 is, however, not actually a loss; depreciation expense, being an estimate based on the best currently available information concerning useful life at the time a depreciation rate is established, would have been 100 greater if the fate of the retired fixtures could have been anticipated, say, a year in advance. We are, therefore, correct in designating this 100 as an added depreciation cost for the year.

Items not yet Identified. We have not yet indicated the interrelationship of the following items:

	Debits	Credits
Cash	—	109,600
Inventories	97,500	—
Payables	105,200	122,800
Salaries	24,700	—
Other expense	5,000	—

Under Purchases we noted that some items might have been paid for in cash on delivery, and thus might have escaped clearance through Payables. If we assume that unidentified Cash Disbursements, 109,600, over the debits in Payables, 105,200, or 4,400, represents this amount, we are then led to a rational explanation for the remaining items: the credit purchases of 93,100 plus the two expense items of 24,700 and 5,000 then equal the credit total in Payables, thus indicating that salaries and expenses were first credited to Payables when the charges were entered on the books. We may note in passing that most accountants would probably prefer to run *all* purchases through the accounts-payable account to avoid the need for the separate forms which cash purchases would otherwise entail.

As we have indicated before, precise determinations of this kind are not practicable in actual situations where usual methods of keeping accounts are followed; adjusting entries and other types of transactions scattered through the accounts might make any such backward analysis of interrelationships yield only approximate results. The object of introducing them here is to enable us to have a closer look at accounts as transactions subassemblies. As we have noted previously: accounts can be understood by us only when we can clearly comprehend the nature of the transactions of which they are composed.

A public accountant engaged in examining a general ledger often finds it somewhat helpful to extract a trial balance following the form shown on page 71, but he would likely expand the form by providing breakdowns of total debits and total credits by transaction sources.[4] He would trace opening balances to the closing balances in his papers for the preceding year to make sure, for one thing, that all adjustments called for in the preceding audit had been given expression and that no further adjustments of such balances had been added; moreover, a comparison of the debit and credit totals by sources with the corresponding items of the earlier year would give him some idea of variations in transaction volume and would supply him with initial clues as to unusual items during the current year.

Divided accounts

Previously we have noted that a need exists for a running analysis of certain, and, in some cases, all general-ledger accounts. This may be readily accomplished by splitting each general-ledger account into as many parts as there are classes of transactions affecting it. A split ledger page may be provided for this purpose, or, more simply, several new accounts may replace a single account. If the latter alternative had been followed in the general ledger which provided the items making up the trial balance of page 71, the Dec. 31 account balances would have been as shown on p. 74. If some or all of the items normally appearing in a general ledger were maintained on this basis, the number of accounts would of course be multiplied. Against this possible inconvenience would be weighed several advantages: a running analysis would be available for statistical tables in internal reports—particularly those for which volume comparisons are required, and the details would automatically appear for various reports, such as statements of cash flow or

[4] Such an analysis is called a "spread sheet."

	Account total	Trial-Balance subtotals
Cash, opening balance	21,500	
Cash receipts, cash customers	10,200	
Cash receipts, credit customers	112,300	
Cash, other receipts	1,600	
Cash disbursed, vouchers	−105,200	
Cash purchases of merchandise	−4,400	36,000
Receivables, opening balance	16,800	
Receivables, charges to customers	125,500	
Receivables, collections	−112,300	
Receivables, bad debts removed	−200	29,800
and so on		

of application of funds.[5] A further advantage might lie in the possibility of more readily locating inaccurate postings where a trial balance has failed to balance. Many, perhaps most, accountants would regard the increased bulk that split accounts would add to a general ledger of minor consequence, especially where modern bookkeeping machines are in use. The author has always favored divided accounts in both large and small installations, for both general ledgers and expense ledgers.

The items that make up published balance sheets are general-ledger accounts or, more often, totals of groupings of general-ledger accounts. The mechanics leading up to the production of a finished financial statement are, as we have said, infinitely varied, and the choice of methods is always a matter of convenience; efficiency is usually a minor factor since any basic gain or loss in efficiency by adopting one method as compared with another is likely to be very small indeed.

General-ledger accounts

Accounts finding their way into balance sheets and operating statements usually appear in the general ledger in financial-state-

[5] These are statements, described in Chapter 14, in which balance-sheet changes during a period are reduced to a cash or funds basis, "funds" being any or all of the items normally classified as working capital. The point of interest here is that the cash components of general-ledger accounts are of importance in preparing these statements, and, if not read directly from a trial balance, might have to be obtained from each account by analysis. A split-account trial balance will be found on page 212.

ment sequence: assets, liabilities, revenues, and expenses. The following categories of general-ledger accounts are the most common; for any individual category we display here, there may well be several general-ledger accounts; but as a rule only one item will appear on the financial statements unless some subcategory is judged to be important enough to warrant a breakdown into a number of items:

1) Cash: commercial and savings accounts with banks; petty-cash funds; cash on hand awaiting deposit; cash in transit to bank; special (temporary) deposits.

2) Cash investments: temporary investments of surplus cash awaiting uncommitted future uses other than the liquidation of specific current liabilities.

3) Receivables: accounts with customers including installment accounts and notes; interest receivable on notes; allowance for uncollectibles (a credit account).

4) Inventories: items purchased or manufactured and held for sale to customers; factory work in process; raw materials to be converted into salable products.

5) Prepaid expense: factory and office supplies; unexpired insurance premiums and similar costs benefiting the immediate future.

6) Fixed assets: land, buildings, machinery, equipment, fixtures, all held for use rather than sale; accumulated depreciation (a credit account).

7) Current payables: unpaid creditors accounts and notes; accrued interest and maturing portions of long-term obligations; taxes, usually subdivided into local and Federal; accrued payrolls and other incurred expense—all usually payable within 12 months.

8) Long-term liabilities: mortgages, bonds, and notes payable after 12 months.

9) Net worth: investment of owners; retained earnings.

10) Sales: amounts received or receivable from customers representing goods delivered or services performed during the accounting period; for example, a year.

11) Cost of sales: (retail organizations) cost of merchandise covered by sales above; (manufacturing establishments) raw material consumed, direct labor, shop overhead, in each case that portion applicable to product sold.

12) Sales expense: salaries, salesmen's transportation and other travel costs, displays, sales-office expense.

13) Administrative expense: officers' compensation, office salaries, general office "running" costs, bad debts. (The last-named is often classified as a sales expense or even as a deduction from sales.)

14) Depreciation: additions to fixed-asset writedowns; if small, this item may be included in some other expense account; minor losses and gains on equipment disposals.

15) Financial income and expense: interest and discount (other than cash discounts which are a reduction of merchandise or materials costs).

16) Federal income tax: the tax applicable to business done during the accounting period, but often including minor or even major adjustments for past periods.

Only the broadest aspects of these sixteen categories need be understood at this time; they will be amplified in succeeding chapters. They are presented here so that as our accounting language and concepts are developed, we may relate them back to this initial classification. Of course, not every business or other organization has all of these categories; on the other hand, many will have additional categories. But those listed here are common to most types of commercial operations, and, once a knowledge of the practices surrounding the accounting for the items cited has been acquired, the meaning of the average financial statement will be more readily apparent.

Summary

General ledgers are key records in all accounting installations, and all other records tie in with or are subordinate to them. The routines of adding to their content almost always involve periodic (e.g. monthly) postings of transaction summaries, accompanied by adjustments that make possible the preparation from the general-ledger trial balance financial statements relating to each accounting period. The accounts which together constitute the general ledger will usually be found to fall under the sixteen major classifications we have just cited, and their sequence in the ledger will very likely follow the pattern shown—commencing with cash accounts and concluding with expense accounts.

CHAPTER SIX

Depreciation & Fixed Assets

Depreciation is lost usefulness. In income statements it is displayed as an expense: a periodic allocation of fixed-asset costs. Accumulated allocations appear in balance sheets as a deduction from such costs. The traditional and generally accepted accounting standard is a straight-line allocation. Deviations from this standard, as, for example, those adopted in the interest of reducing income taxes, require disclosure when carried into financial statements. Depreciation may be identified with individual assets or with asset groups and may be charged or credited with what is sometimes regarded as losses and gains on assets retired. Depreciation practices call for top-level judgment and approval, and they may be presumed to reflect management policy.

77

The term "depreciation" is well known to everyone. A man buys an automobile for $3,000. A year later he finds he can sell it for $1,800 cash or trade it in on a new car for $2,000. He tells us his depreciation has been $1,200 or $1,000, depending on whether he happens to be considering a sale or a trade. If he uses the car for business purposes, perhaps he will be permitted by the IRS to deduct depreciation of no more than 20% ($600) from his business income in figuring his yearly Federal income tax. Or, being a thrifty individual, he plans to keep the car for a period of five years at the end of which time he thinks he should be able to dispose of it for $800; he would then probably tell us that under these circumstances the depreciation on his car will be $440 a year. Or, perhaps his accountant informs him that in view of past experience with this means of travel, the new car should be good for 100,000 miles and that thereafter there may be an estimated scrap or junk value of $200; hence, if during the first year the car is driven 12,000 miles, 10.8% of the investment (or 12% of the depreciable base) will have been consumed in depreciation. We thus have annual depreciation figures ranging between $216 and $1,200; and assorted percentages, each being designated "depreciation," relating to the same automobile and to the same one-year period.

The language of depreciation

Depreciation is basically expired utility:[1] a function of assets and asset ownership. All fixed assets other than land resemble the

[1] "Utility," here interchangeable with "usefulness," may also carry with it

automobile in that they have limited periods during which they can be economically employed. Utility is often regarded as a bundle of services. Loss of utility arises, as we shall see, from a variety of causes, several of which may be present at the same time. Depreciation attributable to certain factors other than use is referred to as *obsolescence* or *inadequacy:* terms we will discuss shortly.

In its current employment by accountants, depreciation generally means *loss of cost*. It can also mean a rate expressed as a percentage, as when we say that the depreciation on a given asset is 20% a year, meaning that the asset may be expected to yield services over a period of five years.

A *provision* for depreciation is the portion of the cost of a fixed asset or fixed-asset group that is judged to be an expense for a given period of time; we often refer to such a provision as "depreciation expense" or "depreciation charged off" for the period. We debit expense, and instead of crediting the asset account, we credit an "accumulated-depreciation" or "reserve" account. And when we dispose of the asset, its cost is removed from the asset account along with the sum total, estimated or actual, of the provisions we have been accumulating; if the provisions plus whatever can be recovered from resale or scrap are less or more than the cost, some accountants speak of the difference as the loss or gain from the asset retirement. Thus, if an asset which two years ago cost us $1,000 and has been depreciated at 10% is sold for $700, a "loss" of $100 has been realized if we follow this concept. We have commented in a preceding chapter on the nature and disposal of this so-called loss or gain; further comments appear later in this chapter.

Causes of depreciation

An automobile, as every owner knows, can depreciate from a great variety of causes; there are even more causes for this erosion of cost when we consider the conditions surrounding the uses to which factory machinery and other commercial assets are put. Deprecia-

---

a restricted meaning: usefulness in satisfying the particular need of a particular owner rather than any of the possible needs of an average owner. Thus, a machine may be useful for several purposes; but, in its present position and to its present owner, if none of these purposes are to be served, its utility, expressed in dollars, is no greater than its sale, trade-in, or scrap value.

tion provisions are attempts to match services performed or lost with the portion of the asset investment representing the cost of these services. It is important that those responsible for establishing and maintaining depreciation policy be fully aware of these causes so that periodic depreciation provisions may reflect the present level of consumption or service loss, and so that these provisions may be decreased or increased as changed conditions arise. Sometimes depreciation policy is limited to the following of rules of thumb which when applied over a period of years lead to gross misstatements of operating costs.

The following are the most common causes associated with the depreciation provisions we encounter in practice:

1) *Use*. Assets are, of course, purchased for the use that may be obtained from them. A two-shift employment of a machine would almost certainly increase depreciation as compared with a single-shift use, thereby making necessary a higher depreciation *rate*.

2) *Disuse*. An idle or partly idle machine depreciates also, often as fast as, sometimes faster, than a busy machine.

3) *Maintenance Policy*. The useful life of an automobile, as we all know, is prolonged by careful maintenance. Often a choice must be made between costly maintenance and rapid depreciation attributable to lack of maintenance: the former may be substantially more expensive than the latter. But a low standard of maintenance may, of course, give rise to costly shutdowns and may adversely affect the quality and quantity of a machine's output. This has been a problem of long standing among taxicab owners; in some companies the policy is to dispose of vehicles after 12 months of service and during that period to perform a bare minimum of maintenance work. Comparable policies often govern the maintenance of factory machinery. It is in this judgment area that accountants and engineers can profitably join hands and come up with a common recommendation.

4) *Obsolescence*. Progress of science and the arts prematurely ages many machines. Changes in styling alone impel many people to buy a new automobile each year; in their view, if they were to use the language of accountants, the old car becomes *obsolescent* a few months after its purchase and *obsolete* by the time new models are announced. Automobile manufacturers call this "style"

obsolescence and, as might be expected, do their best—through advertising and "shows"—to promote the idea. For more substantial reasons, one might hope, machinery is regarded by factory managers as becoming obsolescent when new devices appear on the market that are capable of producing improved, faster, or less costly outputs.

5) *Inadequacy.* Loss of usefulness to the owner, which is the usual meaning of inadequacy, may be brought about by numerous causes. Changes in production are a frequent cause; a machine useful in one type of operation may not be readily adaptable to shifts in production methods or to changes in product; or it may be too costly to operate if adapted, and thus become unsuited to a new environment.

6) *Reduction of Use.* A machine may continue to be fully efficient and capable of economically performing its intended function, but where production falls off because of changes in demand, a scarcity arises in the availability of raw materials that can be fed into it, or some unfavorable situation develops over which the owner has no control, the machine may become an unwanted asset, having no more than disposal value to its owner.

The ordinary use to which a fixed asset is put—the use for which it was originally acquired or to which it has been efficiently converted—is often referred to as giving rise to *normal wear and tear.* The other depreciation factors we have just described are by contrast regarded as the cause of *extraordinary* wear and tear. Moreover, "normal" wear and tear as usually conceived includes a "reasonable" factor for obsolescence, since, in this era of rapid scientific development, change—which underlies all obsolescence—must always be reckoned with.

Background for depreciation

The history of depreciation practices offers a tempting field for research that no one has as yet adequately explored. We do not have the space here to attempt any elaborate analysis of how our present-day notions of depreciation have evolved, but since survivals of older depreciation practices are still being encountered, a brief reference to some of them should serve to place our present conventions on the subject in sharper relief.

At the turn of the century, few firms were providing for depreciation; most of those who did made irregular, lump-sum provisions from retained profits which remained in summaries of owners' equities and did not appear as a fixed-asset offset; they were called "reserves." This practice was primarily a precautionary measure designed to assure the retention of earnings within the business and, appositely, the building up of cash balances so that replacements could be purchased.[2] Reserves were thus designed to provide for replacements rather than to measure expired costs.[3] The next step, which carried through the First World War, was to provide regularly for depreciation by applying a "standard" percentage to book costs. Tables of standard rates were published by the Federal Internal Revenue Service and were often quoted in accounting texts. A rate of 5%, for example, was presumed to signify a *life expectancy* of 20 years for a particular asset (rather than a class of assets). But it was not until the middle 30's that it was recognized that the first essential for a depreciation *base* should be a carefully maintained record of the cost of "live" fixed assets, and, still later, that "standard" rates should be recognized as no more than average rates and hence frequently not applicable, in view of the special problems, nearly always present, which tend to make them of limited importance in practical situations.

Today the character of the depreciation problem is recognized as one that may well be found to vary in vital respects from one industry to another and even as between concerns similarly financed and operated within a single industry. Present intent with respect to future use, disposition, and replacement of fixed assets is a matter demanding top-management consideration and control: a matter that involves methods of capitalization, rates, and administration.

[2] Railroads in the nineteenth century had been in the habit of financing replacements through new issues of securities, and not removing items replaced, thus pyramiding fixed assets—and liabilities as well. Few maintained analyses of property accounts that would enable adjustments for removals had it been the desire to do so. As a result, "inventories" of properties were required when, subsequent to 1905, uniform accounting procedures, including periodic "accruals" of depreciation, were instituted by the Interstate Commerce Commission.

[3] An echo of this venerable practice is heard today in statements by the advocates of current values as a depreciation base; but the motive today is the hope of obtaining larger deductions for income-tax purposes, and is thus quite different from that current in 1900.

Capitalization of asset costs

Although current conventions with respect to fixed-asset cost-ing have been discussed elsewhere in this book, it will be of interest to us here to bear in mind certain optional procedures that affect depreciation:

Capitalization Standards. In most concerns it is helpful to set up *capitalization standards,* especially where, as in the case of build-ings and machine tools, small changes are constantly taking place. Such standards generally provide for the capitalization of costs only where they have the effect of enlarging physical dimensions, in-creasing productivity in some substantial way, lengthening future life, lowering future costs, or involving major replacements. At one time the practice was to designate costs of alterations meeting any one or more of these standards as *extraordinary repairs,* and to capitalize them by charging them against accumulated deprecia-tion. This practice is now only rarely encountered, since on finan-cial statements fixed assets are always carried "net," and the result would be precisely the same as charging them to the asset account: for in either case, increased provisions for depreciation would be required in future years to make up for the writedown of the re-serve account, or to provide for the eventual absorption of the fixed-asset addition.

Cost going into fixed assets is the invoiced cost of purchased assets, less all discounts, plus cost of transportation and of installa-tion, the latter made up of direct labor and materials. The cost of fixed assets constructed by the user is ordinarily limited to the outlay for direct labor and direct materials—that is, costs that would not otherwise have been incurred. Overhead on construc-tion is occasionally added, but we will defer further consideration of this item for a later chapter.

Interest on Investment. During an acquisition or construction period public utilities generally capitalize interest on their invest-ment in plant construction, and sometimes other acquisitions, up to the point of time when the item or project is "dedicated" to productive use—a practice followed even though during the period no counterbalancing interest expense has been incurred. This prac-tice, approved by most Federal and state regulatory bodies, harks back to the point of time when this was the custom of some industrial concerns; but private industry discontinued the practice years ago. The result of following this all-but-abandoned theory is a credit to income during the construction period,[4] countered by added depreciation costs totaling the same amount during the years the facility contributes to production. Most accountants consider that this smoothing out of income as between years, although usually minor in amount, is no longer good practice, even where interest is paid during the construction period on sums that are being invested in the construction. Interest is a cost of financing, so the modern view runs: a general expense of carrying on a business, regardless of the purpose for which the money is spent.

Minor Acquisitions. Many concerns do not capitalize fixed assets that cost less than $10, $100, $500, or some other agreed-on figure. Several reasons support this seeming violation of the principles we have been describing:

1) The cost of keeping records for small items outweighs the benefits to be derived from any possible gain in accuracy.

2) A rough equality exists between the outlay for small items and the periodic depreciation on them—adjusted by losses and gains on retirements—that would otherwise be charged to expense. Because no residual costs are carried forward into following periods, there is always an understatement of assets in the amount of the cost of these items, less accrued depreciation. Most accountants hold that this understatement is a minor one which has no material effect on the significant figures of a balance sheet or income statement; some will say that the understatement is a kind of insurance against a possible overstatement through failure to provide for full accruals of depreciation and obsolescence on capitalized items.

3) Assets having but a *short* durable life are often put in this category; small tools having a useful life, say, of two years or less are an illustration. The justification here, even though the amounts may tend to be substantial, is that replacements are constantly being made and that a two-year period is too short a period: that is, if 50% is to be charged off immediately why not 100%? Not a good argument, perhaps, but one often heard.

[4] Such a credit is actually an anticipation of the future earnings that the completed construction supposedly makes possible.

4) Items such as those mentioned in the preceding paragraph have in some instances been given permanent capitalization equal in amount to the average depreciated cost (e.g. one-half) of such items on hand at any moment of time. The figure remains unchanged until a new "inventory" is taken; the old figure is then brought up—or down—to the new level, and the difference is carried to depreciation expense.

Depreciation methods

Depreciation discussions among accountants and management executives are likely to center about rates and "reserves" (accumulations): the former expressed as a percentage to be applied annually to asset costs in determining current depreciation provisions; the latter the repository to which successive depreciation provisions are credited and to which the cost—or a part of the cost—of fixed assets retired is debited. There are many variations in computing and reporting depreciation; and while many of the methods in current use produce during a period of years only minor quantitative differences in overall results, the particular method employed at a particular time and for a particular asset or asset group may be of considerable importance. Whatever the method, it should be applied *consistently* from year to year: a maxim we must respect in considering a selection from among admissible alternatives in accounting procedures generally.

All methods recognize the wasting character of fixed assets other than land, and endeavor in some equitable manner to spread consumable wasting-asset costs over the periods in which the wasting or consumption takes place: during each operating period a portion of the asset cost becomes an expense.

It is always important that every organization have a depreciation policy as well as a capitalization policy which top management actively (not tacitly) participates in establishing. The purpose is to assure consistency, consider tax advantages (if any are to be gained from the way in which the books are kept as compared with practices adopted for purposes of income and property taxes), regulate the studies to be made and the methods to be followed by those responsible for depreciation computations, and provide a basis for the interpretation—by both insiders and outsiders—of recorded and reported amounts. A management-accounting-determined depreciation policy can be a useful management tool in reaching decisions on acquisitions, maintenance, and replacements.

Straight-Line Depreciation. The simplest as well as the most common method of computing the periodic provision for depreciation is the straight-line method: expected life in years is divided into the asset cost (sometimes less the portion that is expected to be recovered through sale, trade-in, or scrap), and the quotient is the amount of depreciation to be provided for each year of the asset's life. One-twelfth of this sum is then taken up each month. The debit to expense is annually eliminated along with other expense accounts, and the monthly or annual credits build up the accumulated-depreciation account until an amount equal or nearly equal to the asset cost has been accumulated. When the asset is disposed of, the amount thus reserved plus whatever is realized from its disposition is set off against the cost, the result being a gain or loss from disposal.

Such is the typical depreciation-recording process. There are numerous differences in application, among them the following:

1) Depreciation commences (a) on the day following acquisition, (b) midmonth during the month of acquisition, (c) at the beginning of the month following acquisition, (d) midyear in the year of acquisition, or (e) at the beginning of the year following acquisition. Correspondingly, depreciation ends (a) on the day of retirement, (b) midmonth during the month of retirement, (c) at the end of the month of retirement, (d) midyear in the year of retirement, (e) at the end of the year of retirement, or (f) before retirement when the full amount of cost has been accumulated as depreciation. Perhaps methods (c) are the easiest to defend; they have obvious practical advantages, are readily understood and applied, and are in common use. We have no theory that would give preference to any of these methods; but once the method selected has been in use several years, both the annual depreciation expense and reserve balance will differ only in negligible amounts from their counterparts under any of the other methods.

A variant of the straight-line method is the "production" method. Here an estimate is made of the total number of production units a machine is capable of turning out over its useful life, and a unit cost or rate is determined; the unit rate is then applied to the machine's production to arrive at depreciation expense. In practice this variant is rarely applied because of the virtual impossibility of determining a machine's total prospective output; where it has been put into effect the results have been found not to differ materially from those obtained by the application of ordinary straight-line methods.

2) Accumulations of depreciation may be made by individual assets. The characteristic method by which this is accomplished is to maintain a card (punched or hand-kept) for each asset: details of acquisition, identification, location, use, and other physical data on one side; and details of cost, repairs, and accumulations of depreciation on the other. The latter three elements supply the detail of an equal number of controlling accounts; and, when retirements are made, the amounts available from the card support closing-out entries including the gain or loss from retirement. Where the number of fixed assets is large, property records of this type involve a volume of clerical labor that many accountants consider unnecessary, since substantially the same results can be secured through group methods.

3) Group methods of depreciation call for collective provisions and collective reserves or accumulations, the latter being limited in number to, say, three or four for each location or plant: one for buildings, another for machinery or each principal type of machinery, another for fixtures, and so on. The *rate* is an average, commencing with some overall engineering or appraisal estimate, and continuing with periodic—yearly or less frequent—studies of the resulting reserve adequacy. Where a rate is carefully determined in the first instance and, thereafter, periodic studies indicate the rate is too high or too low, an adjustment of the accumulated depreciation provisions is *not* made, but a *new rate* for future periods is computed that will spread undepreciated costs over the newly determined average of useful life.[5]

4) Retirements where group methods are followed are disposed of basically in either of two ways. The first is to determine the portion of the reserve pertaining to the retirement along with the salvage yielded by the asset and then to charge any excess of cost or credit any excess of reserve to loss or gain from retirements,

[5] A method for arriving at such a redetermination which has been employed by the author is illustrated in his *Auditing,* 2nd ed., pp. 410-411.

the general practice previously described. This loss-and-gain account is usually best merged with the regular depreciation provision rather than shown separately in the income statement. As we have previously noted, the difference is actually not a loss or gain but the result of providing too little or too much depreciation during the periods the asset has been in use. A few accountants may even regard the difference as an adjustment of past years' profits for the same reason; this practice, however, is now largely discredited in view of the general recognition that a depreciation rate is an average and that a shortage or overage of the type described will normally be offset by "opposite numbers" in the current year's percentage-depreciation provision.

The second group-method retirement practice is merely to offset the cost of the retirement (i.e. original cost less receipts from resale, trade-in, or scrap) against the reserve, with no recognition of gain or loss and without regard for the length of time the asset has been in the depreciation base. This practice has strong statistical support: a "shortage," for example, in any individual case is likely to be offset by an "overage" on some other item; and since the base is larger than that reflected in an annual provision, this practice is superior to that described in the preceding paragraph. The author has advocated this method for many years and in addition has observed over extended periods of time its successful employment in both private business and governmental organizations.[6]

5) Group methods operate best where the number of depreciable units covered is relatively large. They can still be applied to a small number of units—several buildings, for example—but the review of depreciation adequacy must be more frequent, since an unexpected retirement, as through fire, of one of only a few units might require the recognition of a much larger provision during the period of that event.[7]

Depreciation for Income-Tax Purposes. In Federal income-tax returns, amounts greater than straight-line depreciation are per-

---

[6] Where this method of disposing of retirements is followed, periodic reviews are instituted for the purpose of correcting (if correction is found necessary) the rate to be used in determining future provisions; past provisions or accumulations are not modified.

[7] The same result can be reached by charging a portion of the loss directly to depreciation expense.

mitted under existing law. These include, among others, the declining-balance method and the "sum-of-the-years-digits" method. This concession by the Congress has been attributable to the demand for business tax reductions and to the assertion on the part of many businessmen that the provision for depreciation is a provision for replacement without which capital might be impaired. The validity of this approach we have already considered and need not again examine. Many concerns have applied one of these bases for tax purposes but have recorded depreciation in smaller quantities on their books of account. The law does not require that this cause of tax advantage be incorporated in the accounts, the practice differing in this respect from the concession extended taxpayers through the use of certain methods of inventory valuation where the books and tax return must be in agreement.

Computations on the declining-balance basis are the greatest in the first year of ownership and are projected to be the least in the last year of anticipated use. Under current law, the permitted rate may be as high as 200% of what straight-line depreciation would require, except that for property in use before 1954 and used property acquired from 1954 on, the rate may not exceed 150% of the straight-line rate. These rules are likely to change from time to time.

Under the sum-of-the-years-digits method each year is given a weight corresponding to the years that will elapse before the estimated end of useful life. For an asset useful over a five-year period the depreciation that might be taken during the first year would be determined by first computing the sum of the years $(5 + 4 + 3 + 2 + 1)$,[8] then determining the ratio applicable to the first year $(\frac{5}{15}$ or $33\frac{1}{3}\%)$. On the amount remaining for the second year the rate would be similarly computed $(\frac{4}{10}$, or 40% of the new base equal to $\frac{2}{3}$ of original cost; or $\frac{4}{15}$ $[26\frac{2}{3}\%]$ of acquisition cost).

Some accountants do not favor expressing on the books and in reports depreciation in excess of that based on the straight-line method; others prefer (as do many businessmen) to have the books and tax returns on the same basis. In some cases the excess is referred to as "amortization."[9]

Current-Value Depreciation. The urge to secure larger deprecia-

---

[8] Or $1/2n(n + 1) = 5/2 \times 6 = 15$.
[9] This is a general term for any systematic process of diminution.

tion deductions for income-tax purposes has in recent years led to numerous proposals that seek economic justification for regarding accumulated depreciation as a replacement fund, as we have previously mentioned. This movement we will consider further as a current—and unsolved—problem of accounting in Chapter 16.

Summary

Determining the depreciation policy of an individual organization calls for the establishment of judgment factors based on past experience, intended future uses, and possible recoveries from sale, trade-in, or salvage. The group method for accumulating straight-line depreciation is generally favored, but, like other methods, this method requires frequent review and occasional reestimates of future rates: it may even be regarded as a standard. In published financial statements accountants often set forth the depreciation basis and, if it differs in any material way from the straight-line basis, they may convey, in a footnote or otherwise, some idea of the amount of the deviation.

CHAPTER SEVEN

The Balance Sheet

In this and the next two chapters we review principles and practices to which we have already given some attention; we consider also a number of procedures that have primary significance when we are looking at financial statements as reporting devices. Here the whole can be greater than its parts; for when financial-statement components are displayed in close proximity to each other, the impression emerging—the "central" effect—may well be something distinct and apart. In discussing statement components, therefore, we will need to interpret them as sections of a composite picture, and to consider the varied opinions that readers of such statements are in the habit of establishing for themselves and others. Financial statements contribute importantly to our understanding of organizational accomplishments, but they tell only a part of the story. Because of their limitations, we must employ them intelligently and be careful not to read too much out of them. They furnish us with historical data on past performance, but they reveal no more than a surface indication of what to expect in the future.

Informative, easily read financial statements are earmarks of good management as well as good accounting. Financial statements of business concerns tend to be public documents because of their inclusion in reports to stockholders, credit agencies, and regulatory bodies; in the case of a nonprofit enterprise, because of the need of displaying the source and results of its financing; in the case of a governmental unit, because taxes levied must be justified to taxpayers in the form of costs of public activities. In all situations, the basic structure of financial statements is the same: a balance sheet displaying cash, investments, receivables, inventories, prepaid expenses, fixed assets and depreciation accumulations, contributions from outsiders and a surplus or deficit resulting from operations; an operating statement containing gross income, an intelligible breakdown of operating costs, and the excess of the one over the other; and an analysis that links the present balance sheet with its predecessor and with the operating statement covering the intervening period. A fourth (flow) statement is now often added, its object being an overall summary of financial changes during the period covered by the operating statement; because of its close association with forward accounting as well as historical accounting, our consideration of flow statements will be deferred to Chapter 14.

Our object in this chapter will be to describe the more important of the current practices involved in the presentation of published balance sheets. Changes in standards of disclosure have been common in recent years, and more experimentation is to be expected. These have been largely changes in titles, arrangement, sequence, description—all representing differences in emphasis; changes in substance have been few. Perhaps the most important improvement has been in the attention accountants have given to the inclusion of descriptive detail, especially in informative footnotes: mostly embellishments of sideheads providing supplemental information on items having some nonstandard character or subject to some pending change.

Better to picture the relationship of the descriptive material contained in this and the following two chapters, the reader should have at hand copies of two or three annual reports of business corporations to their stockholders. These can be readily obtained without cost from companies any of whose securities are listed on a stock exchange. References from time to time to these reports will provide practical illustrations of common reporting standards observed by accountants and the various forms of disclosures that accompany departures from these standards.

General features

The balance sheet, we must remember, presents us with a vertical cross-section of an organization's assets and equities at a particular moment of time. From another point of view we may say that the amount of each balance-sheet item, without a disclosure to the contrary, is an *average* of transactions that one might expect to find in progress at any point within a short period of time—say a month or two—before and after the balance-sheet date. Published balance sheets are now preferably presented in comparative form, dated at the beginning and end of the period covered by the accompanying operating statement. This practice gives emphasis to the average character of the item amounts that show little change, and prominence to amounts that have changed, the latter of course calling for footnotes or other indications of the reasons for their unaverage character. A balance sheet's characteristics cannot be expected to extend beyond the range of a month or two. Volume growth, market trends, general business conditions, and other factors may cause it to lose its representative character rather rapidly.

If the organization's operations are highly seasonal, the balance sheet may not reflect an average financial condition; for, at the peak of the season, inventories, receivables, and liabilities may be substantially greater in amount, and cash may be reduced to a fraction of its off-season level. Comparative annual balance sheets of business concerns that have adopted a "natural business year" do not bring out the often widely varying employment of capital during the year. A natural business year is one that ends at a time when business activities are at their lowest point in the annual cycle: a point that permits a more leisurely survey and determination of present position and a point where corrections and other adjustments of the accounts are likely to be at a minimum and can be more readily and accurately made.[1]

A consolidated balance sheet, the character of which we will examine in Chapter 10, always bears that title. Without such a designation it may be presumed that a balance sheet represents but one organization.[2] Occasionally a balance sheet is called "Statement of Financial Condition" (or "Position") in an effort to give it a more descriptive label. But the term "balance sheet" has become well established both inside and outside the financial world.[3] In corporate reports to stockholders the balance sheet sometimes follows the income (which we at times will call "operating") statement. Some accountants favor this practice on the ground that the income statement has been described as the more important and "meaningful" of the two statements. But both are minimal essentials to the depiction of an organization's financial affairs; the author has found that some readers look at the income statement first, but that others, possibly an equal number, turn first to the balance sheet.

The arrangement and sequence of items on a balance sheet vary occasionally from that already indicated. The usual form is called the "account" form, assets (debits) being on the left side and

---

[1] An intracycle balance sheet, prepared in the midst of heaviest business activity, and sandwiched between the customary beginning-and-end-of-year balance sheets, would reveal the uses to which working capital has been put and the amount and character of working capital (often supplemented by short-term bank loans) required for peak operations. An interlarded statement of this sort, though adding significantly to financial information furnished stockholders and analysts, is a stranger to annual corporate reports.

[2] The inclusion of unincorporated plants or branches, which does not call for "consolidated" in the title, is also to be presumed.

[3] The term is often applied by persons having little or no acquaintance with accounting to nonmonetary summations of situations involving favorable factors (assets) and unfavorable factors (liabilities).

liabilities (credits) on the right.[4] In this form the total of assets and the total of liabilities (equal in amount, of course) occupy the same horizontal line on the same or facing pages. Occasionally we find balance-sheet sections arranged in the vertical sequence we have already illustrated: current assets followed successively by current liabilities, long-term liabilities, and stockholders' equity. This "statement" form gives the opportunity of displaying the amount of working capital (current assets less current liabilities), but where there are several blocks of additions and subtractions, this form tends to confuse the reader.[5] In the material that follows we will be concerned with the items as they appear on the account form of balance sheet.

Current assets

Similar subdivisions of current assets may be looked for in nearly all balance sheets: cash, temporary investments, receivables, inventories, and prepaid expenses, in that order—the more liquid assets followed by the less liquid.[6] Each asset group can change daily, likewise their relative proportions. Where the custom of paying bills at specified intervals is followed, recurrent drops in the current-asset total may be expected, followed by periods of accumulating profits[7] included in receivables and cash. In a business organization this cycle of intra-current-asset conversions repeats itself every 60 or 90 days or at some other interval to which the operations of the business have become habituated. On the balance-sheet date, therefore, the *mix* of current-asset items is likely to be of little importance when compared with that on a preceding date or with that of a similar enterprise.

A rule of thumb sometimes included in the definition of current assets is that every item to be so classed must, in the ordinary run of

---

[4] We have already commented on this practice in Chapter 3.

[5] The statement form fails also to bring out two important characteristics of financial position: the often complex interrelation of assets and liabilities other than current, and the total of all assets—a figure frequently quoted in the financial press.

[6] "Liquid" in the sense of rapidity of turnover from their present state into a more liquid state (as from inventory to receivables).

[7] Profits, not sales; *costs* of sales result only in transfers from one current-asset classification to another.

events, be liquidatable within a year. Most accountants today take the position that it is the *operating cycle* rather than the year that should dominate this rule—and this may be less or more than one year.[8]

A general standard of valuation applies to current assets: cost, except where evidence (which includes past experience in the case of receivables) exists that realization will take place at a lesser amount.

Cash. Balances of bank accounts, cash on hand awaiting deposit or in petty-cash and change funds, short-term certificates of deposit, and cash in transit to banks or from branches to home office are types of items underlying the single figure labeled "cash." Usually no detail on the makeup of the total is given, and none is needed. The simple word "cash" is always understood to include the items we have cited. Like other current assets, a certain minimum balance of cash is always expected to be on deposit in the bank, but we cannot determine from a balance sheet the amount that would likely be necessary under wholly off-peak or depression conditions, nor can we determine the amount required to tide over peak periods.

Cash balances are sometimes restricted. Accumulations or allocations of cash that may legally be used *only* in paying off an existing long-term indebtedness are not available for everyday operations; they usually appear between current and fixed assets.[9] A similar treatment would be accorded cash from the sale of the organization's bonds or capital stock, whether or not on deposit with a trustee, that legally (or by Board resolution) may be applied only to the purchase of fixed assets, to the retirement of other indebtedness or of equities, or to any other non-working-capital purpose.

Cash advanced to others for various special purposes is generally not classified as such, but rather, if conforming to the character of a current asset,[10] as a receivable.

---

[8] See *operating cycle* in the author's *Dictionary*.

[9] But if the portion of a long-term debt that is maturing within the following 12 months appears as a current liability (a preferred practice), cash to be applied to its liquidation is merged with other current-asset cash and is not earmarked.

[10] That is, likely to be converted into cash within the operating cycle. An illustration may be found in a deposit required on contract bids, returnable when the award is made or at the contract termination. But a deposit re-

Advances of cash in the nature of prepayments for goods or services not yet received are generally included with inventories, less frequently appear as a separate item following cash or as prepaid expenses. If such advances are repetitive in character and within a few months are transformed into goods or services, their inclusion under inventories raises no question of propriety.

Investments. Investments in government securities or in readily marketable stocks and bonds are accorded a position in current assets following cash. To warrant this position, the component items of investment must not be of a permanent nature and must be capable of immediate sale. If the amount of these investments has been irrevocably committed for some purpose, the balance-sheet position will depend on the purpose, as in the case of special cash items already referred to. Investments in sales outlets or other related organizations are not current assets.

Investments classifiable as current assets follow the usual standard of current-asset valuation: cost except where a lower market price is quite certain to be realized; the item caption should always indicate the market valuation, whether higher or lower.

Receivables. Without qualifying details in captions or footnotes, the unqualified term "receivables" as a balance-sheet caption is understood to consist of unpaid customers "30-day" or "60-day" accounts. It may contain customers installment accounts if minor in amount. But if the total of the latter is substantial,[11] they appear as a separate item. In some concerns it is important to list amounts due from the U.S. government, since receipts from such accounts are often long delayed and subject to downward adjustments.

Pledged, assigned, or sold accounts receivable require separate disclosure and description. In all such cases the effort has been to transform the accounts into cash assets by any of the numerous commercially available devices, ranging from selling the accounts outright without recourse to putting up the accounts as a pledge but without transferring the collection function. Here are some typical

---

quired as a condition precedent to doing business in a given community, and not likely to be returned for at least several years, falls outside the current-asset concept and is classified under some other asset category such as "miscellaneous."

[11] For example 20% or more of the receivables total.

captions for this type of account with the author's comments in brackets:

"Equity in installment accounts pledged of $_____" [In this instance the amount carried into the balance-sheet total was 10% of the amount thus shown as "pledged," 90% in cash having been advanced, the creditor acting as collector; the 10% was also paid to the seller (less commissions and other charges) as, if, and when collected.]

"Installment accounts of which a total of $_____ has been pledged as security on bank loans, contra." [Here the bank loans, appearing as a current liability, were about 20% less than the accounts pledged, the latter being earmarked on the seller's books; and as old accounts are collected (by the seller) new accounts were earmarked in such quantities as may be required to maintain the 20% "margin of safety." In this instance the bank takes over the earmarked accounts and does the collecting only in the event the loans are not paid off or renewed, under satisfactory terms, at maturity.]

"Installment accounts, less accounts sold" [The story behind this display was that the seller, who in this particular instance had disposed without recourse of about half of its installment sales as they were made, sustained a discount of approximately 15% on the face value of the sale after adding 20% to the customer's bill; the buyer of the account, known as a "factor," did the job of collection and, in case of failure of the customer to pay, independently repossessed and disposed of the object sold.]

Many varied relations exist between the buyer, the seller, and the financing agent, but the details of the relationship with those who make advances against receivables or buy them outright only rarely appear—and then in a footnote because of the inadequacy of the sidehead. The main emphasis of the accountant is on the collectibility and timing of the items appearing as receivables, with but a secondary concern for the method by which they are being liquidated.

Customers' notes unsecured are not as a rule brought out as a separate item ("receivables" covering both accounts and notes) since in most situations an unsecured note is little more than a formalized account. Even a "secured" note may be worth no more than an open account. Here again the tendency of accountants is to disclose only possibly adverse factors that may affect normal collectibility.

Accounts—or the portions of accounts—due after one year from the balance-sheet date are sometimes segregated from other receivables and shown below current assets; but the practice today is not to make this separation, and even not to display a total of "current assets" where substantial amounts of such items are involved.

Deferred-payment accounts of a department store may constitute a large portion of its outstanding receivables; if so, a separate disclosure of the amount is sometimes required. But if the outstanding "30-day" and deferred amounts have reached stable levels, the information given to the reader by such segregation is limited to noting the relative current volume of the two kinds of sales.

Pending claims and refunds, classed as receivables and representing insured losses, overpayments of taxes, or any of various other items, are occasionally found on published balance sheets. To be justified in the accounts the general rule followed is that the amount shown should not exceed the amount of claims that have reached the approval stage on the part of the insurer or debtor. Where the claim is of a repetitive character, it may be that its inclusion as an asset can be justified by past experience, even though formal approval of the amount has not yet been secured.

Where a business has sustained an operating loss and is entitled [12] to a refund of Federal income taxes relating to the years preceding the year of loss, the claimed refund may not have reached the approval stage, and the description of the item will so state. There are other income-tax situations where the probability of refund allowances is strong enough to justify the inclusion of the claim as an asset; the language accompanying[13] the item gives the basis for the claim and the point it has reached in recovery proceedings.

Allowance for Doubtful Accounts. In a previous chapter we noted the method of allowing for and displaying the possible loss from bad debts. Where there are several kinds of receivables, there may be several allowance accounts, only their combined amount appearing in the balance sheet. Occasionally where installment or deferred-payment accounts are large as compared with other classes of receivables, a showing of their amounts and the allowances provided for each may be of importance.

[12] Under the "carryback" provisions of Sections 172 of the current Federal Internal Revenue Code. If the loss is not offset by the taxable net income of the two preceding years, the unabsorbed portion becomes a "carryover" applicable to the net income of future (up to five) years.

[13] In the sidehead, a footnote, or both.

Allowance provisions, justified by past experiences, usually cover amounts reported as receivable that have been estimated to be uncollectible—perhaps all of some accounts and parts of others. Costs of collection, as a rule are not significant in amount, and are not usually provided for in advance but are classed as expense as incurred. Allowance accounts cannot be identified with individual receivables, as we have previously noted, but serve as a buffer against the whole body of accounts for which they have been created.

The title "Reserve for Bad Debts" is an equally acceptable but now less-used title for the estimate of uncollectibles.

Inventories. Inventories are often designated by words other than the term itself, and in the case of manufacturers there may be breakdowns by principal classes, such as finished product, work in process, raw materials, and supplies—in that order.[14] Retail stores and retail chains usually describe their inventories as "merchandise." The item "supplies," often in the nature of items that will ultimately be classed as overhead, is sometimes found under "prepaid expenses"; usually its position is not of first importance because of its minor character. The inclusion of factory supplies under inventories is given a slight preference by most accountants.

Inventory valuation embraces widely differing viewpoints. There is general agreement that the valuation basis should always be disclosed, but efforts on the part of certain accountants to increase the acceptance of *lifo*[15] has created much uncertainty concerning the long-established basis of "the lower of cost or market." Thus far, only a minority of American business concerns has followed the lifo ideology and then, only because of the lower income taxes that have generally resulted from its use and the vigorous efforts of lifo proponents urging "general acceptance" as a justification for their position. There is some fear of the effect of a general decline in prices which, should it extend back to the basic year, would lead to

---

[14] This is the traditional order of liquidity. In a few instances we will find this order reversed—possibly on the theory, as explained by one controller to the author, that raw materials have had a "more recent" relationship to cash invested. In most situations, however, there may be equally important and equally recent investments of "cash" in the labor and overhead included in the cost of finished product. Moreover, current assets are almost universally listed in the order of their prospective liquidity rather than their acquisition—which would put raw materials at the bottom of the list.

[15] "Last-in-first-out" as compared with the more usual basis, *fifo*, "first-in-first-out."

higher taxes and a loss of the earlier benefits gained. But a far more important consideration that has hindered the spread of lifo is its fundamental illogic: part of the cost of goods still on hand has been written off, and the result has frequently been a gross understatement of financial position. Where the difference between cost and the lifo basis[16] is disclosed in a published financial statement—which has occasionally been done[17]—we are able to make a quick recasting of current assets and net worth; but most adherents of the lifo basis, claiming that lifo is "cost," have rejected proposals for this disclosure. We thus have in such cases a "secret reserve" [18] the extent of which is not indicated to the reader, if, indeed, it is known at times to management itself. Proponents of lifo, in their eagerness to win a tax advantage, minimize or neglect entirely the balance-sheet understatement.

Cost, from which for present purposes, anyway, we may exclude lifo, is the predominant basis of inventory valuation. It takes on different forms such as fifo, average, standard, and retail-method costs, but the application of any of these bases would in most cases yield approximately the same results, the choice of method being largely determined by custom and convenience. The "lower of cost or market" is still cost that can be fairly attributed to the inventory on hand, but the discounting of cost where "market" has been applied to certain items, will be minor in times of stable or rising prices and will normally be limited to items, no longer usable or salable, that can be disposed of only as scrap or its equivalent. Where a sharp drop in prices has occurred, the writedown attributable to the use of lower market figures may be significant and, therefore, an amount deserving of at least a balance-sheet footnote.

Other causes may justify the valuation of specific inventory items

[16] Some proponents of the lifo basis refer to that basis as a variety of cost. Where purchase costs of inventory items have been steadily rising and the inventory has been disposed of at sales prices that are also ascending, the effort to "match" costs and prices has supplied a surface justification for lifo. But this does not carry over into the balance sheet. The lifo method also has the effect of actually concealing profits realized from the sale, for example, of merchandise that has been purchased at prices substantially less than market prices.

[17] Of course, where the difference is substantial, it *should* be revealed, since the reader's interpretation of both earnings and financial position might be materially affected.

[18] A "secret reserve" is said to exist wherever assets are understated or liabilities overstated, thereby giving rise to *under*stated retained earnings.

below purchase cost; these may in some instances take the form of undisclosed writeoffs; in others, they may be expressed in an inventory "reserve" or valuation account. Common justifications of inventory writedowns include overstocking, defects, deterioration, outmoded items, changes in product, and other causes that would make future disposals at past prices unlikely; but any writedown or reserve that would have the effect of providing a "normal" gross profit in a succeeding period is in the nature of a future possibility rather than a condition deserving present recognition.

Prepaid Expenses. When classified as current assets, prepaid expenses consist of goods and services the benefits from which are shortly to be received, "shortly" implying their absorption as operating expense within the ensuing current-asset cycle. Most types of prepaid expenses are recurrent and may be expected to display little variation from one period to another. Unexpired insurance premiums, amortized on a straight-line basis as we have already described, is the item most often encountered. Factory and office supplies, as noted above, are occasionally included under this caption. Other, less frequent, items are prepaid rent and various sorts of expense advances. The latter at one time often included advertising and sales expense pertaining to a forthcoming "season"; but such items have virtually disappeared from published balance sheets, not only because of income-tax advantages from immediate expensing, but also because much of the preparation for an oncoming season is ascribable to customer (goodwill) maintenance— the keeping open of channels of communication with customers: hence a current cost. Where only minor outlays are required for insurance premiums and other prepayments, many business corporations no longer follow the practice of deferring them, especially in case of insurance where a part of the risk is borne by the organization itself.

Before the advent of the U.S. Securities and Exchange Commission, prepaid expenses were classed as a current asset. But the initial SEC standard was a "deferred-charges" section at the bottom of the asset presentation; this included all items of cost, not represented by visible properties, that were being carried over for absorption in subsequent periods. At the time the standard was adopted, a variety of deferred charges could be noted in published balance sheets: fire losses, operating deficits, unusual ("nonrecurring") expenses of all sorts which if charged against current income would purportedly result in an unfavorable showing of profit-making ability, or if carried to retained earnings would have reduced that account to an amount that would leave no margin for dividend declarations. Since then accountants have consistently discouraged loss deferrals; and the reemergence of profitable operations following the Depression has done much to strengthen their position.

Prepaid insurance premiums plus other prepaid expense, normally not involving significant amounts, are now likely to appear as a single total among current assets, with a minimum of accompanying description.

One "deferred charge" still occasionally met with is *unamortized debt discount*—the amount by which the proceeds derived from long-term indebtedness have fallen short of the face value of the evidences of indebtedness. It is usually amortized [19] (by charging expense) over the life of the debt in proportion to the interest paid; on indebtedness payable in installments this would mean a larger writedown in the earlier years of the issue, and a smaller writedown in the later, in step with interest paid.

Long-term investments

A corporation having one or more domestic subsidiaries will nearly always present consolidated financial statements in its reports to stockholders and the public. A common yardstick for determining whether a consolidation is to be made is the ownership of at least 50% of the voting stock. Foreign subsidiaries, even though fully owned, are often not consolidated, although, as exchange rates have become stabilized and restrictions on remittances to parent companies in the United States have been liberalized, the inclusion of foreign subsidiaries in the consolidated picture has become more frequent.

A more or less permanent holding of minority interests of common stocks of other corporations is a fairly common practice where the aim has been to acquire a large enough interest to insure a

[19] Perhaps a better way of describing the periodic charge to expense over the life of the obligation is to regard it as a gradual writeup of the original proceeds to the full amount of the obligation at maturity. An attempt by the American Accounting Association in 1936 to promote the acceptance of this point of view failed, however.

source of supply or a market outlet that would stabilize or provide
a minimum outlet for sales. Here the standard of value is the cost of
the investment, usually without reference to the current market,
where no disposal of the investment in the immediate future is intended; moreover, in holdings of this character, it may be that no
market exists for the stock, or the "free" shares with which a quoted
value is associated are too few in number to have established a truly
representative price.

Fixed assets and depreciation

In the preceding chapter we discussed the various valuation problems associated with fixed assets. The established accounting and
reporting standard accepted by most accountants is cost less straight-
line depreciation: which means that outlays for fixed assets, save
for residual scrap value, are divided into a series of period-expense
items—a span of time-periods extending over useful life. Because of
the desire to maximize tax advantages, the straight-line amortization
of fixed-asset costs has often yielded to accelerated provisions on
tax returns; some concerns, especially those having substantial earnings, have given expression to these amounts in their books of account and reports, although not required by the income-tax law to
do so. We would expect to find the justification for such variant tax
and reporting practices detailed in corporate reports to stockholders, along with the amounts of the excess over straight-line
costs in annual provisions and the accumulated amounts of depreciation. Where these disclosures do not appear, the reader is left with
the speculation of what, if anything, these excesses really represent.[20]

Indicating the basis of both fixed-asset valuation and depreciation
accruals is a minimal standard of disclosure; and where there has

---

[20] A security analyst of the author's acquaintance puts the normal accumulation of depreciation by long-established companies at one-third of cost, the
ratio of any excess amount beyond that fraction to the total accumulation
giving him a basis for reducing the current years' provision to "normal" cost,
and for increasing net income (to aid his estimate of "earning power") by
the same amount. This rough-and-ready calculation cannot be recommended,
however; in some instances, a two-thirds or even greater accumulation of
depreciation can be justified in terms of a remaining *economic* life much
shorter than physical life.

been a departure from usual standards of capitalization, valuation, and depreciation accruals, we would expect that accompanying information—a footnote, for example—would clearly describe the extent of the departure.

Fixed-asset detail on published balance sheets is typically confined to three or four major classifications, priced at cost:[21] e.g. land, buildings, machinery and fixtures, and automotive equipment; there may be an equal number of items of accumulated depreciation with a net amount shown for each in a three-column display; or, less desirably, but one figure for depreciation may be subtracted on the balance sheet from total fixed-asset costs. If the basis of valuation is not disclosed, cost is assumed.

Long-term Leases. Where an important share of the fixed-asset requirements of an enterprise has been financed by outside agencies and has been leased from them, no values will appear within the balance sheet unless the "lease" for practical purposes can better be described as a purchase contract. However, standard practice requires a footnote disclosure of annual rentals, the average lease period remaining, and the aggregate amount involved in any agreements or options to repurchase at the end of the lease periods.[22]

Intangibles. Patents, trademarks, goodwill, and occasionally other forms of intangibles may sometimes be noted on corporate balance sheets, although less frequently in recent years. It is now generally recognized that most forms of intangibles have only speculative value for the future, and that what appears to be an earning power over and above a "normal" interest return on the investment in tangible assets[23] may have been mainly attributable to efforts the

---

[21] Occasionally it will be noted that containers, small tools, and other short-lived, constantly renewed items, for which formal property records have not been deemed necessary, are reported as having been inventoried or perhaps even estimated, the standard of valuation being "depreciated" cost. Without further description or qualification, it may be presumed that the quoted figures would not differ materially from what would have been revealed by quantity-control records. Because of the short lives possessed by such assets, they are sometimes classed as current and included with inventories, especially where they constitute a direct cost element in the determination of inventory values and have been included in billings to customers.

[22] AICPA, Opinions of the Accounting Principles Board No. 5 (1964).

[23] What is meant here may be clarified by an example. Suppose that *A*, a proprietor, has been enjoying an annual net income, after allowing himself

costs of which have been incurred in the year of the excess; in other words, any "excess" profits in the future may point to factors then in existence rather than something inherited from the past. It is for this reason that for Federal income-tax purposes the amortization of purchased goodwill has often been recognized as a cost of doing business: what was paid for is quickly dissipated; what remains is that which is built up and renewed each year.

So-called goodwill from consolidation—the excess of the price paid over book value[24]—has largely disappeared from published balance sheets because of the practice of reducing the investment in a subsidiary to the latter's book value at the date control became effective. The reason behind this practice is the same as that just described: the "premium" over book value which was paid for the subsidiary's stock is a value associated with yesterday's earning power; tomorrow's earning power, whether equal to or greater or less than yesterday's, will flow from the effort then exerted or from conditions that will not be identical with those obtaining in the past.

In some instances the goodwill or other intangibles previously reported will be found to have been written down to the nominal

---

a salary, of $20,000 on a tangible-asset investment (net worth) of $100,000. The *B* Company purchases his business for $180,000 on the following basis:

Fair value of tangible assets, as appraised		$150,000
Annual interest return thereon at 6%	$9,000	
Added management cost above *A*'s salary allowance to himself	5,000	
Excess of profits, which, considering future risks, is capitalized at 20% by purchaser	6,000	30,000
Total price paid		$180,000

B takes up on its books the tangible assets revalued at $150,000 and the intangible, goodwill, at $30,000; immediately after the purchase, the management of *B* finds that *A*'s sales volume cannot be maintained, or that if it is maintained, rising costs (other than those of management) will lower *A*'s rate of net income by an amount as yet undetermined. Under these circumstances the decision is made to amortize the intangible as expense in three annual installments of $10,000 each.

[24] When the balance sheets of two or more related organizations are joined, the investment (asset) of the top organization cancels out against part or all of the net worth (credit) of the one or more owned organizations. But if the cost is greater than the applicable net worth, a "goodwill [or "excess"] from consolidation" arises, as we will again observe in Chapter 10.

figure of $1. The idea has been expressed that this serves as an assurance to the reader that no intangibles have been hidden in other assets. Under modern accounting standards and both internal and external audit procedures, this form of assurance seems hardly necessary.

Except for instances where the items have been reduced to a nominal value, intangible sideheads are expected to indicate the valuation basis (and sometimes the source), together with the amount that has been amortized.

Current liabilities

The principal items among current liabilities that we would expect to find repeating themselves most often, in the sequence usually followed but with much variation in titles, are the following: bank loans, trade creditors (accounts payable), long-term-debt installment obligations falling due in ensuing year, dividends payable, amounts due to employees, income-tax liability, and deferred income. The meanings of these details are largely self-evident, and need little amplification here. They ordinarily represent prospective payments during several months following the balance-sheet date that are ascribable or related to transactions completed on or before that date.

The income-tax liability may not agree with the income-tax-expense item on the income statement for several reasons: it may contain a holdover liability from a preceding year or be a net figure after deducting advance payments during the year. Moreover, the expense item may contain adjustments of taxes of preceding years. Occasionally the liability will include an accrual of income tax on income not subject to tax until some later date, but if this is substantial in amount, and the time of payment extends into the indefinite future, that portion of the liability may be shown as noncurrent.[25]

Deferred revenue is occasionally found on published balance sheets; usually its character is described. Examples are unearned

[25] An example may be found in the amount of current tax savings attributable to substantially larger deductions for depreciation than the depreciation expense as expressed on the books; these savings are set up as current liabilities and currently amortized over the years when depreciation for tax purposes will fall short of book provisions.

profit on installment contracts receivable, unearned finance charges, customer-service prepayments, unearned interest, and periodical subscriptions unexpired. Where the amount deferred has not yet been collected, it is regarded as a valuation account and is normally deducted from the related asset, the asset being shown net.

Long-term liabilities

There are many forms of long-term indebtedness, ranging from unsecured bank loans to first-mortgage bonds and having an interest-bearing characteristic in common. The interest rate, due date (or rate of installment payments), and nature of the security are normally a part of the descriptive sideheads accompanying each such item.

Amounts of long-term liabilities coming due within the 12-month period succeeding the balance-sheet date are usually shown as current liabilities.

Owners' equity

Owners' equity, consisting of capital paid in and undistributed profits from operation, is the final grouping of balance-sheet items. In proprietorships and partnerships the equity of each contributor of capital is usually shown together with his share of undistributed profits. In a corporation the contributed capital will be found under capital-stock and capital (or, better, paid-in) surplus accounts; the following chapter is devoted to the consideration of these accounts.

Summary

The balance sheet is the first of the two most important financial statements prepared from accounting records. It displays the basic elements of the accounting process which we described in Chapter 3: assets and the equities in assets which characterize the existence of artificial persons. The basis of asset presentation is cost less portions of cost that represent the partial consumption of service-yielding assets. Headings, titles, and footnotes play an important part in conveying to outsiders the meaning of assets and equities.

CHAPTER EIGHT

Stockholders' Equity

Contributions in exchange for capital stock, together with profits earned and retained, are the usual components of the owners' equity in business corporations. Our effort here will be to place in perspective the items most often encountered on corporate balance sheets that make up the stockholders' equity. Some practices have survived from periods of less rigorous accounting and no longer serve their intended purposes. The present trend is in the direction of not only clear explanations of whatever form this equity may take but also the simplification of the net-worth structure.

"Stockholders' equity," or *net worth*, the latter a term long (and still) in use by accountants, is made up of capital paid in (contributions by owners) and accumulated, undistributed profits (which, in terms of the source, as we have previously noted, are contributions[1] by customers). Occasionally other items reflecting asset acquisitions or newly developed asset values are included. Net worth is a term no longer in universal use, as it once was, as a balance-sheet subhead, since, under normal accounting procedures, it does not mean the value of the business to its owners, but rather the owners' interest in asset costs. During periods of rising values, such as the present, the substitution of current values for asset costs would in many cases swell the net-worth figure by a substantial amount; hence the search for a more descriptive title. Some accountants feel that progress in this direction has been made by adopting the caption "stockholders' (or shareholders') equity." But as in other situations where word changes have been suggested, the proposed substitution may prove to be an unhappy one: in time, a new crop of implications will begin to be associated with the altered label, and the move to change will be on again. It is possible that "equity," like "worth," will lead to inferences of "value." But our interest here is not to engage in splitting hairs on word preferences, but to know the kinds of items we may expect to encounter in

[1] "By "contributions" of owners to a corporation we mean payments by them to the corporation in exchange for shares of its capital stock. "Contributions by customers" means purchases of goods or services by outsiders which by yielding a profit to the corporation have increased its net worth.

110

corporate practice where these terms appear, and to understand the meaning behind them.[2]

At first thought, the aggregate of contributions by stockholders and retained earnings should present no important problems. But if the reader will examine a few examples of balance sheets and income statements appearing in annual corporate reports to stockholders, he will discover numerous subdivisions and other variations in their presentation that deserve comment. These we will discuss under the headings of paid-in capital, reserves, dividends (cash, in-kind, and stock), and retained earnings (earned surplus).

Paid-in capital

It will not be within our scope here to discuss differences between the legal requirements under state corporation laws as to the necessity for differentiating between amounts paid in by stockholders and other credits to which the equity of stockholders falls heir. Rather we will set forth four standards sanctioned by accountants, the Federal Securities and Exchange Commission, and financial authorities generally with regard to these amounts.

1) Contributions by stockholders (amounts paid in) should remain intact: which is to say that dividends, losses, and other charges should be absorbed in retained earnings or if exceeding retained earnings, be carried forward (as a reduction of stockholders' contributions) for absorption in subsequent periods.

This standard is now seldom violated, although in pre-SEC days it was not difficult to find examples of the charges of the kind we have mentioned deducted from amounts paid in by stockholders, especially where an effort was being made to initiate or maintain periodic dividend payments and no other net-worth accounts with credit balances were available, or to dispose of operating losses in

[2] One is tempted to add that the investor one is fearful of "misleading" by the term "net worth," or, for that matter, "stockholders' equity," or any other term that may be suggested, will undoubtedly have many other, and much greater, difficulties of interpretation to overcome before he can understand a balance sheet. Accountants would be on safer ground by agreeing to rigorous definitions of old terms rather than searching for and hazarding ostensibly descriptive language having a meaning so transparent as to make definition unnecessary. Here, as elsewhere, no precisely applicable term can be found to cover all possible situations.

the early years of a corporation's existence so that the way might be cleared for dividends out of the earliest earnings.[3]

> 2) *The same standard still holds where stockholders' contributions have been in excess of par or stated value,[4] and the excess has been credited to a "paid-in-surplus" (or capital-surplus) account.*

"Paid-in surplus" like "net worth" is a term in common use among accountants, but on published balance sheets we are likely to find any of numerous descriptive phrases taking its place, such as "additional (or other) capital," "capital paid in in excess of par [or stated] value," and "capital surplus paid in." However, the reader should expect to find the same content no matter which caption appears.

> 3) *Stockholders may contribute unequal amounts per share, especially where a period of time elapses between contributions. The standard here remains unchanged, and an altered average of paid-in value per share obtains in such instances.*

Assume that a certain number of shares brought in $12 per share, of which $10 (the par or stated value) was credited to capital-stock account and $2 to paid-in surplus; a year later the issuance of an equal number of shares yielded $16 per share, resulting in a credit of $6 to paid-in surplus.[5] Both old and new shares now have an average paid-in book value of $14 each, and no separation of the two groups of stockholders is made, either in the books of account or in published balance sheets. The justification occasionally offered for this alteration of paid-in-value-per-share is that the original stockholders have "gained" by disposing of a portion of their future prospects to newcomers while the latter have paid a "premium" for buying an equity in an established enterprise. Of course, both the gain and the premium are wholly imaginary; what the shares will

---

[3] Maintaining paid-in capital intact is sometimes referred to as the "trust-fund doctrine" imposed on corporate management.

[4] By "stated" (or "declared") value is meant the amount as determined by the corporate charter or bylaws (occasionally, if permitted under state law and the corporation's bylaws, by the directors) which, in the case of no-par-value stock, serving in lieu of par value as a credit to the capital-stock account, may often be a fraction of the amount paid in. If stockholders' contributions are to be maintained intact regardless of where credited, no useful purpose is served by this split, but the practice continues.

[5] This procedure is not affected by the presence of previously accumulated retained earnings, if any.

earn in the way of dividends or what they might bring if sold on the market (or even if redeemed by the issuer) are dependent on other factors, most of them unknown to present observers.

> 4) *The cost of a reacquired share if less than par or average stated value is charged to the capital-stock account, and the excess of par or stated value pertaining to that share is transferred to paid-in surplus; if greater, the excess of repurchase cost is charged against paid-in surplus, any excess of the latter on an average-per-share basis remains in the paid-in surplus account; but any cost not thus absorbed on an average-per-share basis is, in effect, a dividend and hence chargeable against retained earnings.*

The standard as thus stated applies to both treasury stock[6] and redeemed (and canceled) shares.[7] Basically there is but little difference between the two. Legally, "treasury" shares remain "issued" or "alive" although fully owned by the corporation (the issuer); they can be sold at any price as compared with shares of original issue, which under most state laws would have to be sold at not less than their par or stated value or under various other restrictive conditions. The original notion of treasury stock dates from the days of wildcat mining ventures of the nineteenth century when authorized par-value shares would be issued in their entirety for property or mining rights, thus establishing a "value" for these assets equal to the par value of the stock issued, and then—to raise working capital —part of the shares would be "donated" back to the issuing company for resale to outsiders for whatever cash price or prices could be obtained for them, despite a usually high par-price ratio. Donated shares are now a rarity, but we may still observe repurchased treasury stock in balance sheets, though much less often than formerly.

If treasury shares are being held specifically for resale or for future bonuses, their cost is not divided between capital stock, paid-in surplus, and retained earnings, but is reported as an asset,[8]

---

[6] As employed here, "treasury" stock is any reacquired stock (repurchased or donated) held "alive" prior to its cancellation or held for reissue upon resale or for reissue in payment of, say, an executive's bonus.

[7] By "redeemed" shares we mean any reacquired shares (repurchased) not held alive "in the treasury"—that is, shares canceled as they are received by way of repurchase, payment of a debt by a stockholder, or exchange for a share of a different class. Redeemed shares are not generally reissuable.

[8] Some justification for this point of view may be seen where the number of shares held is small and the stock has a quoted market value; but the

or, more often—and particularly where the repurchase cost has been large—as a deduction (on the face of the balance sheet) from the total of stockholders' equities. At the same time, under numerous state laws, it is necessary to disclose the unavailability for dividends of a corresponding portion of retained earnings (in a footnote to the balance sheet, for example) because of the prohibition against the use of contributed capital for stock-repurchase purposes.[9] This qualification or prohibition has the effect of making retained earnings unavailable for dividends in the amount of the repurchase cost as long as the shares retain their status as "treasury" stock.

Paid-in capital, whether we find it credited to "capital-stock" account alone, or in part to a "paid-in surplus" or "capital-surplus" account, thus retains its "identity" and remains unchanged as long as the capital stock giving rise to it remains outstanding. On the balance sheet it is itemized by classes of stock, but if paid-in surplus has arisen from the issuance of two or more classes of stock, a single figure for paid-in surplus is likely to appear; or, better, the paid-in surplus is eliminated and added to the capital-stock account(s) and the total simply labeled "Contributions of [or Paid in by] Stockholders."

Reserves

The word "reserve" has already made its appearance in these pages, but we have not stopped to explain all of its varied meanings. It has many. Accountants have too often tolerated the confusion it has created and only in recent years have efforts been made to limit the application of the term. In practice it is still being applied to the following types of accounts:

---

practice of displaying treasury stock as an asset, although still adhered to by General Motors and a few other publicly owned corporations, is strongly condemned by accountants generally.

[9] The basic reason for this common legal restriction limiting stock repurchases to an amount not in excess of retained earnings is that contributed capital should be applied only to the continuing business of the corporation, thereby providing a buffer that would afford some measure of protection to creditors. Without this rule it would be possible for a company that has suffered losses or has just "broken even" and thus has no retained earnings to pay out its liquid assets to stockholders, with amounts owing to creditors offset by less liquid assets or perhaps no assets at all. A few states prohibit the repurchase of capital stock altogether.

1) Valuation reserves are offsets to asset costs that would otherwise be overstated; we have encountered reserves for bad debts and depreciation for which some accountants would substitute "allowance for bad debts" and "accumulated depreciation." The reduction of inventory items from cost to market (or salvage) or from cost to a lifo basis may be recorded in an "inventory-reserve" account, with the debit half of the entry creating it winding up, of course, in cost of sales. Occasionally we may observe a reserve for an accumulated loss on a foreign branch the investment in which is carried as an asset. There is some tendency to call these "allowance" accounts also.

2) A provision for income taxes, called a "reserve" for income taxes, may sometimes be noted among current liabilities in published statements. Here, as in the case of asset reserves and in other applications of the term, "reserve" carries with it the implication of being an inexact amount: an estimate that may differ from amounts that will ultimately be determined. Because the year-end balance sheet of a corporation may be prepared before its income-tax return is completed, "reserve" has been applied to the tax liability in the belief that it would convey the notion of a fair estimate. Under the general caption of "current liabilities," however, the unadorned phrase "income taxes" has satisfied the majority of accountants.

3) Some corporations (e.g. General Motors) have a "reserves" section on their balance sheets, standing between liabilities with well-defined due dates and net worth. Items appearing in this section are often substantial and their meanings, never obvious, and the methods by which they have been accumulated and are being disposed of, are not always revealed. Upon inquiry, we may find that sometimes additions to these reserves are charged to current expense, sometimes to retained earnings, sometimes they represent cash or other assets received. Charges to the reserves may be offset by cash disbursements, assets writedowns, losses and other current expense, and additions to retained earnings. Reserve balances may suggest remote, possibly never-to-be-incurred obligations, or perhaps obligations that will in all probability be covered by the current provisions that are being added to it. Probably most accountants would take the position that if this class of reserve is to continue (a) any item falling under it should be a definable long-term liability (e.g. a pension reserve), (b) additions to the reserve should be charged to current expense, and (c) the reserve's transactions should be summarized and explained in reports to stockholders.

4) Funded reserves are balance-sheet credits offset by balance-sheet assets, usually of equal amount. Best explained as temporary allocations of retained earnings, they relate to prospective debt retirement and sometimes to the prospective retirement of all or a portion of outstanding preferred stock. Further examples of "surplus

reserves" may be found in provisions for an impending lawsuit. This reserve, included in the retained-earnings section of the balance sheet, is maintained intact and ultimately returned to its source when the need for it has passed. Sometimes called the only "true" reserve, a surplus reserve succeeds in being no more than earmarked retained earnings; for if a loss occurs against the possibility of which the reserve has been created, the loss is cleared through the income statement and is never charged direct to retained earnings.

For the first two classes of reserves we have described, the term may be passing into disuse, particularly on published financial statements, although it will continue possibly indefinitely to be used by accountants themselves. The term seems likely to persist for the latter two classes of accounts. Standards for the third class of reserve have been difficult to establish, for many of these reserves have been carryovers from periods when bonuses, losses, and other costs would, for a variety of reasons, be charged against them.

Perhaps most accountants are of the opinion that the reader of a balance sheet is justified in assuming that a prospective loss or liability attaches to reserves appearing immediately above net worth[10] but that a reserve should be so placed only when its identification as a liability has been established and must be recognized.[11] Where the reserve covers a remote, contingent loss, prudent management may demand its recognition but this it can best do by earmarking retained earnings or by disclosure of the possibility in a balance-sheet footnote. If, as we have said, an accountant speaks of a "true" reserve, he could mean such an earmarking: one that takes the form of shift within—and no change in the total of—stockholders' equity. Sometimes the purpose served by this kind of earmarking has been to explain a buildup of retained earnings that supposedly might otherwise lead to a demand by stockholders for more dividends or to raised eyebrows in the Internal Revenue Service that might suggest an assessment on undistributed income.[12]

---

[10] This practice may lead to the somewhat deceptive conclusion, however, that the company's liabilities are larger than they should be and that the assets normally available for paying off obligations are inadequate.

[11] Recognition, as we have previously observed, involves inclusion in the income statement as well as in some non-net-worth balance-sheet item.

[12] Under Section 531 of the Internal Revenue Code. Needless to say, the attention of the IRS would not be easily diverted by the creation of a provision against some wholly hypothetical future contingency.

Some examples of reserves

Let us consider several reserve classes that we may find in current corporation reports:

1) *Employee Benefits.* The varieties of employee-benefit plans are almost limitless. Some plans are voluntary and relatively simple. Others are the result of bargaining and involve many complex features; the determination of provisions for them in the accounts may baffle controllers and public accountants. Some benefits have been funded, and the employer's contributions for retirement pay and other benefits are in the hands of insurance companies or independent trustees. Where, for example, the employer's provisions for benefits have been voluntary or by agreement, contributions are to remain unfunded in the business (but sometimes drawing interest), the reserve provided may represent estimates of the present value of future payments; hence provisions creating and maintaining the reserve would be a charge to current income, and the result would be a recognized long-term liability. In some cases, although the future obligation pertaining to past employment may be determinable within tolerable limits, employers have insisted on remaining on a "pay-as-you-go" basis; benefits when paid are charged to current operations, thus avoiding the creation of a reserve. Regardless of the method in force and the financial plan accompanying it, appended footnotes to published financial statements are required under current practices to reveal essential details and disclose—if not in the form of a fully accumulated reserve —present estimates of future costs pertaining to past employment.

2) *Leasehold Obligations.* In the preceding chapter we gave attention to certain aspects of this subject. A number of accountants advocate that a lessee's accounts should include a reserve for the present value of leases of buildings and equipment along with future rental payments thereunder, especially where the property passes to the lessee (under varied conditions) upon the expiration of the lease. The author has taken the position in several instances that until—if ever—title passes, only footnote references to long-term leases are required but that these footnotes, as we have already noted, should be as informative as possible; annual and total rentals,

the lease period remaining, acquisition intents and conditions, and cancellation privileges are among the items of information that are often included; but that where a lease in form and intent is a purchase contract, the lessee's balance sheet should reflect the full purchase price, with the obligation yet to be paid appearing as a long-term obligation. In neither case would a "reserve" be required.

3) *Guaranties and Warranties.* Goods and services are often sold under conditions that may require further outlays. Usually such added costs are nominal in amount, and accruals or reserves are considered unnecessary. If added costs are incurred at a later date, they are absorbed as expenses at the time of their incurrence and not before. Guaranties are a normal accompaniment of all sales, and uncompensated service work is a normal expectancy of current operations. Reserves of this sort rarely serve any useful purpose; where they do appear, one is likely to look for some material errors of past production for which the future must make good. Costs incurred after the completion date of, say, a long-term contract belong to this category. However, major defects involving known costs of a material amount at the balance-sheet date are a direct, and not a contingent, liability. But unascertained imperfections and hypothetical service calls belong to the future and not to the past. Costs of services performed after the closing date of an installation which is one of many are sometimes described as "goodwill-maintenance" expenses and hence matters for the future rather than the present.

4) *Self-Insurance.* Because the cost of carrying one's own risks may be less than the cost of having some one else assume them, "self-insurance" is a common practice among companies having a large number of risk units. It is not uncommon, therefore, to find reserves created against such risks, and to encounter arguments favoring the recognition of the alleged liability that exists on a balance-sheet date, notwithstanding the absence of any event or condition that would give rise to a loss. Here again, many accountants would regard the creation of a reserve against future events and conditions wholly unnecessary, but they would doubtless urge disclosure, in a balance-sheet footnote, of the existence of the risk where the absorption in the future of a possible loss as a current expense might have an important effect on operations.

5) *Plant Replacement or Construction.* Reserves are occasionally found that attempt to reflect the cost that is about to be incurred

for replacing all or a part of existing plant, or the cost of substantial plant additions. Sometimes the amount is limited to costs above the level of prices reflected in the existing property account: that is, costs attributable to inflation or to an increase in capacity that are not being provided for through current charges to expense. But the information conveyed by any such segregation of retained earnings is, indeed, meager, and often proves to be wholly inaccurate by the time replacement becomes a matter of the immediate future. A far better practice is followed by companies that restrict such information to footnotes or to a report accompanying the financial statements where a more detailed and orderly account of prospective replacement possibilities can be outlined.

6) *Contingencies.* A *contingent* liability is a *possible* future liability arising out of a past event or condition; the term is often associated with a remote—but not yet probable[13]—uncompensable loss. On published financial statements we will find speculative losses ranging from unspecified hazards to existing lawsuits (as for patent infringements or back taxes) provided for in reserves for contingencies. At one time it was the practice to create contingency reserves by a segregation of retained earnings (rather than a debit to current expense) and to charge against such a reserve the loss if and when it occurred, thus keeping it out of the income statement and, as a result, overstating the earnings stream. This practice, commonly followed after World War II in an effort to cover possible unknown costs facing the restoration of business assets from wartime production to a peacetime basis, has now been abandoned and probably under similar circumstances would never again be resumed. It had the effect already indicated: of keeping a variety of operating costs and losses out of current operating expense, thus inflating profits. Moreover, it proved to be impossible—because of wartime advances in technologies and other causes—to distinguish between rehabilitation costs and other costs.[14] The tendency in recent years to maintain a "clean" surplus (retained-earnings) account has largely eliminated this kind of accounting, although

---

[13] If the likelihood of a future loss becomes a certainty, an *actual* liability exists which calls for recognition in both balance sheet and income statement.

[14] Some justification existed for rehabilitation reserves in that estimates of future plant-restoration costs had often been included in contract-settlement agreements and were ultimately compensated for; there was thus a moral compulsion, if not a legal one, to account for such costs when actually incurred.

surplus charges for extraordinary or unbudgeted costs are still being made, as we note below.[15]

Reserves of the nonliability type are for the most part actually unnecessary. The prospective hazards or losses in anticipation of which they have been provided are better identified and evaluated for the reader in accompanying reports or attached footnotes. Where they still appear, we should expect a clear description of their purpose; when the usefulness of a reserve as a signpost has served its purpose, it should be returned intact to its source, and the loss or costs, if any have been incurred, should be carried into operating expense or capitalized as an asset in accordance with the character of the item.

"True" reserves are thus subdivisions of retained earnings. Occasionally we will find such a reserve as a part of the equity acquired in the purchase of a going business; should an actual liability develop, most accountants would probably approve a charge against such a reserve. With this one exception, however, the preferred disposition of a "true" reserve is its eventual return, intact, to its source when the emergency is over, any loss or cost incurred being cleared through the income statement.

Dividends

A dividend, unqualified, is understood to be a *pro rata* cash distribution of corporate profits to stockholders. Other varieties of corporate dividends are:

> *stock dividend:* a distribution to stockholders of the issuing corporation's own capital stock accompanied by the transfer of retained earnings to paid-in capital.
>
> *property dividend* (or *dividend in kind*): a distribution of profits in the form of some asset other than cash.
>
> *liquidating dividend:* a distribution of cash or property or both, charged to some paid-in capital account.

---

[15] Contingency reserves were discussed in AICPA's ARB 50 (1958), a distinction being made between *general* and *specific* reserves. The former were held to be mere subdivisions of retained earnings; the nature of the latter was not considered. It is the author's opinion that the distinction is a purely artificial one, and that all contingent reserves should be classed as subdivisions of retained earnings.

Related to dividends and sometimes classified as such are the following:

spinoff: a transfer by one corporation to its stockholders of the capital stock of a second corporation it has just established (a property dividend) by a transfer of (net) assets to it.

splitoff: the same as a spinoff except that the transfer to stockholders does not become a property dividend but an exchange—which means that the stockholders surrender a portion of their holdings in the first corporation in exchange for the capital stock of the new second corporation. Both the spinoff and splitoff are devices aimed at avoiding income tax.

splitup (usual definition): an issue to present stockholders of additional shares of the same class of shares without modification of the amount of paid-in capital.

splitup (definition for income-tax purposes): a conveyance to two or more new corporations of all of the net assets of a previously established corporation, accompanied by a distribution of the shares of the new corporations to the stockholders of the old corporation in exchange for their holdings.

Consideration of the tax effects of these confections for tax purposes are not within the scope of this book. We may note, however, that in all these cases the result is a recasting of the units and issues of capital stock outstanding without any change in total paid-in values and total retained earnings. The first type of splitup (which is not a tax device) simply increases the number of outstanding shares, its primary purpose being to dilute the market price of the stock[16] and thus spur stock trading. A cash dividend is the simplest and, of course, the most common of all dividends. Three important dates are involved in every Board resolution authorizing such a dividend: the date of declaration (of the resolution) marks the point at which it becomes a current liability (with a corresponding charge to retained earnings); the date for closing the stockholders' records which follows the declaration date and has no effect on the books of account or the financial statements but marks the point at which the identities of the stockholders who are to receive the dividend are determined; and the date of payment, as we might suspect, is the time the liability is reduced to zero as cash in the form of dividend

[16] A 100% splitup or a 100% stock dividend in the case of a stock having a market price of 50 would have the theoretical effect of reducing the price to 25, but the increase in the availability of the shares to a larger body of traders often causes the new price to exceed the theoretical one.

checks goes out to stockholders. Commonly these dates are separated by two or three weeks.

What happens to unclaimed dividend checks? If undeposited by the recipient after, say, six months or a year, the cash is customarily brought back into the accounts along with the unpaid liability in order to simplify the control over the item; but it does not ordinarily appear (except, if important in amount, possibly as a footnote) on a balance sheet. Practice varies. All corporations with numerous stockholders have such items; some stockholders disappear, and neither they nor their heirs can be located. If a bank has acted as the payer of the dividend (on behalf of the corporation), the cash and unpaid amount may never be reclaimed by the corporation, and may ultimately revert to the state.

In declaring a stock dividend, standard practice calls for the capitalization or transfer from retained earnings to paid-in capital of an amount equal to the paid-in value of the previously outstanding shares of that class. This or any other amount called for in the dividend declaration is credited to the capital-stock account or spread between that account and the paid-in surplus account at the time the dividend shares are issued.

A splitup (usual definition) resembles a stock dividend, and many stockholders in receiving the distribution would be unable to distinguish the one from the other. Neither involves the creation of a liability or the diminution of assets; a splitup requires no entries on the books of the distributor, but a stock dividend involves the shift between the surplus and capital-stock accounts we have just described.[17]

Retained earnings

Agitation in recent years to maintain a "clean-surplus" account has reduced capital-surplus and earned-surplus charges and credits to comparatively rare events in corporate accounting. Changes in surplus accounts are now generally limited to net-income credits

---

[17] A stock distribution of under 25% (that is, 25% of previously issued shares) is often regarded as a "true" stock dividend, always involving the capitalization of earnings, sometimes in lieu of cash; but if the percentage is greater than 25%, a stock "split" is the more usual interpretation since its purpose is very likely a movement to increase the distribution of the issuer's shares by lowering, through dilution, of their market price.

and dividend debits and to transactions associated with reorganizations or restatements of capital stock. In published reports to stockholders we may note a few survivors of the theory that surplus charges and credits are items omitted from an income statement so that the latter may display only "earning power," debit items will consist of such things as extraordinary losses from fires, liquidations, and possibly other "once-in-a-lifetime" noncash costs, and of cash items such as tax adjustments and other prior-year costs, and initial charges for the creation and external deposit of employees' benefit funds.

In corporate reports to stockholders a separate statement of the surplus accounts reconciles the amounts of surplus (paid-in and earned) last reported with their present balances. Where earned-surplus details are uninvolved, changes may be appended to the income statement, or reported on the face of the balance sheet.

Summary

Net worth—stockholders' equity—can best be understood only after we have become acquainted with the elements that go into it. Paid-in capital and accumulated earnings are usually its only components, the transactions affecting net worth during a fiscal period being confined to a single credit for earnings (or a debit for a net loss), and one or more debits for dividends. Confining the income statement to items that are thought to reflect earning power and the desire to "make a showing" sometimes lead to surplus charges, but this practice, disapproved by most accountants, is rapidly becoming a thing of the past.

CHAPTER NINE

The Income Statement

Income statements are compilations of transactions which do not carry over into a succeeding period as do those making up the items appearing on the balance sheet: that is, transactions brought forward from past periods and now "expiring," as well as transactions beginning and ending at least in part during the current period. Published income statements are briefer in form and content than balance sheets, and in reports to stockholders are usually limited to less than a dozen items. As in the case of balance sheets, income statements may require footnotes supplementing individual items, their purpose being to disclose and describe unusual transactions or to indicate the particular methodology in disposing of certain transactions where any of several alternative methods might have been followed with equal propriety. Comparative income statements, featuring many corporate reports, provide standards of comparison.

The income statement of a business concern shares equal honors with the balance sheet as the accountant's most important financial resumé. In annual reports to stockholders it sometimes precedes, sometimes follows, the balance sheet.[1] Both statements are essential to an understanding of the past operations of an enterprise. The balance sheet reflects an inventory of the physical and financial tools with which the organization has been conducting its affairs; the income statement reflects transactions affecting operations, output, and profit: activities which these tools have made possible. The stories told by the two statements are, of course, not complete because they embody only activities in which a flow of money has taken place or will be required; the character of management practices, market conditions, dependence on the state of competition, and economic trends on the crests or in the valleys of which the business may be riding are illustrative of the nonaccounting chapters of the story that we must consider in appraising the past success of any enterprise, or in projecting, as best we can, its likely performance in the future. But the limitations attaching to the endproducts of accounting in no way minimize the importance of accounting as a tool of management; nor do they subtract from the use of financial statements as a principal device for both internal and external communication. Of the various factors we have mentioned, the two financial statements alone provide a quantita-

[1] Some accountants hold that the former of these alternatives is to be preferred because of the greater attention now being given to the income statement. However, the intelligent reader of financial statements will seek out the income statement regardless of its position.

tive survey of concluded events and surviving conditions; their combined compass is the whole spectrum of the organization and its flow of transactions. When the management of a business corporation reports to stockholders and the world at large, custom has long dictated that the financial statements form the hard core of the presentation, and any supporting narrative or supplementary schedules are always painstakingly woven around them.

This overlook has particular reference to the income statement. In addition, the income statement has meaning for future projections if we assume that performance characteristics are to remain unchanged or, where change is likely, if we can project what the effect of the change will be on the pattern established by past performance. We must, therefore, be able to identify the normal and abnormal elements of which the income statement is composed. Our effort now will be to acquaint ourselves with these elements as we find them in most published statements.

An income statement is sometimes called "statement of profit and loss," "statement of revenues and expense," or "earnings statement"; we have often referred to it as an "operating statement." Whatever its name, the content is the same, and the objective is to depict the total flow of revenue and the total expense incurred while that revenue is being produced, whether or not directly related to it. The period covered by the statement—week, month, or year— always forms a part of the title. In quarterly and annual reports to stockholders comparative statements are customary: the figures of the corresponding period of the preceding quarter or year alongside those of the current period. Often comparative income statements for a series of past periods are supplied in reports to stockholders for the purpose of indicating what past trends have been. Occasionally a column for "increase or decrease" is provided for the two-period comparison, but this is now generally considered unnecessary, since significant amounts[2] are readily determined even by the unpracticed eye.

Sales

A typical income statement starts out with sales of products delivered to customers or revenues from services performed. These

[2] In financial statements *significant amounts* rarely extend beyond the first two or three digits.

are the credits arising from charges made to customers during the period and are usually net of cancellations, returns, adjustments, and discounts, although discounts, if of the cash variety, occasionally appear separately or are merged with "other" expense. Sometimes several classes of deductions from sales are provided in short; most accountants take the position that in reports to the public these items mean little[3] and are best omitted as unnecessary detail.

Income statements of British corporations often begin with a species of *net* income called "operating profit": a single figure representing a combination of sales, cost of sales, and selling and administrative expense, with no disclosure elsewhere of sales ("turnover") or the other elements mentioned.[4] The reason for this lies in the belief that the volume of business done is something to be withheld from one's competitors: a confidential figure for management's eyes only. But competitors have numerous ways of arriving at approximations of their rivals' sales volume, and the American style of income statement is gradually taking over. No one has been able to demonstrate that the disclosure of sales figures has actually damaged any business organization.

A single sales figure, however, in the income statement of an enterprise producing several different products or services having different profit margins has its principal significance in making possible only a limited number of measures and comparisons. Financial analysts may compute such ratios as sales to inventory, sales to receivables, sales to net worth, and sales to working capital, regarding them as factors in measuring present efficiencies when compared with similar ratios of competitors, or in measuring growth or trends within the business over a period of years. Occasionally we may observe in report narratives one or more clues as to the breakdown by class of business or product, but without any such indication, the reader has no way of determining sales by product lines, the portion of sales arising from government business or foreign trade, or the trends of these classes of sales. Here again we ap-

---

[3] Provided, of course, that the percentage relationship to sales falls within the range of experience of past years or as met with elsewhere.

[4] This was a common practice in the United States before the advent of the reporting standards imposed by the national Securities Act of 1933. Pending amendments of the British Companies Act would, with some exceptions, require the disclosures of sales.

proach the area of alleged confidential information: information at present deemed to be of value principally to management, or information that might lead to the asking of questions difficult to answer. But in many situations sales breakdowns are regarded as details in which the average reader has evinced little interest; besides, these and other income-statement details are almost always available to anyone requesting them. Possibly we may look forward to more sales data in annual reports, but there is no present movement in that direction.

Contractors, heavy-equipment manufacturers, and other producers of any commodity or service requiring more than a few weeks for its completion and delivery are faced with the problem of how to report their sales. One shipbuilder may wait until the delivery date, in the meantime adding production costs to an inventory account; if he has but one ship under construction, he will be unable to report the completed sale until that date has arrived. Another shipbuilder, facing the same problem, will report for each fiscal period during the construction process a portion of his eventual selling price, computed under any of several methods in common use: for example, cost thus far incurred divided by total expected cost (fraction of completion) times total firm selling price; or the numerator of the fraction may be the cost to date which has been audited and approved by some third person such as an independent engineer responsible to both buyer and seller, or a representative of the buyer. Again, the reported sales may be the amounts billed (or collected) when certain stages of the construction have been completed as defined in the contract between the producer and his customer. A third builder will credit periodic billings to his customer to the account he maintains for production cost. No one of these methods can be said to govern all situations.

Whenever the basis of reporting the sales of a contractor or other producer is a shorter period than the period required for production, a full statement of the basis is required in every report.[5] This would include not only the basis for setting off costs against revenues, but also the basis for carrying forward on the balance sheet an inventory of incurred costs not yet absorbed. We are quite justified in concluding that reliance on the income statement of such a con-

---

[5] Such a statement is held by accountants as serving in lieu of a standard procedure.

tractor is dependent on a full knowledge of how his revenues and costs have been computed.

Other income

"Other income" in most situations is not detailed, but some accountants follow the rule of thumb that where more than half of this figure comes from one type of transaction, the sidehead should include the mention of that type; thus a sidehead reading "interest and other income" might well mean that the bulk of this item *is* interest. Usually "other income" is a small fraction of both sales and net profit and hence is not large enough to have a material influence on earnings. But if a substantial profit is realized from, say, the disposal of a plant, the normal practice is to display it as a separate item on the income statement.

Among the incidental items one might find in "other income" of a manufacturing enterprise are, in addition to interest: rents, commissions, and special services.

Cost of sales

Cost of sales is sometimes merged with selling, administrative, and other expense, only a single figure appearing for the whole of these items. But cost of sales is always an important figure for stockholders, analysts, and the general reader as well; without a breakdown, its importance cannot be measured. Costs making up the total are a manufacturer's factory costs that have gone into finished product sold, or the invoice (and transportation and occasionally storage) costs of a retailer's sales.

A useful type of a manufacturer's cost-of-sales presentation is to display material, labor, and overhead costs: the incurred costs of these items modified by the corresponding breakdowns in opening and closing inventories.[6] The trend revealed in the items when compared with those of preceding periods, and discussed in management's letter in an annual report to stockholders, would be of great value to investors. Should inventories be valued on a direct-costing

[6] An alternative is to show in this section of the income statement both opening and closing inventories with the three elements of incurred manufacturing costs between them.

basis, the overhead shown in a cost-of-sales breakdown will be the actual overhead for the period, while the materials and labor items will be inventory-adjusted. Comparative statements containing these breakdowns will then make possible a much more intelligible idea of where costs are going. An increasing number of accountants favor this kind of presentation.

Texts of annual reports to stockholders usually include comments on changes in the components of costs of sales, but if no breakdown by class of products is indicated, the real significance attaching to these changes is likely to be lost. The ways and means by which the cost of sales can be set forth in a more rational, and yet brief, form has not yet been fully explored by accountants; basic information is usually available in internal reports, or in the detailed reports in much more elaborate form which one may secure from the reporting company.

When compensation to employees appears as a separate item, it has now become customary in many instances to include supplementary costs, such as insurance, retirement provisions (or payments), and social security and other benefits. These additional costs, often labeled "fringe" benefits, have become an important element of labor costs and as a rule are no longer classed as an overhead item.

Depletion and depreciation

The amount of depletion and depreciation appearing in the expense accounts is practically always disclosed in published financial statements even though it may be a minor figure having no material effect on profits. It will generally be greater than the increase in the accumulated-depreciation accounts as revealed in beginning and ending balance sheets since the reserve accounts are likely to have been charged with adjustments made necessary by retirements during the period. In a footnote or elsewhere in the report the method of computing depletion and depreciation will usually be given. As we have indicated previously, both the amount and method of depletion and depreciation are important disclosures, since so many methods of determining the periodic provisions are in use. We have already stated that the straight-line basis is the one that we may presume has been followed if nothing to the contrary appears. Where some method of accelerated depreciation is in use, we should look for an explanation of the method and also for a disclosure of the portion of the provision which is in excess of the amount that the straight-line basis would have yielded. Again, any divergence between depletion and depreciation reflected in the report and the amount claimed for tax purposes should likewise be disclosed, since this difference may become important in years of few property additions, at which time substantially smaller deductions may be available on tax returns.

We have already commented on judgments concerning the adequacy of provisions for and accumulations of depletion and depreciation. Most readers of financial statements have no way of reaching conclusions on adequacy, for the reports of public accountants accompanying published statements are usually silent on such matters. The attitude of public accountants is that the adequacy of the periodic writedowns for depletion and depreciation is within the realm of judgment ordinarily associated with engineers or appraisers. At first thought this seems to raise grave doubts as to the worth of this section of the accountant's report. But the accountant has reviewed the methods of property accounting that have been followed, and, without qualification in his reports, it may be assumed that these methods include acceptable standards for capitalization, retirement, and expensing, whatever the basis of accumulation.[7] Gains and losses on retirements[8] are adjustments of the current provision, and over a relatively short period of years depletion and

---

[7] This follows if the method of depletion or depreciation has been consistently applied to all assets. For example, where a sum-of-the-years-digits method has been followed uniformly, newly acquired assets may be overprovided for, at the same time that depreciation for older assets is being underprovided. A perfect balance between the two that would yield a total provision for the period substantially identical with a uniformly applied straight-line method is not to be expected, but the difference in situations familiar to the author have been found not to be of a material character.

[8] Losses on retirements, produced by a failure to provide enough depreciation during the useful life of assets, are sometimes erroneously treated as direct charges against retained earnings. In practically all situations, depreciation is treated as a period cost; hence writedowns, whether of the percentage variety or "losses" from retirements, belong to the same category of expense, and no portion of such cost should be omitted from the income statement. A substantial writeoff from an unanticipated retirement might, of course, rate as an extraordinary deduction for depreciation on the income statement, but this can be explained in a footnote.

depreciation provisions will probably average the same amounts, whatever the basis of accumulation has been, provided it has been a consistent one.

Production overhead is the usual repository of the bulk of depletion and depreciation provisions; and if it is desired to let them remain there, the amount of the provisions can be reported in an income-statement footnote; at the same time the method of determining the provision may be outlined. Where some cost-of-sales detail is provided in the income statement, the depletion and depreciation provision may appear as a separate item.

Occasionally we will encounter a separate provision for plant replacement as an expense in the income statement. This, of course, is an amount in excess of depreciation based on historical cost, not only not deductible on an income-tax return, but also not an expense if we are to adhere to traditional accounting methods; it is, instead, an appropriation of accumulated earnings which *may*, at some future date, according to somebody's present estimate, be reinvested in fixed-asset replacements. Including such provisions as an expense would be regarded by most accountants today as decidedly improper; but where it appears, the safeguard of full disclosure might serve as a palliative.

Provision for income tax

An income-tax provision will always be found in any corporate income statement which winds up with a profit; and because of the current rate of tax on corporate earnings (roughly, 50%), the amount of the provision will approximate the final net-income figure. The principal exception is found in situations where there has been a carryover of an operating loss from a past year; under such circumstances, a disclosure of that fact would appear, if its importance warrants, in a footnote. Another possible cause would be accelerated depreciation appearing in the tax return but not on the books, or an additional tax arising from an under- or over-provided tax for a preceding period; these situations too would demand a disclosure of the cause.

Occasionally an additional tax for a past period is charged against accumulated earnings. Comments on this practice appear in the preceding chapter.

Including in the current provision for taxes an amount that will not be payable, if ever, until some point of time beyond the forthcoming year, although bearing the approval of an AICPA committee,[9] must still be regarded as a practice of doubtful merit.

Extraordinary expenses

Extraordinary losses and other expense, where they have occurred during the reporting period and have not been anticipated by expense provisions of prior periods, are costs that must be absorbed by current operations.[10] Items most often appearing under this head are losses from fixed-asset retirements (which in most cases, as we have previously observed, would be better classified as adjustments of current provisions for depreciation), from sales of investments not associated with everyday operations, and from foreign-exchange transactions; writeoffs of intangibles including amounts paid for interests in subsidiaries that have exceeded the book value on the subsidiary books of account at the time of acquisition; inventory writedowns such as those occasioned by discontinued lines and overstock; and fire losses.

We would expect in each such case where the item exceeds, say, 5% of net income, a fairly detailed explanation of the item and some indication of whether similar losses might be expected in the future.

Operating results

Results from operations are expressed as "net income," "net profit," "(net) earnings," and similar designations, with, perhaps, a general preference for the first-named; if extraordinary items we have just discussed have been substantial in amount, the words "after special charges" may be appended to the designation by some accountants.

The net-income figure is now often followed by a net-income-per-share figure which would be calculated after deducting preferred-dividend requirements, if any, and would be based on the number

[9] *Restatement and Revision,* Chapter 10, Section B.

[10] The steadfast opposition by accountants to "surplus charges" has reduced the number of charges of extraordinary expense to retained earnings almost to the vanishing point. For a further discussion of surplus charges see the author's *Dictionary* under *net income.*

of shares outstanding at the end of the period. If comparative income statements have been presented, the same divisor would be applied to the earnings of the preceding period in order as nearly as possible to make the net-income-per-share figures comparable.

Summary

There are many variations in the form and content of income statements. Seven principal items of information are expected on income statements: net sales, cost of sales, depreciation and depletion, other operating expense, unusual income or losses, income taxes, and net income; also, perhaps, some form of disclosure of the more important trends that appear to be extending into the future. It may well be that the future holds many more demands for information. Conceivable additional demands would put no strain on existing accounting methods, however, and would largely involve making public information which is already compiled and available for internal purposes.

CHAPTER TEN

Consolidated Statements

A single economic entity may take the form of two or more legal entities, each with its own books of account and with nominally independent management. Whenever it is desired to present the overall financial position and joint operating results of the group, accountants overlook the separateness of the legal entities in such a way that the combined figures of the several organizations will appear as those of a single unit. Custom has provided fairly well-established methods for this breakdown and resynthesis, and an example is set forth in which a number of the accountant's customary problems are dealt with.

135

A corporate entity may be less than an economic entity. A factory or sales branch can be and often is separately established as a wholly owned corporation. A competing producer, or a supplier of an important component, may be acquired by a purchase of its outstanding capital stock, sometimes with minority interests remaining. A branch may be instituted in another state or in a foreign country, often with substantial equity interests owned by residents of that state or country. Or, one company or one person, acting as an investment medium for a group of persons, may acquire dominant interests in a number of otherwise unrelated business enterprises. In all these situations, the desirability of some form of a combined showing is required whereby the financial picture of the group may be viewed as though there were but one organization.

A somewhat similar form of relationship exists in the case of an unincorporated branch. Some branches do not maintain separate records, and under such circumstances no question arises concerning the combining of its affairs with those of the home office. But where the operations of the branch are of a substantial character, and a considerable degree of autonomy has been delegated to its management, more-or-less independent bookkeeping records are likely to be regarded as essential. In such cases the branch may even issue its own financial statements; but its affairs will be combined with those of the home office—always in the case of annual reports, often in the case of monthly, quarterly, or other interim reports.

136

In this chapter various types of problems that surround the preparation of combined statements will be considered. Numerous optional procedures are recognized in current practice, and on certain points some controversy may exist. It is always important that decisions on procedural matters in individual situations be based on policies shared by the controller with top management and that these policies meet with at least the tacit approval of the firm's external auditors. Here, as elsewhere, procedural differences may not give rise to significant variations in the overall financial showing. Consistency from period to period is most important, however, particularly in the treatment of items in the income statement, in order that the affairs of one period may be directly comparable with those of another.

Where consolidated statements involve departures from usual methods, or selection has been made from among a number of acceptable alternative procedures that have a material bearing on the information that the statements have been designed to convey, an expression of consolidation policy will normally accompany them, especially those given general circulation: a practice followed by numerous corporations in their annual reports to stockholders.

Some definitions

Combined financial statements is a generic term applicable to any joining of the financial statements of two or more independent or quasi-independent organizations, corporate or otherwise. Included are *consolidated* statements: the combination of the statements of one organization and those of one or more incorporated units owned *or* controlled by it; and *group* statements: the combination of the statements of organizations having a common ownership or *control.* "Control" here means the presence of such factors as a single management or the direction of management by means of policy determination or other device, effective domination in the election of directors, a contract governing the volume, price, and direction of major output, and the like.

Controlling companies may be either *parent* companies or *holding* companies. A parent company is the usual designation of a corporation that owns or controls one or more subordinate or *subsidiary* companies and is itself an operating company. A holding company has no operations of its own aside from devoting its efforts to the management and control of its subsidiaries. A subsidiary (-company) relationship is usually recognized where more than 50% of the subsidiary's voting shares are owned by the controlling company, and often recognized where the percentage is less than 50%, but where, nevertheless, *control* over management and operations is present.[1]

Group statements

The concept of group statements is a simple one. They are employed where there are two or more subsidiaries whose operations are similar and only incidentally related, and where the controlling company's financial affairs, for any of several reasons,[2] are set forth on an unconsolidated basis. An example may be found in the case of an investment company that has purchased a controlling interest in each of several operating companies. The purpose of a group statement would be to show the structure of financial condition and operating results that lie behind what would otherwise be a difficult-to-interpret investment total on the top company's balance sheet. Sometimes the subsidiaries are combined into two or more classes with separate group statements for each.

[1] Among the possible mechanisms through which control is effective, notwithstanding the controlling company's minority interest in outstanding voting stock, are these: a continued ability to secure proxies sufficient to maintain a voting majority; ownership of voting shares by the controlling company's officers, employees, nominees, or other persons having subordinated interests; habitual inactivity of other stockholders who neither exercise their privileges by participating in stockholders' meetings nor give proxies, thus often permitting a small minority to become a majority in stockholders' meetings; possession of a lease or other contract that secures controls over assets without formal conveyance. The Securities and Exchange Commission holds that control includes "the possession, direct or indirect, of the power to direct or cause the direction of the management and policies of a person whether through the ownership of voting securities, by contract, or otherwise." The AICPA suggests a much narrower definition roughly the same as that to be found in IRS regulations: ". . . fifty percent of the outstanding voting shares . . . [and although] there are exceptions to [this] general rule . . . ," it has failed to specify any important classes of exceptions.

[2] For example, where the controlling company is an investment medium, has operations bearing little or no relation to those of its subsidiaries, or has substantial obligations to outsiders which have no claim on the subsidiaries' assets.

There are always serious limitations on combining the accounts of separate legal entities. One is that losses, or the possibility of losses as from insolvency, of the poorer members of the group may be obscured, if not wholly lost sight of, as the result of being joined with more prosperous members. It is generally held that any unusual condition attending any one member of a group may warrant its exclusion; in that event a separate showing of its financial statements will probably be required. Here, as elsewhere, judgment is necessary in determining the relative importance of the exceptional situation. If inclusion might lead in any important degree to unwarranted inferences, or if the accounts of the exceptional member of the group are likely to affect the future financial position or operating results of the combined group, the separation would probably be deemed necessary. The clearest case for group statements is present where the operations of its members are similar and where numerous interrelationships are present.

In some cases there will be intercompany receivables and payables, perhaps other intercompany items. These will be eliminated against each other and omitted from the combined statement.

The 100% subsidiary

Two classes of subsidiary companies fall under the designation of wholly owned: those established by the controlling company in the first instance, and those acquired by it after a period of independent operation.

In the first of these classes the investment account on the controlling company's books—an asset—will be equal in amount to the paid-in capital—an equity—appearing on the books of the subsidiary. In combining the balance sheets of the two organizations, these items, canceling each other, disappear. Remaining in the subsidiary's net worth, however, would be retained earnings (or accumulated losses) since inception, and this amount would be combined with the controlling company's retained earnings (or losses) in a consolidated statement. A dividend paid by the subsidiary to its parent would have no effect on the amount of consolidated retained earnings, since there would have been an increase in the parent's earnings through the receipt of the dividend offsetting a corresponding decrease in the subsidiary's surplus: in other words, a shift of retained earnings from the subsidiary's books to the parent's.

Where one operating company is acquired by another by means of a purchase from stockholders of all of its outstanding voting capital stock, the first problem to be considered will be the relationship between the purchase price and the book value of the acquired equity. The price paid for the subsidiary's shares will in all probability differ from their book value (on the subsidiary's records), and determination must be made, before or at the time of purchase, of the cause as well as the disposition of the difference. For example, assume that a corporation has 10,000 outstanding shares with a paid-in value of $10 per share and accumulated retained earnings of $15 per share. This book value of $25 per share contrasts, let us say, with a cash price of $32 per share that is being offered to shareholders by the prospective controlling company. Inquiry reveals that numerous reasons can be cited for this difference, among them the following:

1) Annual net income per share for the past five years has averaged $1, of which only half has been paid out as cash dividends.

2) A contemporary appraisal of land and buildings indicates a cost-of-reproduction-new-less-depreciation value of an amount $25,000 in excess of their book values.

3) The company's product line, as a supplement to the purchaser's own production, could be marketed by the purchaser's sales staff at a combined saving of $5,000 per annum as compared with present selling costs.

4) A portion of the company's building and machinery, now not fully utilized, could be put to use producing parts the purchaser is now buying from outsiders; the annual savings could be as much as $10,000.

These reasons are typical. There are usually numerous benefits that the purchaser believes will flow from the acquisition of another company. Most of them cannot be precisely or even roughly evaluated; a purchase figure is ordinarily somewhere between bid and asked prices—prices premised on a wholly different set of values. None of the items described here need be a cause for adjustment of the subsidiary's books after the shares have been acquired; but when the accounts are brought together in consolidated statements at a later date, the investment account of $320,000 on the controlling company's books will be divided into four parts: $100,000 will offset and thus eliminate from the consolidated picture the subsidiary's capital-stock account; $150,000 will do the same for the subsidiary's retained earnings up to the date of acquisition; $25,000 possibly will be added to the consolidated cost of fixed assets, or with the balance of $45,000, will be regarded as the *consolidation excess,* to be carried into the balance sheet as *Goodwill from Consolidation,* or, better (and more descriptively) *Excess of Acquisition Cost over Book Value of Subsidiaries.*

The consolidation excess of $45,000 (or $70,000) may (1) be separated out of the investment account on the controlling company's books and appear as a charge to extraordinary expense in the year of acquisition,[3] (2) remain in the investment account unchanged, or (3) be amortized by charges to expense over a period of several years. The tendency in recent years to eliminate intangibles from balance sheets has spread to the investment in subsidiaries, even in situations where consolidated statements are not prepared. As we noted in Chapter 7, there has been a growing conviction that all intangibles have limited lives; that today's goodwill exists by virtue of today's management effort exerted from day to day; and that the cost of its creation and maintenance is inextricably commingled in many different types of current expense. Past-years' goodwill, under modern competitive conditions, is soon dissipated, and, if purchased, deserves to be expensed as quickly as possible.[4]

Where the subsidiary's shares have been purchased from the old stockholders in several blocks over a period of time, how much of the subsidiary's retained earnings, prior to the point at which control has been secured, should be carried as such into the consolidated balance sheet? Opinions differ here; the procedure preferred by the author is to permit in consolidated retained earnings only amounts that have previously been cleared through consolidated income statements and to permit in consolidated income statements only earnings ascribable to the several blocks *since* control has become effective. Assume the existence over a given period of a 40% interest without effective control, followed during the cur-

---

[3] Or, less desirably, as a charge to retained earnings.

[4] There is no settled rule here, but a writeoff over a five-year period is a not uncommon practice.

rent year by the acquisition of the remaining 60%. No consolidation of earnings would be permissible until this year, and then only the subsidiary's profits dating from the final acquisition would be included in the consolidated income statement. The same amount would be the subsidiary's total contribution to consolidated retained earnings.[5]

Intercompany profits on construction, inventories, or other items prior to the date control is effected, usually presumed to be the product of arm's-length transactions, would continue undiminished in consolidation. Intercompany exchanges of goods and services would be eliminated in their entirety only in the consolidation process, although remaining on the books where they have been recorded. Profits would be eliminated to the extent that any remained at the date of acquisition in inventories, in undepreciated portions of fixed assets, or in other assets not realized through sales to outsiders;[6] the eliminated profit would, of course, increase the consolidation excess. Henceforth depreciation expense relating to intercompany construction would have to be reduced proportionately.

Less than 100% ownership

Where a less-than-100% ownership exists, the procedures already referred to remain, in general, unchanged. An additional procedure is involved, however: the assignment of a portion of the retained earnings and periodic net income to the minority interest. The subsidiary's earnings—sales, less cost of sales and expense—are

[5] A less satisfactory basis is to include retained earnings on each block dating from its acquisition (AICPA, *Accounting Research Bulletin* 51, paragraph 10). This has the effect of building up the acquired consolidation excess and showing as available for dividends earnings during a period in which no control existed; moreover, an addition would suddenly appear in consolidated retained earnings that has not previously been recognized as income: an addition not logically tenable, contrary to the assertion sometimes made that this situation does not parallel the conditions surrounding the *pooling of interests* (ARB No. 48) in which two or more organizations are joined together with no effective elimination in whole or in part of either paid-in capital or retained earnings, and with no changes, except for pooling, in either ownership or control.

[6] AICPA ARB 51 would also permit the capitalization, in the case of intercompany construction for a public utility, of "a reasonable return on investment"; however, see the author's comments on this point on page 83.

adjusted and consolidated as though a full 100% of the voting stock were owned. At the end of the earnings statement the amount allocated to the minority interest appears as a deduction from consolidated net profit. How much should this allocation be: should it be based on the net income of the subsidiary before eliminating intercompany profit or the net income as adjusted? The procedure favored by the author is to show as a deduction from the consolidated net profit the portion of the *un*consolidated net income attributable to the minority interest, that amount (less minority dividends during the reporting period) constituting the net increase or decrease in the minority-stockholders' interest since the beginning of the period. This means, of course, that the full accumulated amount of the minority interest would be stated on the basis reflected in the subsidiary's accounts and would not be diminished by its share of the profits earned by the subsidiary but not earned by the parent and subsidiary considered as a single entity.

On the consolidated balance sheet, the preferred procedure is to display "minority stockholders' interest" above the net-worth section of the balance sheet, and, if the amount is substantial, to provide a breakdown between capital stock and retained earnings. On many published financial statements, the interest of minority stockholders, especially where minor in amount, is buried: that is, included with other items of net worth or even added to some item of current liabilities.

Illustration of consolidation

Worksheets and explanations displaying several of the techniques of consolidation appear on pages 145-146. Following are explanations and suggestions for the reader's study of the worksheets and accompanying journal entries:

1) Ames Manufacturing Company has two selling branches, one wholly owned and unincorported (Crawford), the other a corporation (Bass) 80% of whose outstanding shares of capital stock and 90% of whose outstanding mortgage bonds were acquired three years ago (July 1, 19-0) by a cash purchase from the then owners for a lump-sum consideration of $200,000. Shortly thereafter the purchase price was allocated as follows:

Book value, per Bass records:

Bonds, due in seven years—		
Face value—90% of $50,000	45,000	
Unamortized discount—90% of $3,500	3,150	41,850
Capital stock and surplus—		
Par value—80% of $100,000	80,000	
Retained earnings—80% of $50,812.50	40,650	120,650
Balance: acquisition excess		37,500
Total paid		200,000

2) On the Bass books the discount on the bonds is being amortized at the rate of $500 per year, and on the Ames books the bond valuation has been revised upward annually in the amount of $450. The investment valuation on the Ames books thus offsets and cancels out 90% of the net liability on the Bass records (journal entry *1*).

3) The value assigned to capital stock and surplus at acquisition on the Ames books was fixed at amounts necessary to offset exactly the corresponding items on the Bass books (journal entry *2*).

4) The acquisition excess of $37,500 is being amortized over a period of ten years by equal annual charges to expense. The unamortized portion is carried into the consolidated balance sheet.

5) Equipment sold by Ames to Bass in 19-1, $140,000, includes a profit to Ames of 25% on cost. Depreciation of 5% per annum has been taken on the Bass books over the two-year period; hence $28,000 is removed from the fixed-asset total, $2,800 from accrued depreciation, $26,600 from retained earnings, and $1,400 from current expense (journal entry *3*).

6) Ames manufactures the product sold to its branches and to outsiders, and the selling price to the public is a uniform 125% of its cost. On transfers to the Crawford branch the markup is such as to yield that branch a margin of one-eighth of the uniform selling price; on transfers to Bass, one-sixth. Crawford carries no stock of its own, all sales to customers being delivered by Ames direct. Bass' inventory at the beginning of the year, transfer-priced, was $75,000. From this information and that appearing in the two financial statements, the intercompany sales will be found to be $746,300 and the corresponding elimination from cost of sales, $745,940 (journal entry *4*).[7]

7) Eighty percent of the $10,000 dividend paid by Bass during the year and taken up as income by Ames is eliminated by offset (journal entry *5*).

[7] The arithmetic involved here should be traced into the schedule attached to journal entry *4*. If the reader is able to duplicate this schedule (or its equivalent) and the journal entry based on it, he will have gained a good mental picture of the effects of inventories, markups, and intercompany relationships on sales and costs of sales.

AMES MANUFACTURING COMPANY & SUBSIDIARY

Consolidated Worksheet   June 30, 19-3

(Balance Sheet)

Detail	Parent company	Crawford branch	Bass Products	Adjustments and eliminations		Consolidated
Assets						
Cash	47,200	1,870	33,780	7)	2,000	34,850
Receivables	217,530	44,020	7,460	6)	−24,200	244,810
Inventories	64,410	—	84,000	4)	−3,360	145,050
Prepaid expense	2,500	—	1,060		—	3,560
Fixed assets, at cost	329,290	4,540	153,200	3)	−28,000	459,030
Accrued depreciation	−68,990	−4,310	−21,500	3)	2,800	−92,000
Advances to branch	36,770	—	—	7)	−36,770	—
Investment in subsidiary—						
Bonds	43,200	—	—	1)	−43,200	—
Capital stock and surplus	120,650	—	—	2)	−120,650	—
Acquisition excess	26,250	—	—		—	26,250
Total assets	818,810	46,120	258,000			871,550
Liabilities						
Accounts payable	25,430	350	33,900	6)	24,200	33,480
Payable to Ames	—	45,770	—	7)	45,770	—
Mortgage bonds	—	—	50,000	1)	45,000	5,000
Unamortized discount	—	—	−2,000	1)	−1,800	−200
Minority interest—						
Capital stock	—	—	20,000			
Retained earnings—						
July 1, 19-2	—	—	12,720			
Net income for year	—	—	4,500			
Dividend paid	—	—	−2,000			35,220
Majority interest—						
Capital stock	500,000	—	80,000	2)	80,000	500,000
Retained earnings—						
July 1, 19-0	203,200	—	40,650	2)	40,650	
Net additions to July 1, 19-2	60,800	—	10,230	4)	3,000	
				3)	26,600	244,630
Net income for year	35,380	—	18,000	7)	−11,000	
				4)	360	
				3)	−1,400	
				5)	8,000	57,420
Dividends paid	−6,000	—	−8,000	5)	−8,000	−6,000
Total liabilities	818,810	46,120	258,000		—	871,550

AMES MANUFACTURING COMPANY & SUBSIDIARY

Consolidated Worksheet   June 30, 19-3

(Income Statement)

	Constituent units			Adjustments and eliminations		Con-solidated
Detail	Parent company	Crawford branch	Bass Products			
Sales	1,279,100	329,200	539,100	4)	746,300	1,401,100
Cost of sales	1,129,520	288,050	449,250	4)	−745,940	1,120,880
Gross profit	149,580	41,150	89,850			280,220
Expense—						
Selling	41,930	15,010	34,420			91,360
Administration	69,630	14,910	27,330			111,870
Depreciation	7,340	230	5,100	3)	−1,400	11,270
Acquisition excess	3,750	—	—			3,750
Bond discount	−450	—	500			50
Dividend received	−8,000	—	—	5)	8,000	—
Total expense	114,200	30,150	67,350			218,300
Net income	35,380	11,000	22,500		−6,960	61,920
Less—minority stockholders' interest						4,500
Net income consolidated						57,420
Dividends—						
Ames Company	6,000					6,000
Bass Company			10,000	5)	8,000	2,000

8) The intercompany accounts are eliminated against each other. A number of different practices are illustrated. Ames carries its account with Bass among receivables, that with Crawford in a separate account. Either or both methods are acceptable; convenience governs. Crawford has remitted $2,000 to Ames, but Ames did not record this until July, indicating that this amount was in transit on June 30.[8] Here the item is added to cash simply on the worksheets; it would have been better had an adjustment been taken up by Ames on its books, debiting *cash in transit* and crediting the intercompany account. Also Crawford has credited its account with Ames in the amount of $11,000: the result of clearing off its books the year's nominal accounts. For purposes of the present statement the details behind that figure are displayed on the income worksheet (journal entries 6 and 7).[9]

[8] On a balance sheet of the home office in which the branch-office items

AMES MANUFACTURING COMPANY & SUBSIDIARY

Adjustments and Eliminations for Consolidated Financial Statements
June 30, 19-3

(1)

Mortgage bonds	45,000	
Investment in bonds		43,200
Unamortized discount		1,800
Bass bonds held by Ames at book value		

(2)

Capital stock—Bass	80,000	
Retained earnings to July 1, 19-0	40,650	
Investment in Bass capital stock		120,650
Book value of 80% of Bass' outstanding capital stock and retained earnings at acquisition in 19-0, here offset against Ames' investment		

(3)

Retained earnings—July 1, 19-2	26,600	
Allowance for depreciation	2,800	
Fixed assets		28,000
Net income for year (depreciation expense)		1,400
Original profit on equipment sold by Ames to Bass in 19-1 was 25%, or $28,000; accrued depreciation taken by Bass to beginning of current year included profit of $1,400; depreciation expense for 19-3 includes profit of equal amount		

(4)

Retained earnings—July 1, 19-2	3,000	
Sales	746,300	
Inventories		3,360
Cost of sales		745,940
Sales during 19-3 to related units and inventories remaining therefrom:		

---

have not been combined, this item would appear as "cash in transit"; in a combined balance sheet it would be joined directly with cash, there being an analogy here to checks outstanding which—by convention—are always deducted from the cash balance on deposit in the drawee bank.

[9] The latter adjustment on the Ames books can be a simple one: a debit to the interoffice account and a credit to retained earnings, as in journal entry 7. Or, the various nominal accounts that yield the balance of $11,000 may take the place of the credit to retained earnings, combined with or separate from the corresponding nominal accounts of the home office, and later transferred to retained earnings when all of the home-office nominal accounts are closed out.

Unit	Sales	Transfer price	Cost of sales	Gross profit Ames	Gross profit Con- solidated
Crawford	329,200	288,050	263,360	24,690	65,840
Bass	539,100	449,250	431,280	17,970	107,820
Ames (outside)	532,800	—	426,240	106,560	106,560
Bass inventory adjustment—					
July 1, 19-2		−75,000		−3,000	
June 30, 19-3		84,000		3,360	
Transfers during year		746,300		149,580	
Consolidated totals	1,401,100		1,120,880		280,220
Less portion of Ames gross profit not realized (column 4)		360			
Included in cost of sales		745,940			

(5)

Net income for year (dividend received)	8,000	
Dividend paid		8,000
Dividend paid by Bass to Ames included in Ames' income and charged to Bass' retained earnings, and now eliminated		

(6)

Accounts payable	24,200	
Receivables		24,200
Ames-Bass intercompany accounts offset against each other		

(7)

Cash	2,000	
Payable to Ames	45,770	
Advances to branch		36,770
Net income for year		11,000

Advances by Ames included in Crawford's accounts payable; $2,000 remittances not received by Ames until July; net income from branch for year $11,000, closed to Crawford's intercompany account but not yet taken up on Ames' books

Eliminations ledger

If there are a number of subsidiaries, or even in the case of a single subsidiary where various types of interrelationships exist, an *eliminations ledger* supported by an *eliminations journal,* or journal vouchers, is a useful adjunct to the periodic consolidation process. These records contain the items appearing in the elimination column of a consolidating worksheet. As changes occur in equity holdings, formal journal vouchers with supporting data are prepared, and entries and postings are made to record them. The result is a more systematic procedure and a documented record; moreover, it can then be said that all details that find their way into consolidated statements are taken from formally maintained and controlled accounting records. On the consolidating worksheet a trial balance of the eliminations ledger would take the place of the seven journal entries now appearing, for example, in the eliminations column of the illustration on page 145. The classification of accounts for the eliminations ledger would be a mixture: a combination of accounts or account groups to be modified by consolidation as they are reported by the units whose affairs are to be put together.

The coverage of the eliminations ledger may extend to unincorporated manufacturing and selling branches and other subdivisions maintaining self-balancing accounts. Explanations or vouchers supporting entries in the eliminations journal supply a convenient, often more orderly, vehicle for making a permanent record of and ready reference to reasons, sources, approvals, occasional recomputations, and various other details that underlie reconciling items between separate and sometimes differently maintained ledgers.

In the illustration, a selling branch appears whose sales are delivered out of home-office stocks and whose balance-sheet components are limited to cash, receivables, fixtures, payables, and inter-office accounts. The last-named account differs from its counterpart in the home office by the two items reported in journal entry 7. Both items may be regarded as necessary adjustments of the home-office books before they are closed for the period; when such adjustments have been made and the branch's nominal accounts have been spread on the home-office books, the remaining reconciling items, the interoffice accounts, will exactly offset each other.

Assume that the $11,000 profit credit has now been placed on the home-office books,[10] but that the $2,000 has not, for the reason that the home-office books will be automatically corrected when the cash is received in July. A variant of journal entry 7 could then be the following:

[10] By a debit to the interoffice account and a credit to retained earnings.

Cash	2,000	
Payable to Ames	45,770	
*Advances to branch	2,000	
Advances to branch		47,770
*Cash		2,000

The items preceded by asterisks would remain open (unposted) until the remittance from the branch has been received and recorded by the home office.

The trial balance of an eliminations ledger that might have been kept by the Ames Company could have appeared as follows just before consolidation:

Cash	2,000	
Receivables		24,200
Inventories		3,360
Fixed assets		28,000
Allowance for depreciation	2,800	
Advances to branch		47,770
Investment in Bass bonds		43,200
Investment in Bass stock		146,900
Acquisition excess (Goodwill)	26,250	
Accounts payable	24,200	
Payable to Ames	45,770	
Mortgage bonds	45,000	
Unamortized discount		1,800
Capital stock	80,000	
Retained earnings	70,250	
Sales	746,300	
Dividend received	8,000	
Bond discount earned	450	
Cost of sales		745,940
Depreciation		1,400
Bond discount expense		450
Dividends paid		8,000

Like other ledgers in which nominal accounts are expressed, the eliminations ledger must have its annual closing entry; the following, or its equivalent, would be required:

Sales		746,300
Dividend received		8,000
Bond discount earned		450
Cost of sales	745,940	
Depreciation	1,400	
Bond discount expense	450	
Dividend paid	8,000	
Retained earnings		1,040

The cumulative adjustment of retained earnings now stands at $58,210; this amount reduces Ames' retained earnings ($293,380, not including the branch profits) and those of Bass ($58,880, net of minority interest) to the consolidated total appearing on the worksheet ($294,050).

Comment has already been made to the effect that a number of variants can be introduced in the keeping of the eliminations ledger. Here again, as we have noted on other occasions, no standards or conventions are involved—only convenience and preferences (sometimes whims!) of the accountant. For example, the second item—the credit of $24,200 applicable to receivables—may be allowed to stand until the next consolidated statements are prepared, at which time only the net increase or decrease in that amount is journalized; or the whole amount may be reversed at the beginning of the new period. Also, the parent company might well have taken up the $11,000 profit of the Crawford branch before the preparation of the consolidating statements.

Other problems

A number of special problems arise in connection with the application of the procedures we have described in this chapter. Among those of general interest are the following:

1) Occasionally the value of a controlling company's equity in a subsidiary exceeds the price paid for the capital stock acquired. Where assets and liabilities have been fairly stated, the result is a negative goodwill or *consolidation surplus* when balance sheets of controlling company and subsidiary are combined. As with a positive excess, the current practice is to remove the excess by amortizing the difference over a brief span of years by building up the investment account on the controlling company's books with a corresponding credit to current income. Justification for this practice lies in the fact that the net assets controlled are being realized and "proven" to be as real as any other asset group forming a part of the consolidated picture.

2) Where any outstanding minority shares of a subsidiary are acquired, the related portion of the periodic profits assigned to the consolidated retained earnings is recognized as accumulating from the date of acquisition on an average basis; thus if a 60%

ownership of the shares of a subsidiary is increased to 70% at the middle of a fiscal year, 5% of the subsidiary's unconsolidated net income for the year would be regarded as increasing the book value of the acquired shares at the beginning of the year. But, in reverse, if Ames' 80% interest in Bass' shares be reduced to 70% at midyear by a sale of 1,000 shares at $25 per share, none of the subsidiary's current net income would be regarded as belonging in the consolidated picture.[11] Assuming this sale takes place on December 31, 19-3, and applying the transaction to our illustration, we would compute the gain to the parent company as follows:

Selling price on 12-31-19-3	
of 1,000 $10 shares to minority stockholder	$25,000
Less—book value (on Ames' books) at	
6-30-19-3—$\frac{1}{8}$ of 146,900	18,363
Gain from sale (on Ames' books)	$ 6,637

Consolidated net income would be credited with $4,109, computed thus:

Selling price, as above		$25,000
Less:		
Book value of minority interest as at		
12-31-19-3 (equal to $\frac{1}{2}$ of $35,220)	$17,610	
Recovery of remaining acquisition		
excess—$\frac{1}{8}$ of $26,250	3,281	20,891
Consolidated gain		$ 4,109

Here we have a gain arising from the sale of an equity in the consolidated enterprise that resembles treasury stock. Ordinarily we would regard the "gain" as paid-in surplus; in this case it is Ames that sold the stock, and the gain does not affect the equity of Bass' stockholders, but becomes an added equity of Ames' stockholders in the consolidated net assets.

3) A stock dividend issued by a subsidiary has no effect on the consolidated statements.

---

[11] The alternative would be for Ames to take up the earnings for the half-year, but this would merely result in splitting the gain of $6,637 into two parts, both of which would be joined in any statement of consolidated earnings.

Summary

We have thus seen that typically the combination of financial statements which produces consolidated balance sheets and income statements requires the elimination of interrelated items. These items include intercompany receivables and payables; capital stock and retained earnings to the date effective control is secured; and intercompany sales, purchases, and profits on construction. Minority interests are preferably set out and valued on the basis of the subsidiary's book values.

The objective of consolidated financial statements is to show the financial position and operating results of two or more legally separate business units as a single entity, wherever in fact a single economic entity exists: a point of view that will be helpful in solving problems growing out of situations, often highly individual, we have not had the opportunity of discussing here.

CHAPTER ELEVEN

Costs and Their Control

Under modern management practices the costs of carrying out the purposes and functions of an enterprise are identified with organizational activities—and activities with persons to whom authority for specified operations has been entrusted. Cost accounting, having a much narrower meaning, has traditionally been associated with factory operating costs, the latter dealing with the systematic allocation of material, labor, and overhead to factory output. Cost accountants, once preoccupied with widely divergent theories of overhead distribution, are now turning their attention to standard costs and direct costing: devices that permit the exercise of cost controls from higher management levels in line with management's expanding function of control. Costs, including cost allocations, firmly linked with planning, forecasting, and a deeper proliferation of operating authority, have made possible the coordinated judgments and decisions now demanded of management.

t is sometimes said that in business enterprise there are three kinds of accounting: *financial* accounting, *administrative* (or *management*) accounting, and *cost* accounting. The conventional definitions[1] are:

> Financial accounting is concerned with the recording and *external* reporting of transactions affecting revenues, expenses, assets, and liabilities: transactions that are normally recorded and summarized in the general offices of a business.

> Administrative accounting deals with the processes associated with the conduct of management: the gathering of information required in decision-making and in the determination of policies relating to such diverse areas as budget preparation, budget administration, the recognition of costs as expense, depreciation policies and methods, the creation and operation of reserves, internal auditing, and *internal* reporting.

> Cost accounting embraces the design and operation of factory[2] cost systems and product cost-finding procedures, the establishing of activities or cost centers and of physical cost units, the determination and interpretation of unit costs, overhead distribution, and other spreads of expense, and the analysis, reporting, and interpretation of factory-cost behavior.

This traditional view of the separability of accounting functions has always involved shadowy distinctions; it is being rapidly displaced by a growing conviction that accounting activities should

---

[1] Adapted from the author's *Dictionary*.

[2] In this chapter "factory" is intended to cover any manufacturing, shop, or other operation in which labor or machines, or both, have an input of "raw" materials, including parts, and an output of "finished product" differing from the input in form, marketability, or other characteristics.

be articulated parts of a single process in which management at all levels participates, and that the determination of basic policies supporting the accounting system devised for any form of collective endeavor is a responsibility to which management, if not its creator, must of necessity contribute.[3] The participation of management in accounting and the penetration of accounting into management functions have become a widely accepted necessity. Cost systems, at one time assumed to be independent of and unavoidably in conflict with financial accounting, are now integrated with other accounting activities; no longer confined to factory operations, they have been conformed to a common set of concepts. And, as we will observe later, the once highly esoteric estimates of a budget director have been transformed into carefully precast standards for projecting and controlling future operations: standards with which concluded operations can be intelligently compared and judged. The effort today is to bring together into a consistent whole the once loose ends of operational organization and control, and to maintain an external outlook wholly congruous with this newer internal look. Financial accounting has become merely a recapitulation within management accounting, which is taking over and reshaping the tenets of cost accounting.[4]

Cost as expense

Costs in a business enterprise are incurred in the expectation that upon becoming expense[5] they immediately or within a short period

---

[3] The responsibility for accounting policies never rests solely with management, however. In practically all countries today the umbrella of the *public interest* now covers various levels in the accounting process: examples may be found in the imposition on public utilities of account classifications, consumer rates, and profit limitations; in the specification of the form and content of financial statements of business corporations whose shares are held by the public; in regulations supporting income-tax laws; in the limitations on costs relating to government contracts; and, in what may be still more important, the climate of critical scrutiny from many quarters to which published reports are now exposed. The role of management, functioning through the controller in establishing accounting policies, is still a broad one, notwithstanding the practical necessity of not transcending standards dictated by the public interest, whether these standards have been legally imposed or have been generally recognized as a *sine qua non* of responsible business conduct.

[4] If we admit the all-embracing unity of *accounting* concepts, *management* as a modifier of "accounting" becomes a pleonasm.

[5] A few types of cost under ordinary conditions never become expense:

of time will be converted [6]—with a profit added—into cash. We considered in Chapter 2 the conditions precedent to the *recognition* of *external* transactions involving costs: their timing, preaudit, classification, and entry in the accounts. Here we are concerned with movements of costs after the initial recording, up to and including their absorption, and loss of identity, upon making their appearance in the income statement where their cancellation against revenues is effected. The positioning of costs in the records and in reports by means of *internal* transactions is a central task of accounting; the purpose is to build up costs that are or will ultimately be related to revenues, it being recognized that most external cost transactions antedate revenue transactions, often by considerable periods of time; and, within practicable limitations, to identify expense (including costs of sales) with revenues. The principal types of cost movements, with some of which we are already familiar, are these:

1) *Attachment to Product.* A substantial number of the cost transactions of a business enterprise fall into this category, as where a retailer buys merchandise and sells most of it within the same accounting period. His purchases, adjusted by opening and closing inventories, become his cost of sales by a single type of movement for the period—from a *purchases* or inventory account to a *cost-of-sales* account. In a manufacturing establishment at least four steps replace this single movement. Conventional procedures call for the recording of raw-material and parts purchases in an *inventory* account; their transfer, at the beginning of a production process, to a *work-in-process* (or -progress) account; thence, at the completion of production, to a *finished-stock* (or -goods or -product) account; and, finally, upon sale, from finished stock to a *cost-of-sales* account. In like manner, labor and overhead costs flow through the accounts: first, an entry in a factory-expense account, followed by successive transfers, along with raw material and parts, to work-in-process, finished-stock, and cost-of-sales accounts. This procedure

---

land is the principal example. Strictly-speaking, losses arising from the liquidation of receivables, investments, and other assets are also expense; however, at this point we are dealing with costs *deliberately* incurred.

[6] *Conversion* means the replacement of one form of property by another; in this sense, a credit sale involves two conversions—the creation of a receivable and its later liquidation.

makes possible a buildup at each stage of costs consonant with the advance of production; the development of unit costs comparable with projected unit costs; and, at all stages, inventory quantity-and-dollar controls.

2) *Benefits Yielded.* We have already observed that the normal function of fixed assets is to supply a continuous stream of services the cost of which is transferred through periodic provisions for depreciation to expense accounts. A similiar procedure is involved in disposing of expense prepayments. Through internal transactions, the various types of costs are spread directly, or as equitably as possible, over the units of output to which they have contributed. Costs classified as factory overhead are from time to time conventionally transferred to work in process through the medium of an overhead rate—as we will see shortly.

3) *Most Recent Costs.* The *lifo* method of identifying merchandise sold and raw materials put into production with the cost of most recent purchases has the effect of transferring costs to expense that may be materially greater or less than actual costs. Here, during a period of rising prices, the objective, as we have seen, is to reap the maximum in the way of a tax advantage.[7] Regardless of whether lifo methods are accepted as good practice, they have been often employed, and for our purposes here must be regarded as a special way of linking costs with expense.

4) *Market Declines.* Valuing an inventory at the lower of cost or market means that we are associating a part of the cost of unsold merchandise or unprocessed raw materials with expense before any physical outgoing movement has taken place. The amount of the reduction is generally not separately reported but is held to be justified as a cost of the merchandise or materials *flow*, since it is a loss arising from the risk involved in forward buying, or, from an alternative point of view which is often cited, a cost of assuring that future operations will have a better chance of enjoying a "normal" gross margin from sales. The author believes that a writedown to market—an interruption of the normal flow of cost—can be justified only in extreme situations.

5) *Losses.* A loss is a cost which through an unanticipated event or condition is not recoverable through sale or through the enjoy-

---

[7] Current Federal income-tax law, as we have already observed, permits the practice provided the same treatment is reflected in reports to stockholders.

ment of a benefit or service. Fire, theft, and acts of God are the most frequent causes. A loss is recognized when a determination has been made that any given cost has no exchange value and can no longer be related to future operations. Minor or repetitive losses incident to a factory operation, because they can be anticipated, are regarded as factory overhead; a larger, nonrepetitive loss is likely to appear as a general expense rather than a production cost.

6) *Minor Asset Purchases.* We noted in Chapter 6 that minor asset acquisitions are often immediately expensed because they lack materiality as additions to fixed assets and thus have little effect on depreciation expense. They may appear separately on a statement of costs or be merged with depreciation expense.

7) *Attachment to Period.* Many costs are designated as *period costs*, that is, as expenses when they are incurred, or where, as through the medium of an equalization reserve,[8] they are allocated over a period of months. Selling costs and real-estate taxes are examples.

Direct-costing concepts, described below, support the proposition that all fixed factory costs, including depreciation, are period costs.

The flow of factory costs

A *product* cost, then, is a cost readily identified with a product; it does not become an expense until the product enters the expense category through sale. In contrast, a *period* cost is a cost identified with a period of time rather than a product; it becomes an expense of the period during which it is incurred.

[8] An *equalization reserve* is a device for spreading costs identified with a given period of time over the operating expenses of subdivisions of that period. In a typical operation, an estimate is made at the beginning of a fiscal year of the total annual amount of expenses of a certain class (e.g., administrative expenses which are to be paid at irregular intervals during the year); one-twelfth of the total is then charged to expense during each of the first eleven months, with a corresponding credit to a temporary reserve or credit nominal account; the expenses as incurred are charged against the reserve; and at the end of the twelfth month whatever remains in the reserve is then written off as a debit or credit to the expense of that month; an equalization reserve does not carry over from one fiscal year to another. However, during the year, the balance in the equalization reserve is carried on monthly balance sheets as a deferred debt or credit.

A manufacturer's product costs consist of processed raw materials, direct labor, and often factory overhead. Direct labor is labor that works on the product as opposed to indirect labor which services the machines and processes that employ direct labor. Examples of indirect labor are watchmen, janitors, maintenance men, cost accountants, stockkeepers, and superintendents. Indirect labor, supplies (indirect materials), depreciation, rent, power, heat, and light are, as a rule, the leading items making up factory overhead.

To understand the internal transactions recording the flow of factory costs, we will need to examine the mechanics depicted in the accompanying illustration of the factory ledger of a small manufacturing company.[9] On page 161 we have a four-column analysis of a single month's transactions that have been charged or credited to 19 factory-ledger accounts. From an inspection of the figures we can read the following:

1) The factory inventory on April 1[10] consisted of raw materials, 2,800;[11] work in process, 17,800; and finished goods, 58,200; a total of 78,800. At the end of April the corresponding amounts were 5,200, 18,500, 62,700, and 86,400, respectively.

2) During the month, costs were incurred and added to accounts 1-6 amounting to 157,500, of which 15,400 was a provision for depreciation, the only internal transaction.[12]

3) April charges of 152,400 to work in process, all arising from internal transactions, consisted of materials, labor, and overhead: the latter, apparently on the basis of 75% of direct-labor cost, with the result that overhead of 2,700 remained unabsorbed. We may assume that the basis of the materials charges was the total of the month's requisitions calling for physical transfers from the stockroom or from a stockpile of raw materials to the factory location where production operations, involving machines and labor, stand ready to transform them into finished product. The labor charges may be the total of time tickets showing that all productive labor was employed on in-process work. If a job-cost system is in effect—which we will discuss later—all of these costs are entered on work orders, each work

---

[9] Employing, perhaps, not more than 150 people.

[10] In this illustration, one month's transactions are being cleared through the accounts. As a rule, however, factory nominal accounts are accumulated over a 12-month period before being carried into cost of sales and closing inventory.

[11] For convenience, dollar signs have been omitted here and on pages following.

[12] Other possible internal transactions: accruals of labor and other expense, withdrawals of supplies from a supplies inventory carried in the general ledger.

BENDER MANUFACTURING COMPANY

Summary of Factory-Ledger Transactions
Month of April, 19-1

No.	Account	Charges		Credits	
		Opening inventory	April charges	Transfers	Closing inventory
1	Raw materials	2 800	81 300	78 900	5 200
2	Direct labor	—	42 000	42 000	—
	Overhead—				
3	Depreciation	—	15 400	—	—
4	Indirect labor	—	11 000	—	—
5	Maintenance	—	4 700	—	—
6	Other shop expense	—	3 100	—	—
7	Portion absorbed (to 11)	—	—	31 500	—
8	Portion unabsorbed (to 18)	—	—	2 700	—
	Work in process—				
9	Material	14 400	78 900	76 900	16 400
10	Labor	2 000	42 000	42 800	1 200
11	Overhead	1 400	31 500	32 000	900
	Finished goods—				
12	Material	22 500	76 900	77 100	22 300
13	Labor	21 000	42 800	40 700	23 100
14	Overhead	14 700	32 000	29 400	17 300
	Cost of sales—				
15	Material	—	77 100		
16	Labor	—	40 700		
17	Overhead	—	29 400		
18	Unabsorbed overhead	—	2 700		
19	Transfers to G/L			149 900	
	Totals	78 800	611 500	603 900	86 400

order reflecting the cumulative costs of a particular job or product batch, entries thereon being made daily, weekly, or monthly, according to the requirements of the recording method in use.

4) Work in process amounting to 151,700 was closed out during April to finished goods; if work orders are in use, this amount is, perhaps, the total of a group of work orders which reflect the completed cost of a series of jobs or product batches; the three-way breakdown between materials, labor, and overhead is simply a recap of the charges appearing, possibly chronologically, on the completed individual work orders. We may presume that we are now in a position to establish unit costs for each item that has been completed and that our unit costs can be stated in terms of the three basic cost components. This enables us to continue the breakdown throughout the accounts—up to and including the items that make up cost of sales on the income statement. The cost of the completed product has now

been transferred from accounts 9, 10, and 11, to finished-stock accounts 12, 13, and 14. At the same time product quantities and costs will be posted from work orders to individual product accounts in a subsidiary stock ledger or to individual stock cards maintained by an inventory clerk.

5) The cost of April sales was 149,900—which included the unabsorbed overhead of 2,700. The breakdown between material, labor, and overhead may be presumed to be the result of multiplying the number of units sold by the unit costs displayed on the stock-ledger accounts or on stock cards.

6) The cost of sales appears to have been transferred in total to the general ledger, leaving open in the factory ledger the same seven accounts with which we started the month. The items comprising the total of 86,400 are, of course, the end-of-the-month inventories of raw materials, work in process, and finished stock, the first and third items supported by detailed stock records and the second by unfinished work orders; moreover, we would expect to find the same overall total in a general-ledger account bearing a title such as "Factory Ledger" or "Factory Inventory," [13] with a debit balance of 86,400 at the month end.

In recording the movements in and out of the work-in-process and finished-stock accounts of our illustration, the following additional points should be considered:

1) The ratios of raw material to direct labor in successive work-in-process inventories (7.2 and 13.7) can usually be expected to vary from the corresponding ratios in finished-goods inventory additions and withdrawals (1.1, .97, 1.8, and 1.9), for numerous reasons: for example, materials ratios are likely to be higher when called for at the beginning of the production operation. Finished-goods ratios may also change; if a variety of products is being produced, the products may differ from each other in the quantities of direct material and labor that have been expended on them; and the relative efficiency of labor may also vary from one period to another.

2) The overhead-labor ratio in opening inventories (.7) and the corresponding ratio in the closing inventories (.75) suggest that last month's inventories of both work in process and finished stock have been disposed of.

3) An overhead-labor ratio of more than 80% would have been required if all overhead had been allocated to work in process. However, changing the overhead rate from one month to another is not a com-

---

[13] We have here an illustration of a control account supported by a ledger, which in turn contains control accounts supported by detailed inventory records.

mon practice since the proportions of both labor and overhead costs will very probably differ as between short periods. It might well be possible to designate account number 8 as an equalization reserve and thus adjust cumulative costs of sales only at the end of the year.

Factory cost accounts are maintained in many ways. Today, cost-keeping is often linked with delegations of management authority. Thus in our illustration a seven-way breakdown of the inventory accounts is maintained in the factory ledger, which may point to the not uncommon situation in which a plant manager is charged with the responsibility for housing and controlling not only the raw materials necessary for production, but also the finished stock until its delivery to customers. If some person who does not report to the factory head has the job of keeping the stock records and has physical custody of the finished stock, accounts 12-19 would likely be found in another ledger.

Job and process costing

Job costing is the term applied to the technique of distributing factory costs over job or work orders as production takes place. *Process costing*, in contrast, involves the accumulation of costs for each type of operation within a factory, or for a factory as a whole, where the output is (or is treated as) a single kind of good or service.

Our example of factory-ledger accounts will serve to illustrate the two methods. Let us assume that seven work orders were in process during the month of April as follows:

Number	Breakdown	Beginning	Additions	Completed	Ending
2632	M	14,400	400	14,800	
	L	2,000	400	2,400	
	O	1,400	300	1,700	
2685	M		11,500	11,500	
	L		2,600	2,600	
	O		1,950	1,950	
2686	M		12,200		12,200
	L		800		800
	O		600		600
4 others	M		54,800	50,600	4,200
(3 com-	L		38,200	37,800	400
pleted)	O		28,650	28,350	300

Assume further that an inspection of work order 2632 calling for 2,800 units of product M at a cost of 6.73 each shows that 2,700 salable units were actually produced at a cost of 7.00 each:

Items	Original W/O Estimate	Actual	% above (+) or below (−)
Units	2,800	2,700	−3.6
Total cost	18,844	18,900	+.3
Materials:			
Weight	910 lbs	925 lbs	+1.6
Cost	14,560	14,800	
Labor	2,520	2,400	−4.3
Overhead	1,764	1,700	
Unit cost	$6.73	$7.00	+4.1
Material:			
Weight	.325 lb	.343 lb	−5.4
Cost	5.20	5.48	+5.4
Labor	.90	.89	
Overhead	.63	.63	

Here we have a situation where production fell short of the estimate while actual costs exceeded projected costs. The reasons? Accounting does not supply them, but it does furnish clues from which management familiar with the particular operation—a foreman, cost engineer, production manager, or the factory's cost accountant—can make whatever analysis may be necessary in determining the cause and responsibility for what has happened and in supplying a guide for future estimates and production controls.[14]

As outsiders, we can only speculate as to the causes for the variation here. The original estimate may have been faulty. The apparent wastage of raw material may have been caused, for example, by careless processing, a change in specifications after the processing had started, or a more-rigid-than-usual inspection after processing that led to a larger number of rejects. Since the labor cost per unit corresponds to the estimate, a more likely cause would be an unanticipated poor quality of raw material. But the analysis before

[14] Many types of information and analysis may be called for on work-order forms so that they may serve as a basis for management review; examples: data on setup time, spoilage, reruns, sampling, overtime, delays, idle time, special costs, changes in specifications—a virtual chronology of the events and conditions affecting the cost, quality, timing, and disposal of the output.

us is not the final answer. Figures furnished by accountants must be interpreted in the light of a background of information about operating conditions: familiarity with materials, the character of the processing, the skill of foremen and machine operators, inspection standards, and the various factors that affect the salability of the finished product.

It may also be that the results in this case will be judged to be within a range of tolerance that requires no search for causes. The differences shown, considering past experience in fabricating comparable quantities of product *M* may be held to have negligible significance. A selling price of $15 per unit of product *M*, with no competitive product available to buyers, may have increased management's tolerance, in this instance, to a point where a unit cost, say, of anything under $8, would be of little concern. However, this is an unlikely situation. Most managements today would raise questions concerning any variance; skilled management and active competition have led to more accurate cost projections, to lowered tolerances, to more rapid reporting of variances, to more rigorous controls, and to searching inquiries for causes and corrective controls.

Increased participation by accountants in dealing with problems of management has often led to adding to the factory-accountant's functions the burden of determining proximate causes of variances. Under such circumstances he is expected to understand the nature of operations, bear in mind past experience in its relation to the present, and participate in management conferences and decisions concerning operating methods as well as costs.

To relate our schedule on page 164 to process costs, we will need to make the following assumptions of fact: for the month of April, a production goal of 150,000 units of product *K* at a cost of $1 per unit had been projected; at the month end, 148,000 units have been completed at the indicated cost of $151,700, or $1.025 per unit. Here again, questions can be asked concerning such matters as the quality of the raw material, possible wastes arising therefrom, and the efficiency of labor. In lieu of work orders, relatively simple periodic reports of production quantities and costs and comparisons with estimates are prepared by the cost accountant for management's review.

Standards for costs

If the significance of costs is to be reviewed after their occurrence, they must be measured against some standard: a standard of comparison. The standard, or cost pattern, may have originated in the past experience of the business or of a particular industry, or it may be a projection of what judgment has suggested that attainable future costs should be, with past experience serving as an aid in forming the judgment. Estimates of future costs are of two basic types: what the costs should be (ideal costs), and what, in view of the operating environment, they are likely to be. Ideal costs, which are habitually lower than actual costs, may differ materially from the realities faced in everyday production and may have little meaning to the practical man charged with the administration of production controls. Thus, it may be estimated that, assuming a high rate of efficiency and no lost time, the labor time of producing a certain unit of product should be four hours. The required operation has never been performed, however, in less than six hours, for various reasons: lack of highly skilled labor, setup time, delays in obtaining materials promptly or in securing access to tools and machines, holdups in transferring in-process items from one operation to another, perhaps even coffee breaks! Could better supervision or the removal of one or more of these loss factors reduce the time to five hours?

Cost accountants are called upon, at one time or another, to deal with these three kinds of costs: ideal costs, past costs, and attainable costs, the last-named being what a realistic management expects costs will be, considering existing working conditions, normal delays, and reasonable labor and mechanical potentials. In the bulk of practical situations today, attainable costs are accepted as *standard costs:* forward estimates of what production costs will be, under all foreseeable operating capabilities and limitations. Subsequent comparisons with actual costs serve to measure relative efficiencies and provide various bases for performance awards, and often for altering production methods. Translated into other forms, they become indispensable aids in determining prices, forecasting financing requirements for productive operations, estimating profits, and establishing a basic process of communication between administrative heads and various echelons of supervisors.

Standard costs are often thought of as the projection of unit-of-finished-product costs, broken down by materials, labor, and overhead. The original estimate of unit cost on page 164 may be regarded as a standard cost. In this form standard costs can be the building blocks for determining the total costs of operating a factory. But estimates of the cost of the whole of a prospective activity or process, where the likely total of units of output are not readily determinable, or where such units might vary widely from one day to another, may also be designated as standard costs; information booths in a large department store supply us with an example.

Past experience plays an important but not a dominant role in establishing standard costs, but they must be painstakingly modified and kept up to date if they are to serve in any realistic way as a measure of performance. Many cost systems employing standard costs are deficient in this respect; once created, standard costs tend to become fixed and hence to fall far short of a periodically reviewed, realistic preview of the actual conditions under which production will take place. The author's experience has been that the best standard costs come from the combined talents of accountants and specialized industrial engineers, with at least annual reviews and corrections—which, of course, does not mean that standard costs should ever be conformed to actual costs.

Overhead

We have thus far observed one example of how factory overhead moves into work in process out of the original classification given to the transactions of which it is composed, then into finished stock, and eventually into cost of sales. Overhead "rates"—the percentage relationships of overhead costs to direct-labor costs—were applied to the direct-labor costs revealed by work orders covering individual jobs; we might guess that the pre-April rate of 70% and the April rate of 75% were derived from past experience, but even 75% was not large enough to absorb the whole of the latest month's overhead. There are various other ways of deriving and applying a factory-overhead rate: the denominator of the ratio-fraction may be total direct-labor hours, material costs, *prime* costs (that is, direct material plus direct labor), machine hours, and so on. The base most often found in practice is direct-labor cost, the general theory—not often easy to justify—being that most factory overhead supports and services direct labor. But a stronger reason for its popularity is the ease of its determination and application. Where the total of factory overhead is materially less than direct-labor costs, the direct-labor-cost basis is probably as good as any other. But in situations where direct-labor costs are a fraction of overhead costs, as in an automated establishment (a modern oil refinery is a good example), a machine- or process-hour-cost basis may yield more satisfactory results.

Overhead costs in a factory having more than a single output are joint costs, and for joint costs there is no answer: no single, universally acceptable method of allocation. Any division of the overhead between products is wholly arbitrary and not an accounting problem at all. It is a problem that only top management can dispose of, if, indeed, allocation is to be seriously considered. In the past, cost accountants often devoted much time to elaborate, sometimes fantastic methods of overhead distribution and redistribution; the more involved the effort, the more *exact* the allocated cost was assumed to be. Textbooks on cost accounting are still very much concerned with the relative merits of the different bases of overhead spreads. But the plain truth is that the fixed costs and many of the variable costs that make up factory overhead have no measurable relation to specific types or items of output.

Direct costing

Because of the impossibility of any realistic allocation of overhead to factory output, except in total and for all products, the idea of *direct costing* has been hailed with enthusiasm by many accountants and by management wherever it has been applied. To accountants, it has come as a logical development: as a device for disseminating information essential to the full operation of organizational controls; to management, it appeals as a device that has made possible a clearer look at delegations of authority to factory supervisors. Direct costing, as a simplified form of factory accounting, provides channels of communication between top management and operating personnel that are invariably clouded by the ramifications of overhead distributions.

Direct costing is usually described as an accounting procedure that values factory output on the basis of costs that can be readily identified with it. This means *variable* costs, mainly raw materials and direct labor, with occasional items of factory overhead which would not have been incurred were it not for a particular product and which can readily be identified with that product; other overhead, or *indirect* factory expense, regarded as a *period* cost, is excluded. Sometimes selling expense can be directly linked with individual products and is treated as a direct cost.[15] But for many organizations that have accepted the idea of direct costing, factory overhead, along with administrative and selling expense, is conceived as not adding to product costs and is regarded as a period cost: an expense not extending beyond the period in which it has been incurred.

Some accountants would tolerate direct costing as an internal device for "administrative-accounting" purposes, but they stop short of approving it as a basis for inventory valuation. A sudden omission of factory overhead from finished-inventory costs would in some instances effect a substantial reduction in current assets and hence in working capital and in the working-capital ratio. But at the time these words are being written, a more compelling reason for their disapproval is that the direct-costing basis of inventory valuation has not been sanctioned by income-tax regulations; nor has it won approval of the AAA, the SEC, and the Accounting Principles Board of the AICPA. The last-named has given no reasons for its negative position—a position which the author—who has advocated direct costing for many years—believes will ultimately be reversed.[16]

The effect of direct-costing-inventory valuation on the income statement would be less drastic than its effect on a balance sheet because of the offsetting effect of the elements that make up opening and closing inventories.[17] Where the operating cycle of the

[15] But only as an allocation of cost to be added to cost of sales on the income statement, not as an addition to unit-product cost.

[16] Numerous direct-costing studies have been published by the National Accounting Association whose committees considering the subject have included both controllers and public accountants having active contacts with direct-costing practices. The case material collected by these committees has been uniformly convincing. See, for example, *NAA Research Report 37, Current Applications of Direct Costing* (1961).

[17] Thus the effect on Bender's opening and closing inventory (see page

business covers, say, a two-year period, the first year witnessing an inventory buildup and the second a rate of finished-product outflow materially exceeding that of manufacture, a loss in the first year and a large profit in the second year might result. To some accountants, this effect of seeming distortion would be "smoothed out," perhaps eliminated, by carrying into the second year factory costs that direct costing would regard as a period cost of the first year. But, as we have pointed out in an earlier chapter and will again consider in our final chapter, the functions of accounting should not include the operation of any device that has the effect of averaging profits. Moreover, an enterprise with a two-year cycle of the type just described is a rare one; and accounting procedures favoring exceptional situations could hardly be justified in determining their suitability for industry generally.[18]

Variances

Analyses of performance are important functions of management. By devising wise organizational policies, choosing competent staff assistants and operations supervisors, stimulating research and development aimed at better and newer products and lower costs, seeking new and improving old outlets, establishing through budgets a governing plan for future operations, and creating a pervasive *esprit de corps* through vigorous personal leadership, a top executive sets the pace for current performance. But he cannot make intelligent decisions on these matters without a background of experience out of which judgments that precede decisions can be developed. He must have information on what has been done as compared with what was originally proposed, and information concerning differences. To the cost accountant this means pointing

---

161) would be to reduce them by $16,100 and $18,200, respectively, while the effect on the income statement would be to reduce the month's profits by the difference between the two, or $2,100.

[18] The use of direct costing for internal purposes need not, however, interfere with inventory valuations for balance-sheet purposes. It is always possible to add overhead to direct-cost inventories in amounts consonant with previous practices. Preservation of the material-and-labor components of work-in-process and finished stock leads to a labor-cost summation which makes the addition of overhead in a lump sum a simple matter: a practice followed in a number of instances familiar to the author.

out significant *variances,* whatever the cost system may be, and the reasons for their occurrence.

The schedule on page 164 and the explanations that follow it supply a simple example of how variances must be studied, provided of course that facts are substituted for the conjectures we have made. Schedules, with explanations, prepared by the cost accountant and depicting the whole range of factory performance, projected and actual, must be in the hands of the factory management within a day or two (in some cases even hours) after the close of each reporting period: most accountants would prescribe internal-reporting periods of not longer than a month.

Further references to management reports on projected and actual costs will be made in subsequent chapters. At present we will need to consider a form of reporting that covers only important variances. Where the accounts to be compared are numerous and the amounts in many of them conform closely to original estimates, abbreviated reports are often prepared in harmony with what has been called "management by exception." The idea conveyed by this phrase is that only unusual differences need management's attention. Such reports are effective in reducing the time required for review. Occasionally, however, an expense or operation needing attention will not be given the review it deserves simply because the projected amount agrees closely with the actual; yet the need for continuing the expense or operation may have passed. Constant alertness on the part of the accountant is required. The author has recommended in certain situations that *all* costs be given some form of positive executive review, regardless of their correspondence with planned costs.

Responsibility costs and *activity accounting* are terms relating to controls over costs under delegations of management authority; we will consider them in the next chapter.

Summary

We should now have acquired a general picture of the flow of costs through the accounts: their origins, the internal transactions transferring them from one account to another, and the principal methods by which expenses are disposed of. The growing popularity of direct-costing methods, in the endeavor to conform costs to lines of authority created by deepening management controls, is likely to continue. And we might readily hazard the prediction that the recognition by regulatory agencies of direct costing as a basis for inventory valuation is probably not far off.

CHAPTER TWELVE

Accounting & Management

Accounting has made much of modern management possible. It has provided a framework of financial information and control upon which it has been possible to expand the domain of management to any desired operating level of an organization. Delegating authority to subordinate levels improves the administrative process by encouraging the development and better use of the skills of supervisors but without subtracting from the ultimate responsibility of the top executive to account for the results of current operations and to plan the organization's future. Transaction classifications, reporting, analysis, projection through budgets, and the institution and maintenance of a variety of internal controls are accounting functions that have accelerated these developments.

173

An accountant does not work in a vacuum; nor does he delimit his procedures with rigid concepts unrelated to the organization of which he is a part. He is not governed by principles that serve some remote professional objective. Rather, he is a functioning sector of an organism of many parts. The subject matter with which he deals has its sources outside his immediate jurisdiction, his responsibility being confined to providing a protective cover. His daily production is accurate records, his endproducts dependable information on which the rational conclusions and intelligent decisions of others can be based. His relations with the rest of the organization are all-important. His is a management service; he, an important factor of the management concept and structure.

Growth of the management concept

Management has progressed notably from what it once was— hardly two decades ago; it was then a highly personalized, confidential area in which people moved mysteriously and unquestioningly, sometimes rapidly; sometimes, where action was most demanded, seemingly not at all. Management decision-making, often the result of canny insights, or almost as often based on no more than hunch, moved haltingly and was unpredictable, but, in a rapidly expanding economy, more often than not, successful. Before World War II the word for management, as we now employ the term, was "administration." The phrase "scientific management" was

174

in use, but it related primarily to the ways and means of promoting labor efficiency by making labor and factory methods more productive and more predictable. Its approach was from the "bottom up." [1] Administration was a sacred precinct, with a karma-like inevitability that anyone less than the top boss could not fathom, least of all question. An administrative head, reflecting an era of small business financed by personal fortunes, was typically unfitted for transferring his skills to a publicly owned, large-scale enterprise facing rapid changes in methods, products, prices, and world outlook. The dynamism that characterizes business enterprises and other organizations today demands a different approach: an approach that seeks out, develops, and utilizes talents from specialized fields. Yet we can recognize in some organizations survivals of the sort of top omnipotence that, if not laid down as an operating principle, was at least assumed as a matter of course. The conversion to modern ideas of management, accelerated by World War II, inflated costs, and the growth of both domestic and foreign competition has been a rapid one. At the same time, accountants who have dealt professionally with both business and governmental enterprise have learned not to be surprised when they encounter what some would term vestigial survivals. In this older order of things accounting was an administrative burden brought about by income-tax involvements. Governmental accounting in some instances was virtually nonexistent except for the recording of cash movements; in others, by laborious processes that supplied wholly illusory controls over expenditures, it had reached a dead end and was in a state of utter confusion.

But this gloomy picture of the past has had to be redrawn. Our object in this chapter will be to focus attention on the direction which modern management has taken and the resulting new importance and responsibilities it has attached to accounting and accountants.

---

[1] Henri Fayol, the French industrialist whose book *Administration Industrielle et Générale* was published in 1916 but remained unnoticed in this country for many years [an English translation published by Pittman (London) appeared as late as 1949], was the first to call attention to the possibility of looking from the "top down"—as in military commands—in any organization; his themes were planning, organizing, directing, coordinating, and controlling: all areas of activity in which accounting plays an essential part.

The trend of management

Organizations—governmental structures, universities, religious hierarchies, nonprofit as well as profit-making enterprises—are created to accomplish things people want. The structure and co-hesiveness of our civilization are dependent on the collective effort of organizations; indeed, our very well-being is a reflection of the way organizations operate. As our society has aged, the number and complexity of the organizational pattern have increased. The specialization, speed, and change that have featured social progress during the past twenty years have profoundly modified organizational functions and the conduct of organizational affairs. Moreover, organizations, whatever their nature, now operate with an increasing awareness of their responsibilities as both guardians and promoters of the public interest.

Organizational problems are recognized as being much the same everywhere. They persist because people working together require dynamic leadership and direction, clear differentiations in their duties, and satisfactions arising both from the exercise of individual skills and from joint accomplishments.

Leadership has meant many things, ranging from the notion of a person of magnetic qualities who is able to sway others to his point of view, regardless of its merits—to the abstraction that management is now on the way of becoming. Direction implies authority; authority requires the existence of broad powers of leadership which in government are known as law, and in the commercial world, top policy. The objective is the same: to spell out the purposes of assigned or assumed organizational effort and to provide a framework of cooperation for the practical, everyday conduct of the organization's affairs.

Today's management in government *executes* laws, and today's business leadership executes policies. But management qua management does not create laws or policies: these are the endproducts of governing bodies; in our national constitution, for example, elaborate precautions were taken to insure the separation of law making and law enforcement. We thus have legislatures and governors, synods and bishops, boards of directors and presidents. Since World War II an extraordinary amount of attention has been given to a deeper exploration of the management concept as applied to business organizations where the separation of policy and administration has often been confused. Much has emerged on the meaning and seemingly endless ramifications of management—textbooks, university departments, executive training projects, refresher programs for executives, industry-wide conferences, management retreats, firms of management consultants, and professional management bodies:[2] all concerned with exploring latent possibilities, providing standards, advancing the cause of improved business techniques, and all giving recognition to the need for substituting methodologies for personalities.[3]

It is in connection with this last development that the accountant's role has been substantially widened and deepened. Playing down arbitrary decisions and building up *decision-making*[4] by management as an art, if not a science, have focused attention on the importance of accounting as a device that can contribute to and influence the institution and maintenance of these newer, now widely recognized management functions.

[2] Interest in professional management development has not been confined to this country where the American Management Association (AMA) has supplied leadership for many years. A European society known as Federation Européen des Associations de Conseils en Organisation (FEACO) was established in September, 1960 as a confederation of member management societies, each from a different country.

[3] While stressing the means and methods of improved executive functioning, management authorities have given little attention to the need, if need there be, for establishing any firm line of demarcation between business policy and business administration; a usual assumption is that the two functions have independent origins. Except in the rarest instances, stockholders of large enterprises no longer have more than a nominal hand in shaping policies, although as a concession to tradition they are frequently called upon to give their unconsidered, uncritical, offhand approval to management policies already established. A board of directors may participate, even lead, in policy-making, but again, in larger organizations, with rare exceptions, it conducts no independent inquiry into possible alternatives to management's policy proposals. Customer reaction, regulation by legislation, the prospect, however remote, of stockholder disapproval, and public opinion do impose, however, effective *limits* on corporate policies; and it may be that these restraining, essentially negative influences will in the long run be judged as adequately tempering, if not shaping administratively determined policies *in the public interest.*

[4] By "decision-making"—an almost overworked term in management circles —we mean simply *action* originating within a defined area of delegated authority.

Management controls

What we will refer to here as *controls* are the methods and practices that serve to promote a smooth, efficient organization. The author has stated elsewhere[5] that, in part:

> . . . control embraces the original wish or idea (concerning a desired goal or plan of action), an understanding of the ultimate purpose and consequences of what is sought, the establishment of a plan, the adoption of a standard of performance, the conception of particular devices of operation and reporting to be employed, and their institution and enforcement . . .

Controls have been described as formal, informal, and implicit. Formal controls include resolutions of a board of directors, directives of management, an approved organizational plan, an accounting manual, written instructions governing an activity or the conduct of a project, and procedures firmly established by professional fiat or even by universally recognized custom. Informal controls consist principally of communications between supervisors and the supervised, ranging from oral instructions to a subordinate on a specific problem at hand, to the varied forms of in-service training that have been designed to increase operating skills. Implicit controls are less well defined and are often subtle in their meaning and effect: an *esprit de corps,* a natural feeling of cooperation between supervisors and individual employees, pride in performance, and the many kinds of human relationships and self-imposed individual standards—all of which, nurtured by wise leadership, are suggested by example or words of encouragement, as contrasted with regulation, command, admonishment, or instruction. Implicit internal controls are powerful agents of management; and the deviser of formal controls learns, often through painful experience, that there are situations best left to the intelligence and initiative of individuals. In drawing up regulations, experience tells us that we must never fail to leave to the individual as large an area as possible of free movement: the opportunity of being able to choose between alternatives, however restricted the defined range between their upper and lower limits may be, or to arrive at a solution demanding the individual's best judgment, however elemental. Many benefits of a diverse character

[5] In *A Dictionary for Accountants,* under *control.*

emerge from the operation of implicit controls: satisfactions to, and hence the improved morale of, the individual; the development and recognition of leadership potentials where wisdom is observable from judgments exercised; improved relations with outsiders; and all the benefits that can flow from shared responsibilities and enthusiasms. Accountants, who often draft regulations, profit from the sensitiveness they develop as to where the boundary lines should be drawn between the formal, the informal, and the implicit.

Internal controls

Internal controls, the core of management's supervisory techniques, are often described as management's everyday working tools. The term is used by accountants to mean the devices employed for the administration and direction of operations, and for insuring orderliness, propriety, and accuracy in the recording and reporting of transactions. We have already considered a number of these controls; at this point we will emphasize their importance as management devices.

Internal controls are usually formal controls, such as those described in an organization or accounting manual, or controls that conform to long-established customs of operation. Our interest here is to examine the kinds of internal controls that more directly relate to the management-accounting relationship. The more technical accounting and auditing aspects of internal controls we have reserved for Chapter 15.

General Organization Plan. We have already commented on the desirability of and current trend toward a strong central plan of organization headed by an executive from whom all operating authority emanates and to whom responsibilities of subordinates point. Delegated authorities require clear definitions of activity and accountability, with neither overlapping nor undefined areas of responsibility. Almost any operation falls short of this ideal, and there are numerous reasons: limitations of executive foresight and capacity, inadequate knowledge of operating conditions, intramanagement rivalries, established habits of employees, modifications in the environment of defined activities, changes in products and methods behind which the pattern of organization tends always to lag, the survival of older modes of operation that have led to complications no one has had the time, energy, or inclination to modernize, and so on. Even with an operation that has moved along with apparent efficiency, small deviations from prescribed practices are likely to be present; keeping operating routines within established channels is always difficult and may at times not even be desirable. The prescribed routines may be faulty in spots; new employees may have adapted procedures to their own way of doing things; or shifts in activity or method within one sector of the organization have a way of affecting other sectors unexpectedly. Public accountants accustomed to surveying systems of internal control as a feature of annual examinations will almost always discover changes, not formally approved, that have taken place between their visits. These may be small modifications in method which if uncorrected may lead ultimately to consequences both important and undesirable.

Perhaps our observations at this point have proceeded far enough to indicate that the installation and maintenance of an organizational pattern are never really completed. No organization escapes being dynamic, and at any one moment of time it will be found to have veered, in some degree at least, from original intent and prescription. The importance of this for our purposes is to give emphasis to the fact that accounting, designed to fit as closely as possible into the going organization, has a role in revealing and assessing these changes as they occur; and it must be prepared to keep abreast of them by adapting its classifications and reports to shifting responsibilities.

Reports. We have already referred to reporting as an essential need of good management; here we must think of reports as an important feature of internal controls. Internal reporting provides the vehicle of communication between persons to whom authority has been delegated and their superiors. To serve this purpose they must tell their stories well and be prompt in their appearance.

Internal Check. Internal check is usually conceived as consisting of procedures instituted as protection against fraud and error, particularly cash irregularities. Actually, the objective of internal check is to insure orderly, reliable procedures that guard against carelessness, inadvertence, or irresponsibility of persons who are involved in any way with the processing of transactions. Since fraud is perpetrated by creating false transactions or withholding or modifying normal transactions, and errors arise from the varied forms of negligence, precautionary measures instituted by top management involve two main features: the cross-control of transactions, and the separation of custody and accounting. These protective devices are normally built into an accounting system, are integral parts of daily routines, and are applied either before or at the time a transaction is consummated. They do not include the *preaudit* and *internal-audit* activities described in subsequent paragraphs which are essentially *post*audit functions. Following are representative internal-check procedures:

> Cash received is listed by mail clerks, and the total of such listings is independently reconciled with daily bank deposits and ledger cash credits. Cash receipts are deposited intact.
>
> Bank reconciliations are made monthly by persons independent of mail room, cashier, and accounting.
>
> Clerks maintaining receivables records have no contact with cash received; where two or more clerks post such records, they may be rotated periodically. Noncash credits bear top-level approvals.
>
> Cashiers and disbursing clerks report to the treasurer or a similar officer; controller's office records but handles neither receipts nor payments.
>
> Copies of purchase orders are sent to the receiving clerk but without quantities showing; quantities appearing on receiving reports are obtained only by actual inspection and count. Independent count is also reported by storekeeper as purchases are received into stock.
>
> Clerks or supervisors at strategic points in the organization, normally serving other functions, and designated property-accountability officers, maintain records of property location, use, and condition, and file periodic reports thereon, but have no authority over acquisition, movement, or retirement of property.

Cross-checking of transactions is as a rule so coordinated that little or no additional handling cost is incurred, and no time is lost in transaction processing. Internal checks that are simply duplications of clerical operations are avoided by a careful analysis and division of functions at the transaction level.

Providing internal checks to insure accuracy and honesty has its limits, of course. Situations are often encountered by accountants where the cost of maintaining a protective check far exceeds the possible loss that might occur without it. In such situations, a restudy of the need may result in an alternative method involving lesser costs. Sampling techniques of testing often provide an effective substitute where transactions of the same type occur in large numbers.

Preaudit. The preaudit of expenditures, which we will discuss more fully in Chapter 15, is now recognized as an important internal control by management. Often regarded as an activity of the controller, preaudit is actually a widespread function within an organization, especially where the idea of substantial delegations of management authority has taken hold. In such situations the initial stage in the preaudit process rests on the person whose authority is exercised at the time the commitment for an expenditure is incurred. Having originally approved the incurring of the transaction, he must now signify that the specifications laid down have or have not been complied with. To the voucher auditor this is required *prima-facie* but not conclusive evidence. He must make sure that evidence from other sources as to quantity, quality, price, and disposition is assembled in the transaction document. Management's interest in this process, beginning with the delegation of authority to incur expenditures of a particular type and within a variety of specified limitations, extends to reports on the general effectiveness of the delegation and on the adequacy of the subsequent steps of transaction processing.

Direct Costing. Direct costing, which we considered at some length in the preceding chapter, although not yet widely recognized as a basis for external reporting but nevertheless a device from which management can benefit, establishes a strong link in any system of management controls by adhering to organizational lines. Delegating authority always carries with it the responsibility for defined areas of expenditure, and each such area under direct costing becomes identified with a particular account or associated group of accounts. Administrative authority, carried direct to expenditures for overhead, looks to those who incur overhead expense rather than to those traditionally burdened with overhead allocations; the accounting process under direct costing, following the organizational pattern, makes no distribution of overhead, thus requiring the same direct reporting to management for overhead functions as for all other organizational activities.

Activity Accounting. Standard costs, direct costing, and—as we shall observe in the next chapter—budgeting-in-depth are devices that contribute to management controls over costs. Collectively, they make possible the institution of authority at "transaction levels": points at which transactions originate and are absorbed. They open up two-way channels of communication that facilitate a) a greater participation by top management in control processes, b) larger delegations of authority to centers of responsibility—the "activity" level, c) substantial increases in both the number and visibility of such centers, d) the interpretation of costs as the responsibility of those who incur them and in terms of their contribution to productivity, and e) feedbacks of accountability to the delegators of authority. *Activity accounting* provides a mechanism that brings together these concepts associated with the functioning of modern management.[6] An *activity* is recognized wherever the work of an organizational unit contributes to a specified function —and this means any point at which there is a coincidence of organization and function. In practical situations this is any point at which the incurrence of transactions has been authorized.

For our purposes here we may limit our further consideration of activity accounting to a number of concepts and practices that have been associated with it:

1) Every activity has a "head" who is held responsible for its transactions and for its operations generally.

2) Every item of cost (and income) within an organization is the responsibility of some one, and only one, activity head. Although the benefit from the cost extends to one or more other activities, the cost remains undivided.

3) An *organizational unit* may house more than one activity but no activity may extend beyond one organizational unit; thus activities become the building blocks which under one arrangement may be functional units that lead to financial statements; under another arrangement they may contribute to an organizational picture of budgeting and other controls; under still another arrangement they may yield objective costs (labor, materials, services, and other items classified according to the original character of the expenditure).

[6] *Responsibility accounting,* sometimes identified with activity accounting and more nearly related to "cost-center" accounting, is generally limited to the fixing of accountability for certain costs at specified levels but is not conceived as being an essential element of the organizational structure.

4) At least one account is maintained for each activity; and a periodic copy of each account is given to and approved by the activity head.

5) The lines of authority (delegations) and accountability (reports) and the flow of information between activity heads and top management are kept as simple and direct as possible.

Forward Accounting. Our comments on forward accounting appear in the next chapter. We will briefly note here that accounting today as a management aid is expected to look ahead to what is likely to happen, in addition to looking behind and recording, summarizing, and displaying past events and conditions. The forward look, although often guided by what has happened in the past, is always a creative management process; to be a controlling service, its projections must be an attainable ideal, not one toward which the organization's management can aspire but never reach. The details of classifications of items making up the forward look should correspond precisely with the classification of accounts that is to be followed in recording subsequent historical events and conditions so that comparisons of actual with projected events and conditions may be made, and differences may be explained on a rational basis.

Internal Auditing. Internal audit is now an important management control over operations in all large enterprises. In smaller concerns having no internal auditor, the principle can be and often is recognized through periodic studies of procedures instituted by personnel within the organization or undertaken as an extension of external-audit procedures by public accountants. Management consultants are also available for this purpose.

The function of internal auditing is to review procedures, records, controls, and management policies to make sure that everything is as it should be. Chapter 15 considers the major features of internal auditing as we know it today.

Controls and People. Internal controls should never ignore the abilities and limitations of persons occupying management posts within an organization. It is generally held to be poor practice to conform procedures to the known capacities of individual executives, yet it would be unfair to the organization if the maximum yield were not derived from their peculiar, often highly creative talents. We can do no more here than call attention to this problem as one requiring a careful weighing of alternative procedures when internal controls are being formulated or appraised. It will be sufficient for us, in acquainting ourselves with the elements of accounting, to recognize that this problem, in varying degrees, is always present, and that its further study must be left to the specialized field of management.

Many people to whom authority is delegated do not take kindly to becoming a part of the administrative machinery involved in operating internal controls. They do not want to become "entangled in paperwork" even though much of such work can be, and is usually, redelegated to assistants. Paperwork, they say, is what the accountant is hired to perform and dispose of. There are several reasons for this kind of reaction. Delegations are often not complete; they fail to include the full measure of authority intended—and certainly responsibility for carrying through on an approved expenditure should always be specifically expressed in such delegations. Again, emphasis in management circles today is being put on the idea that the assignment of authority for any operation is an *undivided* one, and that a *decision* to incur an obligation includes the necessity of approving it for payment and providing assurance that money's worth has been acquired. Finally, the paperwork complained of usually involves only a modest amount of effort: an effort that can be made very nominal indeed with the careful designing of procedures, forms, and timing.

Summary

We have seen that accounting serves management in many ways and that the accountant is intrusted with the creation and maintenance of probably the most important of management's controls over operations. Because of his ability to look forward, as well as being the organization's specialist on matters pertaining to the past, the controller has become a fully functioning member of the top-management staff, occupying a position subordinate only to the top executive. The authority delegated to him may be defined as embracing the field of accounting and reporting policies and procedures, but in practice he counsels and advises with management on a wide variety of matters, and his objective point of view is very likely not only to be highly respected but to establish the basis on which many of the organization's top policies can be built.

CHAPTER THIRTEEN

Forward Accounting

Forward accounting is a device of modern management. It provides a major mechanism for planning, instituting, and controlling an organization's activities. Its function is to make possible two-way communication between levels of exercised authority by establishing operating standards against which performance is reported and critically reviewed. In the form of a skilfully devised budget it sharpens operating responsibilities, demands accountability from those operating under delegated authority, and assures planning that coordinates policy, management competence, and technical skills. In today's budgetary procedures the executive head of an enterprise is the budget director and the controller his aid in devising the budgetary pattern: a combination that assures consistency as between the budget's several parts, the analysis of operating results in terms of advance specifications, and the formulation of conclusions concerning practical accomplishments.

Books of account are historical records; financial statements of the kind we have been discussing are historical summaries of past transactions. But an increasingly important task of the accountant is looking ahead and assisting in the planning for what is to come. This is the function of *forward accounting*. The chief instrument is the *budget*. In this chapter we are concerned with the nature of the budgetary process: how and when a budget originates, who prepares it, who administers it, how it is changed if changes are found to be necessary, and the character of internal progress reports in which budgets figure.

Forward accounting differs in numerous ways from historical accounting. In forward accounting many people are likely to participate—in fact, in varying degrees all management assists in the preparation of budgetary components. There are no books of account, and budgetary items do not appear on historical records. The controller is the key figure in developing the budgetary system, and he plays an important part in its administration; but he is not its enforcing agent. It is top management that assumes the responsibility for instituting and operating the budget.

Growth of the budgetary idea

Budgeting is a natural outgrowth of the emphasis that has been attached to the role of management since World War II. We have already discussed certain ideas currently associated with management functions. Of particular importance to the budgetary concept are (a) the large measure of delegated authority that budgeting makes possible, (b) the acceptance of the responsibilities these delegations require, and (c) the feedback from delegatees to delegators. A budget, the instrument that makes this triangular concept possible, provides a working basis for maintaining it, and enables a top executive realistically to observe and control the conditions under which operations take place. The budget, as a communications device, insures better management relationships and hence improved operations; it provides a common medium for expressing plans, projecting action, and assessing results.

Before World War II, a budget, if prepared at all, was rarely more than a controller's educated guess of what might be expected to happen in the next ensuing year. Often he would do little more than start out with the assumption that the current year's volume of sales would carry forward into the period following; or he would prepare charts of past performance or growth that would point to larger or smaller sales figures for the future. As for expenses: the current year's record was presumed to be at a level that could be duplicated next year; if the net profit for the current year had been satisfactory, no changes, except obvious ones, would be made. Occasionally one found that the principal purpose served by projecting ahead was to anticipate cash requirements which at one or more points during the year might necessitate short-term bank loans for which some advance estimate was essential.

We have already noted the rapid postwar expansion of management practices. Even at its earlier stages the primary emphasis was on the forward look: profiting by the experience—successes and failures—of the past and present, but regarding future activities as calling for a greater skill in planning and direction. It turned out that budgeting, which had been much written about but in typical cases imperfectly put into action, could be utilized as a most helpful and adaptable management tool for this purpose.

In some cases the post of budget officer was created. This was an attempt to recognize not the separate character of the budgetary operation but its newness and the need for developing the budgetary idea and budgetary techniques with some degree of independence. There was a precedent for this: for many years government agencies, particularly Federal agencies, had had budget officers who had operated with notable success in securing Congressional appropriations. Unfortunately these budget officers, usually not accountants and without carefully delineated authority, would make estimates without reference to their agencies' books of account (if any) and through intricate allotment systems would attempt independently to control expenditures, and in some instances to influence if not direct delegations of authority.[1] But with the Budget and Accounting Procedures Act of 1950 came the recognition that budgeting must be linked with top management and that the administrator of a budget should not be a free-wheeling and powerless budget officer but the agency head himself. With the parallel development of the controllership function in government, the budget responsibility was recognized as one in which all management must participate, just as management has become so closely related to accounting. Government was unable to develop a good working model of a budget officer; today, both in government and business, the operating head of the organization has become the focus of ultimate budgetary responsibility, management generally the developer and enforcer of the budget, and the controller an agent for supplying the budget system and methods of budgetary reporting. The functions of the budget officer, such as they were, have been taken over by others.

Budgetary practices in business are still in a period of transition, ranging from situations where a budget is little more than a forward estimate to situations we have come to recognize as the current ideal of the budgeting art. As in all segments of management, however, a budgeting plan can be no more successful in its application to an individual enterprise than the persons who compose the management permit it to be. No two budget systems can be the same: not primarily because of differences in the nature of business done, but because of the human elements which operate them. Some accountants have gone so far as to assert that the strength of any management group varies proportionately with the worth of the budget system under which the group determines how the organization is to function. But at the same time we should remember that

---

[1] In some Federal agencies an "allotment ledger" had been instituted which was operated independently of the general ledger, its purpose being to determine allotment balances (i.e., allotments less obligations) and thus provide the budget officer with enforcement data. Under the government's modern budgetary procedures, an allotment ledger can only serve as a deterrent to good enforcement controls.

there are many facets in the management structure and that budgeting, though an important element, is only one of them.

Varieties of budgeting

Various forms of budgeting are found in the business world. The
commonest variety embraces the five operating goals of the organization as a whole: an attainable sales objective, the desired profit
margin, low operating costs, carefully planned capital expenditures,
and adequate financing. Budgeting looks ahead for a 12-month
period; it is prepared before the period begins and as far in advance as a fair balance between the possibility of realistic estimates
and the preparations for new goals will permit. It is called an *operations* or *planning* budget, and sometimes a *short-range* budget in
contrast with a long-range budget which might look ahead for as
many as five years or even more. A long-range budget does not as a
rule get into the details of an annual or other short-range budget,
and the plans it embodies are likely to involve only major changes
in operations: new products, plants, and locations, development of
foreign markets, changes in capitalizations, and the like.

A *variable* budget contains two or more alternative plans of
action, the one to be followed at any particular time during the
projected period being suited to any of several possible events or
conditions that may arise during the year; thus, substantial changes
in the volume of sales may require a separate operating plan for
each of a number of sales ranges. The term is also applied to a
budget which for any of a number of reasons cannot be on a firm
basis before the beginning of a fiscal period and must be recast from
time to time as the year progresses: a procedure that may have to
be adopted by a new enterprise or by a business subject to major
unknown contingencies. An *appropriation* budget is a term sometimes used in separately projecting additions and retirements of
fixed assets; when employed in this way an *appropriation* is a
planned allowance for a particular building, a new machine, major
overhauls, or even recurrent repairs.

Occasionally the word "ideal" is used as a modifying adjective;
an ideal budget is one that forecasts conditions that cannot in all
probability be attained: its revenues are too high or its operating
costs too low. Originally intended as a spur for attaining better per-

formance and closer controls, or deliberately "idealized" as a basis for determining bonuses or penalties, it has been largely abandoned in favor of the more realistic outlook of the modern operations budget—which projects the attainable, yet provides necessary incentives to "better the work." [2]

An operations budget may be a forecast in terms of *commitments* for expenses and assets as in the case of much governmental planning; more often it is a forecast of expense to be incurred, assets to be acquired, and liabilities to be paid, thus reflecting the concepts of ordinary accrual accounting.

In governmental practices the term *program* or *performance*[3] budget is often encountered. It has the same significance as a planning budget, and the present trend is to put it on an accrual rather than obligations[4] basis.

Our interest here will be limited for the most part to the short-range operations (or program) budget.

A *financial* budget is a projection of financial position (balance sheet) at the end of a future period and an estimate of such interim financial requirements as current borrowings or additional working capital. The principal features of such a projection are generally incorporated in an operations budget. Flow estimates—which we will discuss in the next chapter—put financial budgeting to the practical test.

Conditions precedent

The structure and operation of a budget are dependent on the character of the organization into which it is to be fitted. Ineffective budgetary operations are usually associated with loose organizational patterns. Accountants are in agreement on the general characteristics of what constitutes the kind of organization in which the full benefits of budgeting can be realized. Several textbooks on

---

[2] This change parallels the disappearance of "ideal" costs in setting performance standards in manufacturing operations.

[3] "Performance" as applied to a budget was a term much favored by former President Hoover in the first (1949) of two reports on administrative practices in the Federal government; in his second report (1955) he adopted the term *program budget* which is in general use in the Federal government today.

[4] The "obligations basis," a term met with only in older forms of governmental accounting, adds to the accrual basis contractual amounts for goods and services not yet received.

budgeting, however, are concerned primarily with a form of organization that we do not encounter frequently in the practical world. With the installation of budgetary systems, accountants, through their recommendations, often have the opportunity of bringing about substantial improvements in organizational relationships. For our purposes here we will assume a preferred organizational pattern of a business corporation as a frame of reference, bearing in mind of course that the procedures we are able to follow in any given situation will have to be adapted to the organizational peculiarities we encounter.

What is this ideal management structure in a business enterprise? We have already reviewed in the preceding chapter the present-day pattern of good organization, and the following components of that pattern of importance in the drafting and administration of a budget require no added discussion:

1) Clear statements and frequent reviews and restatements by the corporate board of directors of organizational aims, policies, and structure.

2) A management design established by the board, usually embodied in a president or other designated top executive, in full control of all corporate activities, reporting to the board.

3) Delegations by the top executive, throughout the organizational structure, of carefully defined (and from time to time, redefined) authority for decision-making.

4) Suballotments of authority for decision-making residing in persons supervising units of activity in which function and organization are coincident.

5) Assumption by delegatees of full responsibility growing out of assigned authority.

6) Accountability reporting (feedback) that supplies top management with performance data and demonstrates the practicality of items 3 and 4 above.

7) Activity accounting fortified by budgetary cost standards and direct-costing methods.

Standard costs embodying attainable goals are a natural component of budgetary standards since they represent a kind of planned-cost objective under direct lines of authority; coupled with projected units of production, they become a budget item.

Even where direct costing is not practiced and overhead is distributed—and perhaps redistributed—to processes and products, primary responsibilities recognized at points where initial obligations are incurred can be incorporated as an integral element of budgetary practices.

Budget planning

Whatever the plan of organization, the initial step in putting a budgeting project into motion is to have a well-defined and accepted outline of administrative authorities: the points within the organization where responsibilities reside and have already been exercised with respect to the incurring of costs and other decisions affecting revenue, expense, and financial position. Another preliminary requirement is a timing schedule—setting a final date for each stage in the preparation and adoption of the complete budget. A third preliminary is to provide for the prompt review, correction, and approval of the various budget sections as they are submitted; this is accomplished, as a rule, by establishing a review committee composed of major executives who sift proposals, details, arguments, and criticisms so that final decisions can be made by the company's administrative head, or in some cases, by a budget committee of the board of directors. The latter type of review is usually confined to the determination that proposed operating plans conform to the board's overall policies for the budget period; a committee review is more often a challenging sort of action: a questioning of the bases for estimates, the dovetailing of proposals with overall objectives, the practical ability to carry out an indicated operation that is new or that deviates from the actual accomplishments of past periods, and so on.

Assuming that the setting for next year's budget preparation has been laid, and that a budget committee has been established consisting, say, of the executive vice-president, the production manager, and the controller (there are many variations in membership on such committees), the next step is to understand and present clearly to all who are to participate in the budget project the firm objectives of operations for the period to be budgeted. This will embrace such top-policy objectives as sales volume, markets to be served and shifts therein, pricing policy, current prices and indicated price changes; production schedules (often by months, often in-

cluding inventory ceilings); modifications in quality levels and operating methods as compared with those of the current year; specific
allowances for advertising and research-and-development programs;
changes in benefits and other conditions relating to compensation
for services; net profit and dividend aims; equipment-purchase-and-
retirement proposals. In each case a range may be indicated that
will permit judgments to be exercised at various points in the organization.

In larger concerns a formal long-range plan or an annual revision
of a previously adopted plan precedes projections for the next year.
But in all enterprises some long-range planning will be present, for
no budget period can be ended abruptly without considering its
effect on and the needs of the periods following. Our effort here, as
we have said, is limited to an examination of some of the characteristics of short-range (annual or less) budgeting. The long-range
budget is concerned mainly with foreseeable major changes in
financing, investments, and fixed assets.

Where operating authority has been intelligently diffused throughout an organization, the determination of budgetary estimates follows organizational lines, beginning with the lowest level of authority (an activity unit) at which decisions affecting everyday
operations are to be reached. This is sometimes interpreted as being the level at which revenues can originate or individual costs are
approved. The desirable point with respect to costs, however, is the
level at which firm commitments are made that lead to or result in
expenditures, whether or not, as a matter of form or general control, higher approval is conventionally secured. Some accountants
have been greatly concerned with exploring this point, since it has
been generally conceded in management practice that to begin with
the *formal approval level* is not enough to insure full responsibility
for costs that are being incurred. In a certain manufacturing situation familiar to the author the *incurral* level for maintenance costs
was found to be the individual machine operators themselves, and
budget estimates for maintenance costs in this section were accordingly made their responsibility, subject to review by foreman
and superintendent before formal submission. Ordinarily, prospective minor costs that do not reach *significant* totals are lumped together and a ceiling may be established for them. But in general,
after the budget period's objectives have been announced, the effort

is always to call for budget estimates, conforming to the overall plan, at the lowest practicable level of authority, responsibility, and accountability, with proposed permissible excesses, for example, in the form of designated percentages at specified points only if first approved by higher authority.

Any pattern of operations in a business organization is naturally dependent on prospective sales. The sales level may be established as top policy, but in any case its details are projected and often modified by the sales division of the organization. Often a substantial period of time is required in the firming of these estimates, especially where the projected performance is to differ in material respects from what has been done in the past. Not the least of the considerations in a manufacturing establishment is the ability of production to meet the sales schedule. More complications arise where the product line or production methods are being altered; questions as to the timing of retooling, the production flow, and the ability to keep within prescribed standards of quality and output rates are never easily resolved. During this period of investigation and debate, some other sectors of the budget can be finally determined; but others, dependent on the character of what is to be produced and sold and when, must wait until these basic decisions have been made.

Some accountants hold that the first step in budgetary procedure is to decide what the profit objective should be and then to build the rest of the budget around it. But no business today operates only or even primarily for the purpose of providing returns to stockholders. Corporate enterprise has many acknowledged social objectives which in practical situations require and are given as much weight as profit considerations. The relative values assigned to the varied objectives of business differ from one corporation to another and often unconsciously affect decisions that the framing of a budget demands; but it is safe to say that many objectives today are given at least equal weight with profits.

Establishing the budget

Having made known the organization's proposed scope of operations and other objectives and having collected estimates from the constituted centers of delegated authority within the organization, the budget pieces are fitted together. It is at this point that the services of the controller come into full play. He reviews each estimate for its completeness, accuracy, conformity with top policy and stated objectives, confinement to its particular area of authority, and consistency with the other estimates; his endeavor is to correct obvious errors (with acknowledgment, if not approval, at the source) and to present a complete whole to the budget committee or other reviewing authority, together with notes on any persisting disagreement and his comments on matters he feels need the reviewer's detailed attention. He supplies supporting analyses of summary figures and prepares comparisons with past experience or experience elsewhere. But at no point does he abandon his independence and substitute his judgment for that of the management; necessarily he leaves this to the reviewing authority and ultimately to the board committee or to the president or other top officer to whom the reviewing authority reports.

The work of the reviewing authority often leads to material changes: proposed programs may be too elaborate and work loads overestimated; ranges of activity as in research and development, usually not directly related to volume, may be cut down or even increased; and there may be indicated duplications and overlappings that the reviewing authority will be expected to eliminate or minimize. A characteristic method of review is to work from the current year's actual and estimated [5] figures and to question modifications of these figures in terms of the top-level plan for the forthcoming year. This method does not by itself yield the best results; it may lead the reviewer away from questioning the overall justification of particular departments or activities that already have become too expensive or too ingrown, or that for one reason or another even though showing no increases, need reconsideration by top authority. Of course, a better time for such investigations is not during the budget-development period but before. Management reviews can be midyear, not year-end, problems; yet it may often be the budget-reviewing body that raises the first question in such cases.

Furnishing or verifying answers to many of the reviewing authority's questions ordinarily falls within the province of the internal

[5] Estimated for the balance of the current year since next year's budget must be prepared before the current year has been completed.

auditor. On matters pertaining to capacity, output, unit costs, and the like—both actual and potential—his training and knowledge of operations enable him to supply supporting—sometimes contrasting —facts and figures relating to departmental estimates.

In analyzing a prospective manufacturing operation, standard costs and direct costing are notable aids. We have already observed their usefulness generally in establishing closer working relationships between policy-making and production operations. Direct costing enables top management to look down both organizational and functional lines to individual activities, thereby simplifying and strengthening the structure of intermediate controls and at the same time providing that services performed and their costs be justified by the supplier of services rather than the user.

After top-management review, required changes are incorporated in the budget document and the mutual consistency of the various parts is again tested.

We should recall at this point that the budget is not an operable control until there has been a full meeting of the minds on corrections and other changes instituted during the final review. Those who make changes are not the ones who have to be governed by them; consequently, a change should be a practical one, and until it has been accepted, though perhaps reluctantly, at the operating level, management communication on the budget has not been completed.

Full details of the completed budget document are not, as a rule, distributed throughout the organization. But those who must operate under budgetary restrictions should be fully informed not only of the particulars relating to their responsibilities but also of at least the main features applicable to the operations of other activities with which they are closely related.

Continuous budget

The typical budget is one covering a single fiscal year, as we have noted. Another type of budget has been experimented with in recent years: a *continuous* or *moving* budget. In this form, projections are made by months (or four-week periods) for a full year in advance and as a month is ended it is removed from the projection and a new month—12 or even 24 months ahead—is added.[6] This style of budgeting embodies most of the producers we have already mentioned and can readily be adapted to an organization whose operations are not seasonal and where estimates for a single month twelve months away do not involve substantial unknowns. The continuous forward planning required from all departments may be of benefit to the organization particularly where changes are being gradually evolved over a long period of time, forward financing faces a tight schedule, or, in a special situation, such as one familiar to the author, where the reduction and gradual elimination of a large backlog of orders called for the close planning of monthly output over at least a 24-month period.

Enforcement

Budget enforcement, an organization-wide job, follows down through organizational lines to individual responsibilities at activity levels. We can gain some idea of how enforcement operates if we look in on Adam Johnson whom we will identify as a junior executive of Nickerson Products, Inc. As a result of our questioning, he has given us the following account of himself:

"I run our company's sales development activity, which means that it is my responsibility to keep our distributors happy (all of them independently owned and operated and under franchise from us), cancel violated franchises when necessary, and establish new outlets at the rate of three or four a year. This involves a small office at headquarters and a great deal of traveling on my part. I have an assistant (who does some traveling), a secretary, and an office staff of four people who report to me. We handle a large volume of correspondence, which includes monthly reports from distributors, complaints, special orders, particularly those involving product modifications to suit individual customers, and nontechnical inquiries concerning our product. I report to the sales manager, who reports to the executive vice-president, who reports to the president, who reports annually to the stockholders. Our board sticks to policy statements, budget reviews, and examinations of monthly financial reports; if it gets into operating problems, only our president knows

[6] Divided, for example, into successive periods of one, one, one, three, and six months.

about it. Last year I operated under an allowance[7] of $125,000 for direct costs under my control; this year I was cut to $100,000 because, in our industry, sales are down and we see more than a few hazards in the future. . . . At the planning stage of our present budget, I had turned in estimates of $52,000 for salaries, $35,000 for travel, $16,000 for samples, and $5,000 for office expense; these objects of expense were again authorized, but I was told to cut down my estimates as I might see fit; so I have lopped off one of my staff ($5,000) and reduced travel costs to $32,000; but now, at midyear, I am planning a further change—a shift from samples to travel. This I can do under our procedure; I have merely notified our sales manager of this shift, and he has approved. This approval —and nobody above him is concerned—is virtually nominal; activity heads like myself may make such shifts on their own, provided the total budgetary allowance for the activity isn't exceeded and our overall program isn't modified as a result. I have figured out plans for shifting one of my staff on half-time to another department, saving on travel by teaming up with representatives from other departments on nearby short trips and using one car instead of two, and disposing of my samples, which must be renewed twice yearly, at better prices. These efforts will save at least $5,000 as compared with my record last year. . . . We activity heads receive monthly reports, on the second of each month, of what we have spent for the preceding month and the year to date, and I file a one-page report usually before the fifth, quoting these figures and providing an estimate (within my allowance, of course) for probable expense for each of the next six months, regardless of the overlapping of fiscal years. . . . Two years ago, toward the end of the year, I figured we should have a display at a nearby state fair, but my budget then was as tight as always; so I prepared a brief report on the prospective benefits, asking for $10,000 and got five; but, even so, having looked for and discovered ways of cutting corners, we had a good exhibit, and it brought in quite a number of inquiries and some real business."

Here we are able to observe, at first hand, some sidelights on one form of budget administration and its effect on an activity head.

---

[7] "Allowance," "allocation," "allotment," and "appropriation" could be interchangeable terms here. Each of these terms, however, has a distinct meaning in governmental accounting.

Few departments can be run quite as simply as this one, but the principle, weighed down, perhaps, by the numerous complications that attend management at the "grass roots," can always be followed —of giving the operating administrator (activity head) a measure of freedom in which to move on his own, in some cases providing recognition (often nonmonetary) for budget cutting or taking on an added workload without a budget increase. In this instance, our cost-conscious activity head, in the fourth echelon of management, has reacted typically: he takes pride in his role in the administration of the budget, and has planned some savings of his own; at the same time, one can detect an undercurrent of confidence that if any unforeseen need arises for expanding his program, he will find a sympathetic ear for any proposal he may suggest.

This last comment may be regarded as being at variance with the traditional conduct of persons engaged in the administrative process. Expanded responsibilities too often are assumed to call for increased expenditures, following Parkinson's law, including additional compensation for the activity head. This notion until recently was actually promoted in the Federal government by the Civil Service Commission; the Commission's examiners, often unable to evaluate the relative importance of supervisors by any other means, gave great weight to the number of persons supervised. The urge to add to one's staff was thus very real, and stories of such "empire-building" in the Federal government still persist, notwithstanding recent shifts in the Commission's rating processes.

Reporting

We have spoken of accountability or "feedback" as a necessary consequence of the responsibility that must be assumed when delegated authority is accepted. Basically feedback is a reporting from lower to higher levels of authority—of progress, changes, setbacks, breakdowns, and prospects for the immediate future, most of this of a qualitative character. But under what we like to regard as well-devised and well-administered budget schemes, the report must in all cases include not only dollar references, but other quantitative elements: work performed by units of measurement, comparisons with last year's performance, outside records, top-policy goals or self-imposed standards, and, particularly important to our viewpoint here, comparisons of budgeted and actual dollar costs (revenues, too, in some departments), along with a narrative account of reasons for differences between planned and actual and with a look at the probabilities just ahead. Who prepares this report—the activity head, his assistant, or the controller? There are many variations. The activity head is not expected to be an accountant, and the quantitative portions of his report—those relating to his own controllable costs, anyway—are generally supplied by the controller. Other amounts may issue from the same source, or they may be compiled from informal records kept within the activity. As to outside data: operators nowadays are expected to keep themselves informed, often through trade channels, on what is happening elsewhere and at what cost. Whatever the nature of the activity, there are always numerous possibilities of measurement and comparison available.

Reporting may also be informal, and there may be daily, weekly, or monthly meetings of those having management responsibilities within a given area of operations, these meetings taking the place of, say, more formal methods of reporting. Performance can often be profitably discussed "around the table," differences and mutual criticisms freely aired, and agreement, often promptly reached, on matters that cannot wait on more formal procedures.

Summary

Budgeting, in management's view, requires agreements on general objectives and ways of achieving them, a period of planning at all management levels with a full consideration of all available alternatives, a top review and coordination of planning proposals, delegations of authority consistent with the budgetary goals finally adopted, and controls that will assure the achievement of these goals.

In the next chapter the reader will find an illustration of a budget projection where a flow statement plays an important role.

CHAPTER FOURTEEN

Flow Statements

Balance sheets reflect the present outcome of past financial events and conditions; income statements the revenue-producing transactions of a concluded period. Neither of these traditional statements accounts for past financial operations. Flow statements supply this information and the belief is growing that they should be included in reports of public accountants and be covered by the opinions accompanying their reports. Three types of flow statements have been suggested as suitable for reporting on past financial management; and at least one of them can be utilized in preparing projections of future financial and operating performance.

An income statement supplies information concerning periodic proprietorship changes. We can also describe an income statement as a summary of external-transaction *halves* that constitute the sources of current revenue and expense. But an income statement does not tell us what has happened to the counterpart financial[1] halves of these transactions; and it is wholly unaffected by either half of purely financial transactions (e.g. the purchase of an asset).

To provide a historical summary of changes during a given period in an organization's financial structure, a certain form of analysis has for many years been employed in corporate reports to stockholders and in long-form reports of public accountants to their clients. Known as the *statement of application of funds*[2] and covering a fiscal period, it has been primarily a summary of the net increases and decreases revealed by comparisons of the component items of the balance sheets at the beginning and end of the period. The state-

---

[1] We are already familiar with the fact that each side of every transaction affects one or more balance-sheet items. In this chapter we are using *financial* as referring to assets and liabilities generally, excluding the revenue-and-expense components of retained earnings. Thus, the financial half of an item of expense is a credit to accounts payable or cash; the debit is a decrease in proprietorship.

[2] Or *statement of source and application of funds;* less familiar titles have been *statement of funds, statement of funds received and applied, statement of changes in financial position,* and *summary of changes in working capital.* As used here, *funds* means working capital, one or more elements of working capital, or an issue of capital stock in exchange for an asset (for statement purposes regarded as the equivalent of a sale of capital stock and the application of the proceeds to the asset purchase).

ment has had well-recognized limiting characteristics: in its conventional form it displays changes in working capital as a single figure[3] although the cause of change may lie within; again, for non-working-capital items differences only are set forth without disclosing what may have been important movements, both debit and credit, during the period that has elapsed between balance-sheet dates; and net income for the period has been cleared of certain (but not all) internal transactions such as the provision for depreciation. The result is a display of the *net*-working-capital movement: a condensed and greatly circumscribed version of the period's external transactions.

In recent years various attempts have been made to provide an improved version of this statement and the terms "cash flow" and "funds flow" have been increasingly employed. Also various forms of the statement have been experimented with in an effort to overcome at least some of its shortcomings. We will refer to all of these as "flow" statements.[4]

Illustrations of flow statements

To trace the sources of a flow statement and to provide a basis for judging its significance, we may turn to the two balance sheets and the income statement for the between-balance-sheets period on page 205. Arranged for convenience here in "statement" form, the balance sheets display familiar elements: current assets less current liabilities, or working capital, to which are added net fixed assets; we then subtract long-term liabilities, leaving net worth (stockholders' equity). The last-named is broken down into its components. The year's operating results are supported by an income statement the only unusual feature of which is a summary cost of sales in terms of the three factory-cost elements, excluding, however, depreciation. Depreciation is regarded here as a period cost rather

[3] A comparative listing of the balance-sheet components of working capital is often presented as a supplement.

[4] Two AICPA pronouncements have been concerned with flow statements: *Cash Flow Analysis and the Funds Statement* (1961), and *The Statement of Source and Application of Funds* (1963), the latter an "opinion" of the Institute's Accounting-Principles Board. However, a better background and analysis of flow statements can be found in *NAA Research Report No. 38*, and *Cash-Flow Analysis for Management Control* (1961).

Comparative Balance Sheets

(thousands of dollars)

	December 31 19-1	December 31 19-2
Cash	904	2 822
Investments (cost or less)	1 783	1 862
Customers accounts	2 057	2 245
Allowance for bad debts	−67	−78
Inventories (cost or less)	3 211	2 477
Prepaid expense	131	102
Current assets	8 019	9 430
Current liabilities	2 848	2 246
Working capital	5 171	7 184
Fixed assets, at cost	13 250	17 347
Accumulated depreciation	−7 233	−7 463
5% serial bonds	−5 200	−4 800
Net worth	5 988	12 263
Capital stock	2 000	5 500
Paid-in surplus	100	250
Retained earnings 1-1-19-2	3 888	3 888
Net income 19-2	—	2 725
Dividend paid	—	−100
As above	5 988	12 263

Summary Income Statement

Year ended December 31, 19-2

Sales		27 289
Cost of sales:		
Material	11 241	
Labor	4 290	
Overhead	5 148	
Overhead variance	111	20 790
Gross profit		6 499
Profit from sale of investment		45
Year-end investment writedown		−20
Dividends received		55
Provision for bad debts		−60
Provision for depreciation		−1 335
Selling & general expense		−1 303
Interest paid		−250
Accrued income tax		−906
Net income		2 725

Supplementary information:

1) Proceeds of $266,000 from the sale of a portion of the company's holdings of minority interests in listed common stocks were immediately reinvested in similar securities along with an additional $54,000.

2) Bad debts recovered, $30,000.

3) Inventories consisted of raw materials and in-process and finished stock, the latter at the beginning of the year being broken down into materials $595,000, labor $210,000, and overhead $252,000; and at the end of the year, $933,000, $444,000, and $533,000, respectively.

4) Unpaid-for purchases of raw materials and accruals of income tax (the latter $800,000 at the end of 19-1) make up the total of current liabilities at the beginning and end of the year.

5) Fixed assets purchased in 19-2 were $5,197,000; there were no recoveries on retirements.

than a product cost. Following the two statements are explanations needed for preparing the three flow statements on pages 207 and 208.

Sources of the flow elements

Before proceeding further the reader should now turn to the three flow statements and determine as best he can how each item in the statements was determined, bearing in mind that all needed information has been supplied on page 205. By so doing he will form a better idea of the "backward look" that historical flow statements make possible. He will also be afforded a review of the basically simple interrelationships of accounts that we have been referring to from time to time, beginning with the illustrative "figures" in Chapter 1. Again, he will be better prepared to understand the practical necessity of the ledger-account breakdowns which we mentioned in Chapter 5 and which we have illustrated on pages 211-212 of this chapter.

The reader should have little trouble in reconciling the details of the first two flow statements with the balance sheets; but he may have difficulty tracing to their sources the details of the third statement. The explanations that follow may help:

Collections from customers are obtained by subtracting from sales (27,289) the increase in receivables (188) and the bad-debt writeoffs (79), to which we must add bad-debt recoveries (30); the writeoffs are the result of adding the collections (30) to the bad-debt expense (60) and subtracting the increase (11) in the allowance balance.

Net gain on investment realization is the profit (45) from investment sales less the year-end writedown (20) to the then current market prices.

The sale of capital stock is the sum of the increase (3,500) in the capital-stock account and the increase (150) in the paid-in surplus account; it is reasonable to suppose that this was all one transaction.

To obtain the cash outlay for raw materials, the amount (11,241) appearing in the income statement must be adjusted by two inventory variations and the variation in accounts payable. The first variation is in the raw material in the finished product (933 − 595 = 338), the second in the raw material that has not yet entered

THORPE MANUFACTURING COMPANY

Statement of Source and Application of Funds
Year ended December 31, 19-2
(thousands of dollars)

Funds received:
Income from operations—

Net income	2 725		
Add back provision for depreciation	1 335	4 060	
Sale of capital stock		3 650	7 710

Funds applied:

Purchase of fixed assets	5 197	
Retirement of serial bonds	400	
Dividend paid	100	5 697
Increase in working capital		2 013

THORPE MANUFACTURING COMPANY

Funds-flow Statement
Year ended December 31, 19-2
(thousands of dollars)

Funds were derived from:

Sale of capital stock			3 650
Operations—			
Sales to customers		27 289	
Investment earnings		80	27 369
Total funds available			31 019

Funds were applied to:

Assets acquired—

Fixed assets		5 197	
In-process & finished goods		853	
Added investments		79	
Other, net		42	6 171

Liabilities reduced—

Serial bonds retired			400
Dividend declared & paid			100
Operations—			
Cost of sales	20 790		
Less materials inventory not replaced	879	19 911	
Selling & general expense		1 363	
Interest paid		250	
Income tax accrued		906	22 430
Increase in cash			1 913
Total funds applied			31 019

THORPE MANUFACTURING COMPANY

Cash-flow Statement
Year ended December 31, 19-2
(*thousands of dollars*)

Cash was derived from:		
Operations—		
Collections from customers	27 052	
Dividends received	55	
Other investment income, net	25	27 132
Sale of capital stock		3 650
Total cash income		30 782
Cash was disbursed for:		
Factory costs—		
Materials	10 700	
Labor	4 524	
Overhead	5 540	20 764
Other expense—		
Selling and general	1 274	
Interest paid	250	
Income tax (19-1)	800	2 324
Retirement of serial bonds		400
Machinery and equipment		5 197
Dividend to stockholders		100
Total cash disbursements		28 785
Increase in cash funds:		
Cash	1 918	
Marketable securities	79	1 997

finished product ([3,211 − 595 − 210 − 252 = 2,154] − [2,477 − 933 − 444 − 533 = 567] = 1,587); the third adjustment is the excess of materials payables at the beginning of the year (2,848 − 800 = 2,048) over the corresponding amount at the end of the year (2,246 − 906 = 1,340), or 708. We now have 11,241 + 338 − 1,587 + 708, or 10,700. Cash labor costs are computed by adding to the amount (4,290) appearing on the income statement, the increase in inventory (444 − 210 = 234); similarly, cash overhead costs equal the income-statement amount (5,259 including the overhead variance of 111), plus the increase in inventory (533 − 252 = 281), or 5,540.

The cost of fixed assets retired (13,250 + 5,197 − 17,347 = 1,100) appears to have been charged in full against accumulated depreciation (7,233 + 1,335 − 7,468 = 1,100). Since asset charge-offs and provisions for depreciation are purely internal transactions, the only item affecting our cash-flow statement is the amount of new fixed assets purchased (5,197).

The only other amount in the cash-flow statement differing from its counterpart in the income statement is selling and general expense (1,303) which must be adjusted by the decline (29) in prepaid expense during the year.

Because the investments in stocks of other corporations are "cash investments," and a sale of a portion of the securities was followed by a replacement, we are justified in combining cash and investments into a single item which we have termed "cash funds."

Statement of application of funds

This traditional statement, as we have already mentioned, is of frequent appearance in the typical corporate report to stockholders, not alongside or ranking with the income statement but in the president's letter where it has been referred to in various ways as depicting the year's principal financial events. Occasionally it has emerged as a separate statement, and in a few instances known to the author it has been covered by the public accountant's opinion: a trend that is likely to continue.[5]

Our illustration shows the usual features of this statement: the net income as reported in the income statement to which the depreciation provision for the year is "added back" for the reason we have indicated, followed by the cash proceeds from the sale of capital stock; the total of 7,710 (thousands of dollars) has gone into new plant items, the retirement of this year's installment of serial bonds, a cash dividend to stockholders, and finally an addition of 2,013 to working capital. A glance at the comparative balance sheets would lead one to conclude that more than 95% of the latter amount was still in the form of cash.

Funds-flow statement

In the second of the three flow statements we observe at once that instead of displaying a single figure for net income we have substituted the principal items of the income statement ($27,289 + 80 - 20,790 - 1,363 - 250 - 906 [= 4,060]$), the depreciation provision of 1,335 being omitted (it was "added back" in the first statement); and that instead of the single figure for the working-

---

[5] This is the only form of flow statement referred to in the AICPA bulletin of 1963.

capital increase (2,013), we have substituted the principal items of which it is composed (853 + 79 + a combination of four smaller changes: 188 − 11 − 29 − 106 or 42, −879 [= −1,587 + 708] + 1,918).[6]

The combination of the materials-inventory decrease and the decrease in amounts owing to suppliers for unpaid materials purchases yields the "funds" effect of the inventory decrease. If the materials inventory figure had been larger or smaller, it would have been natural to expect that there would have been a corresponding increase or decrease in unpaid materials purchases.

Cash-flow statement

The second statement differs from the first in that the operating-income figure is broken down into seven component elements, three labeled "funds *derived from* operations," and the remaining four "funds *applied to* operations." Here, "funds" (as described in footnote 2) may be observed in the form of items modifying working capital and embodying the accrual basis of accounting; in both of these statements this is accomplished by displaying balance-sheet differences. Depreciation expense was added back to net income in the first example: an internal transaction that had had no effect on working capital [7] and thus did not affect any fund; likewise, fixed-assets retired during the year, 1,100,[8] by means of one or more internal transactions, had not given rise to any movement of funds.

But just as the first statement can be regarded as a telescoped version of the second, so the second can be regarded as a telescoped version of the third. In the cash-flow statement we further dissect the balance-sheet accounts; we go behind working capital

---

[6] For the reader whose patience does not permit him to trace the source of these figures, let it be said that after he has discovered that 79, 188, 11, 29, and 1,918 proceed directly from the comparative balance sheets the remainder, with the help of the income statement and the footnotes, may be computed thus: 853 = 933 + 444 + 533 − 595 − 210 − 252; 106 = 906 − 800; 879 = 3,211 − 2,477 + 853 − [(2,848 − 800) − (2,246 − 906)]; 1,587 = 3,211 − 2,477 + 853; 708 = 2,848 − 2,246 + 106 = 1,587 − 879.

[7] The adjustments of investments (20) and prepaid expense (29) are not given the same treatment, since they had the effect of *reducing* working capital.

[8] Which in this instance we can derive in either of two ways: 13,250 + 5,197 − 17,347; or 7,233 + 1,335 − 7,468!

and relate balance-sheet changes to major cash movements during the period.

Our cash-flow analysis is thus essentially a recapitulation of cash receipts and disbursements for the period separating the two balance sheets. Most of the items could have been built up through accumulations of cashbook entries covering the same period. We might not get precisely the same results because many balance-sheet figures are *net* amounts, and because of internal transactions representing transfers from primary to secondary classifications (for example, transfers of materials purchases to endproduct accounts); the differences in some situations could be minor and within tolerance levels established for immaterial changes. The main advantage in keeping the analysis close to balance-sheet differences or to amounts readily derived from these differences is that many cash-flow items bear the same labels as items to be found in the balance sheets and in the income statement: difficult-to-reconcile amounts, usually differing in no material way, raise questions not easily answered without becoming involved in discussions of bookkeeping techniques.

General-ledger relationships

The periodic construction of flow statements is facilitated by expanding the general-ledger classification of accounts to include special nominal or adjunct accounts—as many as may be necessary to identify and isolate cross-relationships—and thus supplying, through the resulting enlarged trial balance, in whatever detail desired, the items of financial statements, including any or all of the flow statements. Accounting—the recording and reporting of transactions—and its handmaiden, bookkeeping, can serve many purposes; its special adaptation, as in the schedule on page 214, to the mechanical preparation of flow statements gives a new degree of precision to these statements, accelerates and wholly simplifies their preparation, and widens their use. There can be little doubt that the demand for cash-flow statements for internal consumption and funds-flow statements for external display—or similar analytical statements—will increase, and that the collection and use of transaction totals in an expanded classification of conventional general-ledger accounts will be called for.

THORPE MANUFACTURING COMPANY

Trial-Balance Spread

Year ended December 31, 19-2

(thousands of dollars)

Account Name	Number	General-ledger trial balance Debits	General-ledger trial balance Credits	Sources of statement elements B/S and P & L	Cash flow	Funds Flow	Funds Applied
Cash	101	(0) 904					
	103 104	(3) 31 023	(4) 29 105	2 822	—	1 918	—
Investments	111	(0) 1 783					
	113 114	(4) 320	(10) 221	1 862	1 997	79	—
	116		(11) 20				
Customers	121	(0) 2 057					
	123 124	(1) 28 120	(5) 831				
	126		(3) 27 022				
	128		(7) 79	2 245	—	188a	—
Allowance for b/d	130		(0) 67				
	133 134	(7) 79	(6) 60				
	136		(3) 30	−78	−27 052	−11a	—
Materials	151	(0) 2 154					
	153 154	(2) 9 992	(8) 11 579		9 992a	−1 587b	—
Processed materials	161	(0) 595					
	163 164	(8) 11 579	(9) 11 241				
labor	171	(0) 210					
	173 174	(2) 4 524	(9) 4 290		4 524	—	—
overhead	181	(0) 252					
	183 181	(2) 5 540	(9) 5 148	2 477	5 510	853	—
	186		(9) 111				
Prepayments	191	(0) 131					
	194		(12) 29	102	—	−29a	—

THORPE MANUFACTURING COMPANY *Continued*

Account		General-ledger trial balance		B/S and P & L	Sources of statement elements — Cash flow	Funds — Flow	Funds — Applied
Name	Number	Debits	Credits				
Accrued income tax	200	—	(0) 800	—	800	—	—
	203 204	(4) 800	(2) 906	−906	—	−106a	2 013
Other current debt	210	—	(0) 2 048	—	—	—	—
	213 214	(4) 27 235	(2) 26 527	−1 340	708a	708b	—
Working capital (0 = 5,171)				7 184			
Fixed assets	301	(0) 13 250	—	—	—	—	—
	303 304	(2) 5 197	(13) 1 100	17 347	5 197	5 197	5 197
Accumulated depreciation	310	—	(0) 7 233	—	—	—	—
	313 314	(13) 1 100	(14) 1 335	−7 468	—	—	—
Serial bonds	400	—	(0) 5 200	—	—	—	—
	403	(4) 400	—	−4 800	400	400	400
Paid-in capital	500	—	(0) 2 100	−5 750	—	—	—
Retained earnings	504	—	(3) 3 650	−6 513	−3 650	−3 650	−3 650
Net income for year	550	—	(0) 3 888	—	—	—	—
	554	—	(15) 2 725	—	—	—	−2 725
Dividend	555	(4) 100	—	—	100	—	100
Sales	603 604	—	(1) 28 120	−27 289	—	−27 289	—
Cost of sales	609	(5) 20 790	—	20 790	—	20 790	—
Sale of investments	613 614	(9) 831	(3) 266	−45	−25	—	—
Investment loss	623	(10) 221	—	20	—	—	—
Dividend received	634	(11) 20	(3) 55	−55	−55	−80	—
Depreciation	653	(14) 1 335	—	1 335	—	—	−1 335
Selling & general	663	(2) 1 274	—	—	1 274	—	—
Prepaid writedown	665	(12) 29	—	—	—	—	—
Bad-debt provision	667	(6) 60	—	1 363	—	1 363	—
Interest paid	673	(4) 250	—	250	250	250	—
Income taxes	683	(2) 906	—	906	—	906	—
Net income	699	(15) 2 725	—	2 725	—	—	—
Totals		175 786	175 786	0	0	0	0

Legend:

Point of commencement:
  0 Ledger balances
      December 31, 19-1
External transactions of 19-2:
  1 Sales
  2 Costs incurred
  3 Cash receipts
  4 Cash disbursements
Internal transactions of 19-2:
  5 Allowances to customers
  6 Provision for bad debts

Internal transactions of 19-2 (cont.):
  7 Bad debts written off
  8 Raw materials into finished
      goods
  9 Finished goods into cost of sales
 10 Investments sold
 11 Investment decline in value
 12 Amortization of prepayments
 13 Fixed assets retired
 14 Provision for depreciation
 15 Income and expense to retained
      earnings

Turning to the Thorpe trial-balance "spread" on page 212, it will be seen that in the first two money columns the general-ledger classification has been greatly augmented. With the exception of 16 balances carried forward from the preceding year (keyed with O's) there are 48 accounts containing totals of all of the company's transactions for the year 19-2. Keys *1* through *15* show how the 48 accounts are interrelated.

Thus for cash we have three ledger accounts: opening balance, receipts, and disbursements; together they provide the year-end balance of 2,822 needed for the balance sheet, while the excess of receipts over disbursements (1,918) supplies the balance appearing in the second flow statement. Again, for investments we have provided three accounts in addition to the opening balance: purchases, sales (at cost), and markdown. Combining and extending the four accounts gives us the balance-sheet figure of 1,862; the difference between opening and closing balances (79) gives us the growth figure for the funds-flow statement; and the combined increase in cash and investments (1,997) provides us with the balancing figure in the cash-flow statement.[9]

Flow statements generally

Flow summaries deserve a greater currency in external reporting than they have been getting. [The management of cash and working

---

[9] The reader will note that the parenthetical amount of working capital at beginning of the year (5,171) is the net of the preceding "0" items; that the corresponding figure at the year-end (7,184) is the net of the eight items directly above it; and that the extension into the "Funds" column at the extreme right (2,013) is the excess of the latter over the former.

capital can often be well portrayed by means of these statements, particularly one that covers a span of several years, or by means of a series of these statements in comparative form, especially where there has been a gradual tightening in amounts available for dividends or for purchases of new equipment. Occasionally bankers ask accountants to prepare the equivalent of a cash-flow analysis following a bank loan, it being recognized that the cash acquired through a short- or long-term loan is ordinarily merged with other cash that may be present, and not devoted to a single purpose. A cash-flow projection under such circumstances would cover not only the loan proceeds but other incoming cash as well, unless the use of the loan proceeds has been restricted to specified purposes. Few bank loans provide for such controls.

Perhaps the most important impetus that has been given to the inclusion of flow statements in reports to stockholders has arisen from the practice of many accounting firms of permitting the income statement to be burdened with exaggerated costs. Lifo, accelerated depreciation, and other causes of substantial writeoffs of past costs (mostly inspired by the urge to secure present and ultimate income-tax advantages rather than by the desire to adhere to simpler concepts of expiring costs), and expense provisions anticipating future costs (principally "deferred" income taxes) have not infrequently so obscured the meaning of "net income" that baffled financial analysts, investors, and others seeking information from income statements have been driven to demand something more lucid, more primitive, more consistent, and more directly related to simple income and outgo, and something that could be compared from one period to another and that could put the operating results of similarly situated companies on a common footing. In the expanding use of flow statements covering past operations, we are witnessing an increasing demand for a return of the income statement to a more intelligible accrual basis, or, failing in that, to a still simpler cash basis.[10]

---

[10] In the 1963 opinion we have already referred to (footnote 4), the AICPA Accounting Principles Board recommended that a source-and-application-of-funds statement "should be presented as supplementary information in financial reports" and that its "coverage" in the report of the public accountant be "optional." The opinion gives no hint of other forms of flow statements, makes no attempt to clarify, least of all amplify, existing concepts, and contains no suggestions as to form or method of presentation. Its main purposes

For internal-reporting purposes the cash-flow statement bears more management earmarks[11] than the other two statements but would often be of interest to outsiders. In annual reports to stockholders the *funds*-flow statement is preferred by the author; it corresponds more closely to the (accrual) accounting basis of the balance sheet and income statement; moreover, the author has found that the two major breakdowns it contains—as compared with the time-honored statement of source and application of funds—add to its understanding by nontechnicians.

Cash-flow projections

An estimate of cash flow is of importance in developing a budget forecast, as we have hinted in the preceding chapter. The term "cash estimates" is often used in forecasting the collection and deployment of cash over a future operating period, and in working toward a balance sheet at the end of that period. A statement of cash estimates, whatever its form, is essentially a *forward* cash-flow statement: a cash-flow *projection*.

The procedures required in preparing a forward cash-flow estimate are roughly the reverse of what we have followed in setting forth our historical analysis of past events and conditions. In the illustrative schedule on page 218 we are disclosing a situation that presented itself to Thorpe at the beginning of November, 19-1, at a time when financial statements at October 31 only were available. In preparing the schedule it was necessary to add to the actual figures of October 31 estimates for the balance of 19-1 as well as estimates for the twelve months of 19-2.[12] We will limit our discussion here to the 19-2 projections.

---

were undoubtedly to correct growing impressions among financial analysts by declaring (1) that a "total" cash flow could not be considered available for the payment of dividends, (2) that the importance of the traditional income statement should not be discounted, and (3) that a figure for "net cash flow per share" has no significance for anyone—least of all, the investor.

[11] Because it is more nearly related to original transactions.

[12] The reader will observe that the balance-of-19-1 estimate of transactions will bring the October balance sheet and income statement into only approximate agreement with the final December 31 amounts which we have shown on page 212. This we may presume has required a reestimate for the remaining two months of 19-1, and not one-sixth or other fraction of the forward projections of November 19-0. Forward estimates of what is about to take

In the explanations that follow, we will be reviewing a situation that has been oversimplified to a considerable degree, our aim being to provide examples of forward accounting and a forward-flow statement that have as their purpose a demonstration of a general methodology: an approach to which accounting can and does make an important contribution, and an approach that we might lose sight of in a more involved set of conditions. The preparation of a budget requires not only a thorough knowledge of operating characteristics—the way in which the budgeted organization has functioned in the past and may be expected under similar conditions to perform in the future—but also an imaginative measurement of known and controlled changes that will characterize future operations; and an even more imaginative measurement of the allowances that must always be made for inevitable, unknown, and uncontrolled events that in varied forms will rise to bedevil as well as to benefit the direction of the organization's affairs. The numbered paragraphs below relate very generally to similarly numbered transaction groupings in Thorpe's forward estimates as they appear on pages 218-219.

1) Sales projections based on existing customer relations are seldom enough in any budget preparation. Marketing studies suggesting new domestic and foreign outlets, an improvement or worsening of general economic conditions, new products, restyling and other modifications of old products, price trends, new types and levels of demand, the effects as yet untried of new advertising and other marketing devices: these are among the factors that lead to the all-important beginning (and in many ways controlling) figure of sales. This estimate should be not an ideal projection but one that under duly weighed conditions can be justified as a reasonable, attainable expectation.

Responsibility for the sales estimate usually lies with the sales department of the enterprise. But its estimate, challenged by the top executive (who among other things may demand increased sales activity, authorize new products, and provide new outlets) and pruned by the controller (whose notions of forward planning have been tempered by the realities of past experience), is quite likely to be a composite figure: the endproduct of numerous pro-

---

place can be expected, of course, to be more accurate where there are only minor variations from month to month in production and sales.

THORPE MANUFACTURING COMPANY
Forward Estimates of Financial Position Fourteen Months from October 31, 19-1
(thousands of dollars)

Item	Actual October 31, 19-1	November December	December 31, 19-1	Estimates 19-2 transactions — Debit	Estimates 19-2 transactions — Credit	December 31, 19-2
Cash	852	360	1 212	(2) 30 000 (7) 3 600	(9) 32 110	2 702
Investments	1 783	—	1 783			1 783
Customers	1 832	183	2 015	(1) 30 000	(2) 30 000 (3) 50	1 965
Bad-debt estimates	-90	—	-90	(3) 50	(3) 40	-80
Materials	953	630	1 583	(5) 12 000	(5) 13 200	383
In-process and finished goods:						
Materials	715	-100	615	(5) 13 200	(1) 12 400	1 415
Labor	320	-40	280	(5) 4 800	(4) 4 500	580
Overhead	384	-48	336	(5) 6 000	(4) 5 600	736
Prepaid expense	136	-29	107		(6) 30	77
Current liabilities:						
Materials	-1 322	-500	-1 822	(9) 13 200	(5) 12 000	-622
Labor & overhead	—	—	—	(9) 10 800	(5) 10 800	—
Income tax	-700	-200	-900	(9) 790	(6) 1 000	-1 110
Other expense	—	—	—	(9) 2 500	(6) 2 500	—
Fixed assets	13 100	100	13 200	(8) 4 200	(8) 500	16 900
Accrued depreciation	-7 010	-200	-7 210	(8) 500	(8) 1 500	-8 210
Serial bonds	-5 300	100	-5 200	(9) 400	—	-4 800
Capital stock	-2 000	—	-2 000		(7) 3 500	-5 500

THORPE MANUFACTURING COMPANY *Continued*

Estimates

Item	Actual October 31, 19-1	November December	December 31, 19-1	19-2 transactions Debit	19-2 transactions Credit	December 31, 19-2
Paid-in surplus	-100	—	-100		(7) 100	-200
Retained earnings	-1 880	—	-1 880	—	(10) 1 929	-3 809
Net income for year	-1 773	-256	-2 029	(10) 2 029	(11) 2 430	-2 430
Dividends	100	—	100	(9) 220	(10) 100	220
Sales	-23 670	-4 000	-27 670	—	(1) 30 000	-30 000
Cost of sales	18 328	3 032	21 360	(4) 22 500		22 500
Depreciation	1 000	200	1 200	(8) 1 500		1 500
Selling & general	1 611	272	1 883	(6) 2 250		2 250
				(3) 40		40
Bad debts	28	—	28	(6) 30		30
Interest paid	230	40	270	(6) 250		250
Income tax	700	200	900	(6) 1 000		1 000
Net income	1 773	256	2 029	(11) 2 430		2 430
Totals	0	0	0	168 489	168 489	0

Estimated and Actual Balance Sheets
December 31, 19-2
(thousands of dollars)

	December 31, 19-2		
Assets	*Budget*	*Actual*	*Variation*
Cash	2 702	2 822	120
Investments, at cost	1 783	1 862	79
Customers accounts, net	1 885	2 167	282
Inventories	3 114	2 477	−637
Prepaid expense	77	102	25
Current assets	9 561	9 430	−131
Fixed assets	16 900	17 347	447
Accumulated depreciation	8 210	7 468	742
Fixed assets, net	8 690	9 879	1 189
Total assets	18 251	19 309	1 058
Liabilities			
Accounts payable	1 732	2 246	514
Serial bonds	4 800	4 800	—
Stockholders equity:			
Capital stock	5 500	5 500	—
Paid-in surplus	200	250	50
Earned surplus	6 019	6 513	494
Total liabilities	18 251	19 309	1 058

Income Statement
Year ended December 31, 19-2

Sales	30 000	27 289	2 711
Cost of sales:			
Materials	12 400	11 241	−1 159
Labor	4 500	4 290	−210
Overhead	5 600	5 259	−341
Total cost of sales	22 500	20 790	−1 710
Ratio to sales	.750	.762	.012
Depreciation	1 500	1 335	−165
Selling & general	2 250	1 303	−947
Interest	250	250	—
Other expense, net	70	−20	−90
Total expense	26 570	23 658	−2 912
Net income before Federal income tax	3 430	3 631	201
Provision for income tax	1 000	906	−94
Net income	2 430	2 725	295
Dividend to stockholders	220	100	−120

posals and suggestions from many persons. Where the organization's productive facilities make possible a varied output, it may be that the recommendations of outside consultants on such matters as an optimum product mix may influence the direction of sales and production.

The sales figure shown may be regarded as a *net* estimate, with no separate provision for returns and allowances. Where future uncertainties call for a variable budget, several sales estimates may be adopted, each based on differing assumptions as to future events and conditions, and each calling for differing supporting costs. Here we have confined ourselves to a single sales estimate (30,000).

2) The cash realization from sales can often be a closely controlled figure, not merely through the stimulation of sales for cash or of collection activities, but also by such devices as extending improved discount rates and other credit terms, calling for advances on certain types of sales, or arranging for the outside financing of other types, often at the buyer's expense. In the present case the estimate of collections, which includes the realization of receivables carried over from the preceding period, has been assumed to be an amount equal to the sales figure. A combination of the judgments of the sales, credit, and accounting departments has probably resulted in the amount shown.

3) A provision for doubtful accounts and the probable actual writeoff of bad debts are estimates for which the credit-and-collections staff, aided by the controller, has had primary responsibility; economic conditions, credit terms, and customer classes are contributing factors.

4) Having determined what the sales volume and the realization period ought to be, Thorpe's management next directs its attention to the prospective factory cost of sales. Here, direct standard costs— which means the raw materials, parts, and direct labor entering the product and the various elements making up factory overhead— make possible the participation of top management in weighing the alternatives always present in the determination and review of unit-product and volume-production costs to meet the already determined sales projection. In these days, top management, along with the production and factory manager and the controller, has become fully aware of the part it can play in the critical review of—and the controls it can and must exercise over—product-cost

components. Plant capacity and adaptability, raw-material alternatives and prices, buy-or-make decisions concerning parts, possible
increases in labor rates and extensions of fringe benefits, service
details, curtailments and substitutions involving factory overhead:
these are among the matters for top-management participation
which direct standard costing makes possible in some situations
and gives added realism to in others.

In the present case, consideration of the transfer from inventory
to cost of sales in terms of materials, labor, and overhead may be
presumed to have commenced with the standard costs of the material-and-labor elements of each unit to be sold. Overhead, which
in this instance appears to be running at the rate of 125% of labor
costs (5,600), will be considered not from the point of view of
the adequacy of this rate, but from that of the detail composing
the anticipated expenditure for the year (6,000): the character and
costs of the several factory services of which the overhead figure
is the total, the effect on costs of modifying the qualities and quantities of services provided, of contracting for (rather than producing) certain services, or of adopting alternative services.

5) Closely connected with and at least partly dependent on the
consideration given product costs will be the flow into cost of sales of
the inventory carryover from the preceding year and the question
of how much inventory of materials, in-process work, and finished
stock need be carried at any time in anticipation of sales. During
recent years the minimization of these requirements through mechanical devices and improved purchasing methods, the "smoothing" of production, and the frequent review of operating standards
has featured an important part of the management services public
accountants have made available to their clients. In organizations
the size of Thorpe, these are major problems of a production manager or production vice-president, aided from time to time by outside reviews and by the newer control techniques. Moreover the
factors of which these problems are composed are often in a state
of flux, and the effect of any one on the whole of a productive
process may require the latter's modification.

6) Other operating costs, principally selling and general, more
or less independent of volume, are reviewed on their merits; they
are direct costs and include executive compensation.

7) Having completed our review of operating income and ex-

pense, we turn to the "financial" transactions, the first of these being a proposed sale of capital stock—which is expected to yield a premium over par or stated value. Presumably this premium is a net figure after deducting anticipated selling commissions and other costs such as an SEC registration. From a glance at the next item below, one might infer that the major purpose of the sale was to finance new fixed assets.

8) Three transactions are combined here: the purchase of fixed assets, the retirement of certain equipment, and the provision for depreciation for the year, apparently at a rate of around 10%. The decisions to buy new equipment and to float additional shares of capital stock have probably been made independently of the budget preparation.

9) Prospective disbursements for the year have been summarized in one entry. In practice receipts and disbursements are likely to be broken down by months in order that the need for temporary financing—a 90-day bank loan, for example—might be disclosed and planned for.

The remaining two entries are mechanical shifts designed to provide in the final column the balance of retained earnings at the beginning of 19-2, the year's net income, and the dividend paid in 19-2.

Projected vs. actual financial statements

Fourteen months later we will be in a position to test Thorpe's projected transactions for 19-2 against the actual; for our forward estimates, made in November, 19-1, and summarized on page 218, together with the year's results we have shown on page 213, permit us to place the two together for comparison on page 220, and to lead us to such observations as these:

> Despite a sales deficiency of more than 9% as compared with the 19-1 estimate, and a gross-profit deficiency of more than 7%, the firm's net profit was increased $295,000, or 12%, over expectations, the major cause of this showing having been brought about by a drastic cut in selling and general overhead costs.

> Working capital failed to meet our original estimate of $7,829,000 for the year-end by $645,000 because purchases of new fixed assets ($5,197,000), exceeding the amount originally projected

($4,200,000), could be financed only in part by the profit increase we have just mentioned.

Remarks such as those appearing in the two paragraphs above are, of course, only surface analyses; they call attention merely to the magnitude of certain differences, not to the reasons for them, and the inferences they contain may not be accurate ones. Again, we may surmise: (1) that the reason for selling certain of the firm's investments was to help finance a fixed-asset acquisition, but (2) that the funds were reinvested shortly thereafter because other sources of financing had become available; yet neither of these deductions (which are no more than assumptions) may be related to the actual events that preceded the sale and the reinvestment. No accountant would be content to report the events as we have described them here; the figures we quote we may presume to be accurate, but the reasons for the decisions leading to these events are required to give life to the variances we have noted.

Looking back at our build-up of the flow statement, we find ourselves justified in reaching a number of conclusions:

1) A forward cash-flow statement, commencing with the latest available balance sheet and working toward a balance-sheet estimate at any desired future date, provides a convenient vehicle for participation in program projections at many management levels.

2) By adhering to the classification of accounts portraying historical costs, a complete, realistic picture can be drawn of the financial and operating activities of a forthcoming period that will supply (a) a firm basis for top-management controls during that period, and (b), where at a subsequent date program changes are required, a committed position from which to proceed further.

3) The principles associated with standard costs in factory operations can be applied to all costs, with reports of variances when compared not only with cost projections but with past operations as well.

4) Direct costing and activity accounting when associated with program projections and identified with the endproducts of costs furnishes a realistic view to top management of how responsibilities assumed, following delegations of authority, have been met.

5) As a useful instrument of *forward accounting*, the cash-flow statement, the constructional details of which have been participated in by management, becomes a valuable addition to the expanding concept of that branch of accounting; it further widens the usefulness and understanding of balance sheets and income statements as the short-term objectives of the accounting process and adds substance to the notion that accounting provides an indispensable tool for management's everyday use.

Summary

We have observed the form and utility of flow statements as a framework into which can be fitted not only a picture of past operations but also a picture of what is to come. Because the bulk of a firm's transactions lend themselves to a relatively few basic classifications, the flow statement can be so devised as to present a periodic overall summary of all past or proposed events and conditions within a given period, including, but going far beyond, those making up an income statement. It can be a valuable supplement to the traditional statements to which public accountants have subscribed in the past and which management has presented to stockholders; and it may, with ample justification, surpass in importance the income statement in its present form as a basis for explaining the past and future of a firm's operations.

CHAPTER FIFTEEN

The Audit Function

Auditing is preventive accounting. It is also preventive management. It examines past events with an unjaundiced eye, measuring them against both conventional and prescribed standards of performance, but always with a critical overlook at the standards themselves. It prosecutes its aims not by command, not by persuasion, but by reports that reveal, appraise, and recommend. It has become a powerful instrument for molding as well as testing and correcting management policies. Its opinions, when disclosed, following its explorations, are value judgments heavily weighted with the public interest.

Today the audit function may be observed as an always active, management-supported, persistent ferment at work throughout countless organizational structures; and its revealed attitudes, backed by its wide investigative potential, exert an influence fully as powerful as that resulting from actual investigation and reporting. Moreover, through the medium of professional bodies it has created, it looks within itself from time to time and strengthens its perspective, methods of inquiry, and activities generally, reaffirming or modifying the principles that dominate its labors; by so doing, it strives to provide an answer to the question: "Who audits the auditors?"

Accounting, recording organizational performance, has long supplied the medium for regulating operating practices at transaction origins and for supplying a two-way vehicle of communication between the varied compartments of management. It routinizes, classifies, and disposes of great quantities of transactions, and, without loss of perspective, provides at required intervals a summing-up of past events by means of historical statements of activities and current statements of position that stand as models of comprehensiveness and brevity.

The audit area

Into the accounting orbit, as we have already observed, a management factor has been infiltrating: in many cases, even in large business organizations, almost imperceptibly. It has not always been an unconscious process, but where its implications have been perceived, the new element has sometimes been viewed by those upon whom the added burden has fallen with no little apprehension, but by those among the more knowing in management circles, as an aspect of the evolution of the accounting process: they assert that it should now be recognized that accounting stands as a major force in making top policies more than intentions, management decisions more than directives, and organizational accomplishments more than uncoordinated group activities.

In its traditional role accounting has not been a faultless device. Its best current forms, manual and mechanical, minimize but do not eliminate mistakes. Operated at different organizational levels by individuals exercising varying degrees of authority, leadership, competence, and conscience, its procedural details may be modified, often unconsciously, by them, and thus inch away from predetermined standards of conformity, however well devised the standards may have been. Errors may escape notice or be wrongly disposed of; or, although discovered, their correction may be neglected. New conditions may be carelessly analyzed or may give rise to transactions of a different order which nevertheless are cast into the old molds, and must subsequently be recast. Or, the existing classification may inadequately display an important trend. Ideal in concept, imperfect in practice—these are aspects of the many well-conceived lines of human endeavor of which traditional accounting has been one.

Accounting has at times been subject to abuses. False entries, failures to record losses or to recognize liabilities, deliberately improper classifications, and other conscious acts of commission and omission affecting the accounting records have been known to remain undetected over considerable periods of time; meanwhile, those who have relied on the propriety of financial statements based on inaccurate records may have suffered irreparable harm, while those guilty of building up such records have continued to enjoy the fruits of their dishonesty. Accounting does not automatically supply its own correctives. In its bare essentials the bookkeeping around which accounting revolves is a process of recording and reporting on the transactions that have been fed into it. Uncorrected improprieties attaching to transactions remain in the financial statements that emerge from them.

In this context, we can view auditing as a natural complement of transaction recording. From the days of Pacioli[1] some form of internal or external review has been regarded as an integral, normative element of the accounting process: a critical look at the record of events during a given period of time before releasing a report on what has transpired during that period. Most of the developments that have taken place in auditing[2] since Pacioli's day have been of a procedural character, which the changing economy has made necessary; the fundamental objective has remained unchanged: auditing stands guard against the various forms of accounting improprieties that have their origins in human ignorance, fallibility, or wrongful intent.

But just as the scope of accounting has been enlarged by its proximity to the field of management, so auditing has been acquiring new implications, as yet imperfectly developed, in its responsibilities to management. Some aspects of these implications will be noted as we examine the three distinct but interdependent divisions of the auditing process—preauditing, internal auditing, and external auditing.

Preaudit

Preaudit, also known as *administrative audit,* is sometimes considered as belonging to the area of *internal check,* but its importance is now recognized as primary: a major element in every system of *internal control.*[3] The importance of what takes place in

[1] Pacioli's suggestion (in the 15th century) for an audit program was limited, however, to a "call-and-check" procedure having as its objective the determination of the correctness of account balances before their transfer to a new ledger. Littleton, *Accounting Evolution to 1900* (New York: American Institute of Certified Public Accountants, 1933), p. 259.

[2] Derived from *audire,* to hear, "audit" has by no means lost its original meaning: a "hearing," i.e., on the success, or absence of it, with which a servant has conducted his master's affairs. The modern auditor as well must listen to oral explanations that invariably supplement the written record of most types of transactions.

[3] As these terms are used here, *internal check*—the maintenance of safeguards surrounding transaction processing designed to minimize error, fraud, and irregularities generally—is only one of the elements of the management function of *internal control,* the latter term including also such features as internal audit, forward accounting (standard costs, budgeting, and budgetary controls), both internal and external reporting, and a number of more recent additions such as direct costing.

preaudit is of direct concern to management; it deserves a position in the organizational scale that will insure its functioning with large measures of authority, discretion, and judgment. Responsibility for the development of and adherence to preaudit procedures centers on the controller. He acts as a coordinator since the first steps in the preaudit process are undertaken by persons not under his control. The preauditor, on the staff of the controller, makes certain that these preliminary activities have been carried out before completing the preaudit process.[4]

Preaudit is the final stage in the processing of a transaction. By the time a voucher and the supporting evidence have arrived at the preauditor's desk, the transaction has, of course, been fully consummated; nevertheless, in the preauditor's hands it is subject to review, adjustment, and even rejection. The general purpose of preaudit is to make sure that the elements required to perfect the transaction are actually present before the transaction has become a part of the official record.

Preaudit of an expenditure often involves two steps: the review of the proposed contract or purchase order; and, after the receipt of the goods or services ordered, the acceptance of the liability to pay the supplier.

The extent of the preaudit of contracts and purchase orders by or under the direction of the controller will be found usually to vary inversely as the depth of the administrative reviews already given them before reaching the controller's office. Points that must be covered before or after that event include an examination of the requisition or other authorization of purchase or work to be done: the present need for the item ordered, approval of the proposal under procedures instituted by management, and the availability of funds. There are many other possible avenues of inquiry having as their objectives the determination of compliance with specific limitations on types and modes of acquisition: who may obligate, sources of supply, methods of procuring bids and choosing from among them, satisfactory quality protection, and so on. It is the job of top management (usually upon recommendation of the

---

[4] The controller's preaudit work may be the responsibility of one person or group; in large organizations there may be a voucher auditor, a revenue auditor, and so on, depending on the nature, location, and volume of business done, and the protective devices instituted at points of origin and receipt.

controller) to determine what these protective steps should be before firm orders are placed, and by whom these steps should be taken; the job remaining to the controller: to make certain that these requirements have been met.

After the receipt of the goods or services, preaudit involves comparisons of the details of invoices with the original contracts, or with the specifications of purchase orders; a determination of the adequacy of the evidence that goods or services of the kind and in the amount ordered have been received, fully inspected for quality and quantity, and placed in stock; the verification of prices, extensions, additions, returns, allowances, and discounts; an inquiry into the authenticity of signatures acknowledging the receipt, inspection, and approval.

Revenue preaudit includes such details as the review of the authenticity of the customer's order, the examination of evidences of independent inspection before delivery or shipment, tie-ins with shipping documents and with delivery receipts from the customer; and, in the case of cash receipts, such tests as daily comparisons of register totals with bank deposits.

For transactions other than expenditures and receipts, preaudit responsibilities are often assigned to other persons in the organization such as the treasurer, perhaps the controller himself, or even the top executive. Whatever the arrangement, no transaction should escape preaudit; and this always means approvals by persons other than those who have: (a) initiated the order, (b) handled, stocked, or disposed of the goods or services received, or (c) enjoyed or are to enjoy any benefit derived from them.

Coding is a final major element of the preaudit process: the determination of the accounts to be affected by the transaction.[5] There may be a *coding clerk* thoroughly familiar with the classification of the organization's accounts and with the intended content of each account; for certain transactions, the controller himself may reserve the right to indicate the accounts to be charged and credited, at least in the case of less routine transactions; or the account

[5] Where, as a part of the internal-audit process, copies of, say, expense accounts are distributed periodically to activity heads responsible for them, the coding operation may include the explanation which, with the amount, is to be posted to the account. The aim here, in the effort to assure speed and accuracy in the posting operation, is to make the operation as mechanical as possible, leaving no discretionary authority in the hands of the posting clerk.

designations may be affixed "at the source," and subsequently reviewed for their propriety by the controller or a member of his staff.

As contrasted with the other two forms of audit we have mentioned, preaudit has not been professionalized; it is a process or series of processes tailormade for each organization and often widely distributed throughout the organizational structure. Good management requires that preauditors be given as free a hand as possible, thus acknowledging their quasi-professional status. A frequent observation made by external auditors is that the worth of a preauditor to any organization can be measured by the independence with which he operates.

Internal audit

Internal audit is a comparatively recent development; it was virtually unknown thirty years ago, and only during the last twenty years has it emerged as a distinct branch of accounting. Its full measure of professional standing may be said to date from 1941 with the founding of the Institute of Internal Auditors and the first appearance of the Institute's journal, *The Internal Auditor*. Because of branches in England, it is the only international society of professional accountants.

Internal auditing has been described as an appraisal discipline. It reviews organizational behavior generally, and, in its best forms, having the support of top management, it has few if any inhibitions to limit the depth of its probings or to dampen the critical nature of its reports. As a staff function, internal auditing has become perhaps the most essential element among internal controls; it has no line or operating responsibilities other than to subordinate its activities in a very general way to some top officer in the organization. This supervision is usually the responsibility of the controller; less frequently the internal auditor reports to the president, the treasurer, or even the chairman of the board. In any case the effort is usually made to give the internal auditor a professional status within the organization: to keep him free from pressures and persuasions, and to expect him not to take sides on any controversial issue unless he has had the opportunity of developing an independent opinion based on a full, unrestricted investigation that has yielded the kind of evidence he is competent to weigh.

The scope of an internal auditor's responsibilities is to be found in the formal assignment of authority given him by the management that employs him. Sometimes the language is both broad and brief, the inference being that the internal auditor is to find his own proper metier within the organization, top-management's preferred objective being to encourage and support him, rather than circumscribe him in any way—either expressly or through implications that may so easily be read into a detailed job description—and to leave to his professional training, to the standards of his professional association, and to his own good judgment the practical details of what he should do and the way he should go about it. In recent years, there has been a marked tendency on the part of top management to spare no effort in keeping the organizational paths clear for the internal auditor and to remove or at least minimize obstructions should any appear.

Internal auditing is commonly regarded as an essential part of the accounting activity within an organization, notwithstanding that many of the problems it encounters and with which it is expected to deal have not until recently been regarded as being within the accounting domain. At no point are management and accounting more intimately related than in the activities now normally prosecuted by the internal auditor.

In organizations both large and small we find the internal auditor functioning most successfully where he has been appointed by top management and serves in a staff capacity under the controller. There are a number of reasons supporting this organizational position. First, recognized accounting implications are involved in many of the situations with which the internal auditor must deal; again, the controller is commonly expected to be the best informed person in the organization on management problems with which, sooner or later, the internal auditor will be brought into contact; and finally, the controller serves as a natural buffer between the internal auditor and the persons associated with the organizational areas which are the objects of his probings. The practical effect of this shielding is to recognize the necessity of the internal auditor's unfettered approach to problems in order that his objectivity may be maintained.

Verification and Appraisal. As conventionally defined, the first duty of the internal auditor is to determine the reliability of the accounting records and the accuracy of the periodic financial statements and of the statistics and other information that constitute the system of internal reporting. This involves a more or less detailed verification of several classes of transactions, testchecking of others, and perhaps a scanning of less vulnerable transaction groups. Transaction reviews by any of these three methods are never ends in themselves; they are vital elements in the internal auditor's studies of the operation of prescribed procedures and of their adequacy. Improprieties which his examination may disclose are weighed by him for their importance; some of them may be so slight an infraction of a preset standard that they deserve no reporting. A small infraction, say, of a method of posting by a records clerk might be something that could be corrected at once by the clerk, and the internal auditor might conclude that the error is not likely to be repeated; if the infraction were of a somewhat higher order of importance, he might still not report it, but at a suitable period thereafter look for its correction or continued incurrence. The remedies he can apply involve both taste and good judgment and are at all times flexible; his aim is always to correct and improve, and to firm up delegations of authority and assumptions of responsibility. His own productivity cannot be rated by the number of irregularities he discovers and reports; rather by work betterments and the improvement in the general tone of the business conducted by the organization he serves. He soon learns never to forget that the chief ingredients of the organization are transactions and people and that the happy coexistence of the two is in the last analysis what he must endeavor to promote.

Because of the internal auditor's essential and well-developed skills in dealing with practical situations, he is frequently involved in what one internal auditor has described to the author as "frustrations of men in dealing with and operating under organizational policy, and of organizational policy in dealing with and operating over men." He is often called on by top management to "unkink" organizational problems that cannot be solved by simple disclosure or by applying or even adding to existing rules. He often becomes the organization's "trouble-shooter" under conditions where the traditional concepts of accounting may be only remotely involved.

He has conditioned himself to the business of tracing undesired effects back to basic causes; he has learned to look for the unexpected and to exhibit no surprise when he finds it. As a diagnostician he has also learned that history repeats itself; that like effects may be traced to like causes. Some internal auditors have indicated that special investigations constitute more than half of their daily labors. A few have informed the author that they have very little time for anything else.

Internal Check. Internal check we have already described as the body of protective devices that have been created to forestall *irregularities.*[6] Some irregularities are revealed by routine, periodic transaction reviews; others by studies or procedural reviews[7] involving such activities as the receipt and handling of collections from customers. Both types of investigative activity are usually found necessary by the internal auditor.

When an important irregularity is discovered by or reported to the internal auditor, he must not only seek out the cause, weigh its effects, determine if any property or money loss is involved, and propose the needed correction of a faulty procedure; but, in the light of what has happened, he is expected also to review the assignments of duties to the individuals directly and indirectly concerned, and arrive at conclusions concerning their competence and honesty. He may in the end recommend organizational, procedural, and personnel changes.

Cooperation with External Auditor. To many people there is a surprising lack of conflict and rivalry between internal and external auditors; the writer has encountered no such situation in practice.

---

[6] Here in the sense of wrongful acts, whether unintended or deliberate; we have previously discussed this in Chapter 12.

[7] A *procedural review* by an internal or external auditor normally goes beyond the traditional examination of internal controls by incorporating the testing practice sometimes referred to as a "horizontal" audit, whereby samplings of both typical and nontypical transactions are followed through their historical development, from their sources to their final lodgments somewhere in the accounts, or to their removal from the accounts. The purpose is to establish more firmly the validity of account content, to provide practical insights into the way in which instituted internal controls actually operate, and to reveal the points at which internal controls are nonexistent, weak, or interlock imperfectly with each other. The term has long been in use by the writer in contradistinction to the more typical "vertical" examination having as its aim the justification of an account balance in terms of its immediate supporting elements.

The functions of the two actually complement each other. For example, most public accountants do not undertake any elaborate search for fraud as a part of their periodic examinations. Rather, they may rely on the procedural reviews of the internal auditor, going over his investigative methods and reports with him, and often suggesting "angles" that their wider experience has taught them to look for. In some instances the public accountant will review all of the reports made by the internal auditor for the period, before drawing up or completing his own audit program. In general, public accountants find internal auditors open to suggestions and not infrequently seeking approbation at a professional level of their past year's program and accomplishments. Public accountants often participate with controllers in suggesting items for internal-audit programs for the ensuing year.

Most public accountants make formal studies of internal controls as a major feature of their annual examinations. This may be done anew each year, or their studies may be cycled over a period, say, of three years. In either case it is customary to secure the cooperation of the internal auditor and occasionally to rely on him in developing preliminary answers to various sections of an internal-control questionnaire, particularly the portion dealing with internal check.

Reports of the Internal Auditor. Reports of internal auditors range all the way from informal conversations to detailed documents studded with "accountese," the latter extreme being, of course, the more conventional and the least effective. Where a written report has been decided on, following an investigation of a particular division of the organization or of some general procedure or special problem, the recurrent difficulties of reporting, so often encountered, will likely present themselves. The internal auditor must first of all decide whether he is to include the procedural steps he has taken in making his examination; the answer is usually "no." No one is likely to be interested in what he did to arrive at the conclusions his report embodies; and few are in a position to arrive at any opinon concerning the thoroughness or other professional qualities of the work he has performed. Also he will find little or no attention is given to a listing of any customary audit steps he has omitted. Again, he can only subtract from his prestige by presenting a list of minor errors discovered, especially where the necessary corrections of transactions and correctives in procedures have already been made by the persons responsible. Interest in his report is enhanced when he describes in the briefest way and in nontechnical language the conditions he has found, and the remedies he recommends, as, for example, possible procedural and personnel changes. An important step is to review the draft report wherever practicable with the operating personnel involved; such a review often leads to joint conclusions as to the auditor's proposed recommendations concerning existing practices or proposed shifts in personnel. The review may also lead to a change in emphasis by a careful reexamination of the long-range effects that have resulted from practices criticized, or that may result if certain correctives are applied.

Followup. Not the least important of the internal auditor's duties is to determine what has been done about the recommendations he has made; if his proposed remedies have been accepted by management, have they been actually instituted? And if they have, is the procedure functioning as it should? It is of course possible he may find that his proposals have initially been given a positive and even enthusiastic reception, and that subsequently the second question will have to be answered in the negative.

Followup plans should be automatic; the internal auditor may aid in determining what the revised policies or procedures should be, but the primary responsibility of correction and enforcement should never be his if his objectivity is to be respected. Usually his nonparticipation in administrative action except at the staff level is well understood and consistently supported by management.

Procedures in Small Organizations. In smaller organizations it is both possible and desirable to institute internal-audit practices without an internal auditor. Procedural studies at regular intervals can be made—and often are—by the proprietor himself or perhaps his principal assistant. But within the levels of cost that even a small firm can afford are the services supplied by public accountants. Much of the work of smaller accounting firms and individual practitioners—many of whom have a background of broad experience and are highly qualified professionally—frequently involves monthly and even continuous procedural and transaction reviews; perhaps the whole task of bookkeeping may be assumed by these practitioners, their periodic fees as a rule being much less than the salary of a full-time clerk. Strictly speaking, neither internal auditing nor an independent examination as these terms are ordinarily defined is involved under such circumstances; rather, a single substitute for both, which, considering the size of the business, the nature of its problems, and the proximity of the owner to individual transactions, may operate with equal effectiveness.

External audit

The public accountant supplies the concluding stage in the audit process. His role is unique in that he is responsible not only to the persons employing him but also, as is often said, to the world at large. His representations as to transaction aggregates, imposed by custom and required by law and by the regulations of government commissions and other public bodies, but couched in language of his own choosing, are universally relied on by stockholders and by numerous other elements of the public.

The public accountant is, first of all, an interpreter of an organization's financial affairs. The financial statements with which he associates his name must of necessity conform to certain accepted conventions since readers of the statements may be expected to *interpret* them as they would other financial statements, unless accompanying disclosures or qualifications have had the effect of modifying their point of view.

Another purpose of the external audit is the *protection* given to investors. Under national and state laws and regulations, the annual audit, and the standards that have gone into the making of it, give assurance that the conventions and customs normally underlying the items displayed in financial statements are present, and that their accuracy within these conventions and customs can be depended upon.

A public accountant's established services to management have also come to be of the first order of importance. These include the preparation of income-tax returns, or aid in their preparation or review; and forward planning on such diversified matters as budgetary procedures, costing methods, inventory controls, incentive plans, and pension schemes. Because of the public accountant's contacts with many problems falling under these and similar heads, and his growing specialization in management services, he is in a unique position to pass his experience along to his clients. However, from our point of view here, such services are not auditing but natural consequences of the auditor's developed skills. Their relation to auditing is that they may well contribute to a better background for succeeding audits, as well as to better management.

The External Audit Concept. The author has defined the periodic audit made by the public accountant as:

> An exploratory, critical review . . . of the underlying internal controls and accounting records of a business enterprise or other economic unit, precedent to the expression by him of a judgment as to the propriety of its financial statements.[8]

In practice, periodic examinations by public accountants vary widely in character although some correspondence in their procedures has been gained through frequent considerations of the subject within professional organizations, and the existence of audit texts in which the methods of audit most often followed are presented and illustrated.[9] The American Institute of Certified Public Accountants several years ago adopted a number of basic standards that have shed some light on the meaning of the public accountant's audits and reports; these may be briefly summarized thus:

> *General standards:* (1) The audit must be conducted by a person of adequate technical training and experience. (2) The auditor must maintain an independent mental attitude. (3) "Due professional care" must be reflected in the conduct of the audit and in the audit report.
>
> *Field-work standards:* (4) The audit must be carefully planned, and assistants, if any, competently supervised. (5) Internal controls must be studied and evaluated as a basis for reliance and for the determination of the scope of testing procedures. (6) Sufficient evidence, obtained through inspection, observation, inquiries, and confirmations, is a necessary prerequisite to the auditor's opinion expressed in his report.
>
> *Reporting standards:* (7) The report must indicate whether the financial statements conform to "generally accepted principles of accounting." (8) The report must state whether these principles have been consistently followed and whether they deviate from those of the preceding period. (9) Disclosures in the financial statements, including footnotes, will be regarded as adequate unless exception is

[8] A quotation based in part on the author's definition in his *Dictionary.*

[9] As in the author's *Auditing: An Introduction to the Work of the Public Accountant.*

taken in the auditor's report. (10) The report must contain the auditor's opinion of the financial statements, a qualified opinion, or a denial of opinion, the last-named with reasons therefor.

Several points appearing in these standards, which suggest functional aspects of auditing, call for our particular attention here. The first is that the tests or sampling procedures (which in these days characterize a large part of the field work involved in the public accountant's examination) must be based on a study of the internal controls actually operating in the enterprise, the inference being that the better these controls, the more the reliance that can be placed on testing and sampling (as compared with detailed-audit)[10] methods. If the auditor could be completely satisfied with the methods of internal control, he would have no need even for sampling: a brief scanning might do. But despite a clear and eminently satisfactory set of regulations establishing and ostensibly successfully maintaining a system of internal control, the experienced auditor can be sure of the character of the system *actually in operation* only by testing transactions that supposedly have run the gamut of the various controls of which the system is composed. The auditor's procedure here resembles in some ways quality-control testing in manufacturing plants. Where samples reveal a higher incidence of imperfections than a predetermined maximum would allow, second and third samples are taken; if the imperfections exceed the line of tolerance, a whole output of products may be rejected. As applied to an audit, a certain quantity or type of error might mean a detailed audit and a qualified report or perhaps no report at all.

A second point suggested by these standards is the reference to competent "evidence" to which inspection (of accounts and transaction documents), observation (of methods followed), inquiries (concerning conformance to procedures, by questioning individual employees), and confirmations (from outsiders concerning transactions as yet not completed) have contributed. A public accountant's methods may well differ importantly in his examination of different enterprises. Only when evidence in these varied forms has been

---

[10] By a "detailed" audit is meant a review of every transaction during a given period or every transaction contained in a particular account or group of accounts, as contrasted with a "sampling" audit limited to the examination of a relatively small fraction of transactions during the same period or in the same account or group.

amassed to his satisfaction is he in a position to express his professional opinion—which is, in the last analysis, a *value judgment*.[11]

A third point lies in the emphasis on consistency from one year to another. To form his opinion the public accountant must necessarily have a standard of comparison. This year's financial statements need not closely resemble last year's or those of any similarly situated enterprise; but if they do not, the auditor must determine the source of the variation: a change in the classification of accounts or a major shift in the way of doing business, for example. Whatever the cause, a material variation calls for a footnote or other elaboration, a qualification in which the character and quantitative effect of the variation are disclosed, or in extreme cases a denial of an opinion.

The Audit Report. Public accountants, through their professional organization, the American Institute of Certified Public Accountants, have adopted a standard short form of report that is acceptable to the U.S. Securities and Exchange Commission, the New York Stock Exchange, and other public or quasi-public organizations to which corporations must send financial data. This report passed through a number of stages during the period 1934-47.[12] Now, with minor variations, it can be found in the annual reports of almost all American corporations. Along with other accountants the author believes that the employment of this standard-language report (or "certificate" as it is often called), despite its universality, is essentially a transitory phenomenon. An audit has come to mean much more than any of the possible implications one may gather from such a report; moreover, the expressions one finds in the standard report are awkward, even repetitious, and are as subject to possible misinterpretation by unskilled readers as were the earlier versions. But in its favor it may be said that it has become so well established that its imperfections are overlooked and are not at the moment matters of serious concern. It has, in fact, become a signpost of audit regularity and approval.[13]

[11] That is, a judgment the basis of which is the whole of the public accountant's past training and experience.

[12] For the detail of these changes see the author's *Auditing*, Chapter 16.

[13] This is not to say that simplified language, or perhaps no language at all above the accountant's signature might not lead to a clearer interpretation of the public accountant's function. The author's further comments and proposal for a substitute form can be found in his *Auditing*, Chapter 16.

Summary

A nonprofessional observer of the characteristics of the audit function we have been describing may well be struck by the combination of forward and backward looks that play equally prominent roles in the whole of the social institution we call accounting; he will see on the one hand the planning, projecting, classifying, recording, allocating, and participant-in-management functions of the accountant as controller; on the other hand, the proving and approving function of the accountant as auditor. Ostensibly the one is identified with the inside, subjective approach of the operating executive; the other, with the arm's-length, essentially objective, professional approach of one endowed with a critical wisdom sharpened by hindsight. Both deal with the same subject matter: the standards followed in the two sectors, having a common origin and a common acceptance, differ from each other only in procedural particulars. Despite the influence of public bodies (the SEC, for example) accounting standards, generated almost wholly within the private accounting domain, have been the acknowledged common property of both sectors; and their expressed aims have never failed to include solicitude for the public interest. Moreover, as practiced by both the controller and the external auditor, accounting stands unique among social institutions as its own arbiter of what the public interest is and should be.

CHAPTER SIXTEEN

Endproducts

Financial statements, culminating the accountant's labors, are the raw materials of an extraordinarily diverse array of readers: investors, analysts, economists, reporters, commentators, students, and many others. Although professional standards of disclosure and objective opinions of "fairness," designed to aid and assure readers, fall within the province of the public accountant, responsibility for the propriety of the facts and conditions embodied in financial statements, being the outgrowth of controllable operating policies, is an acknowledged element of the management discipline. Whether accounting data serve as a means of communication between management levels in business or with stockholders and the public, as grist for the mill of ratio analysis, or collectively as an index of the nation's economic health, the possibilities and limitations attending their use deserve a wider understanding.

Having considered the main features of the *accounting process,* we are now prepared to say that it provides

as an everyday operating essential—
1) An orderly method of recognizing, timing, classifying, recording, and reporting transactions: transactions being the expression in universal symbols of known events and conditions.
2) Regularity and accuracy in the conduct of day-to-day operations through designed flows of transaction information.

as a tool of management—
3) A vehicle for the definition, allocation, and delimitation of authority.
4) A basis of communication between management and activity levels that makes possible in-depth delegations of authority.
5) Internal controls insuring the acceptance and administration of policies, including the maintenance of required standards of performance.
6) Accountability (feedback) from activity centers to sources of authority.
7) A technique for the forward planning of agreed objectives.
8) A means for reshaping objectives and policies as new events and conditions are encountered.
9) Comparisons—of operating projections with actual attainments— that aid in determining causes of variances and facilitate the institution of corrective measures.

as the basis of external reporting—
10) Transaction summaries making up long-established conventional displays of financial status and operating performance that feature management's reports to the outside world.

11) Data permitting comparisons of present and past status and performance.

as a model for assembling economic data—

12) A flow pattern that can be adapted to the depiction not only of overall industry operations but also of national income.

Preparing financial statements

In reporting on a financial statement the public accountant, as we have already observed, studiously avoids any expression of opinion of financial condition as revealed by the statement as a whole, of trends indicated by comparative statements, or of any other inference that only the reader of a statement may be expected to extract from it. He abstains from interpretation because what is to happen in the future—an unavoidable accompaniment of interpretation—he regards as a purely subjective concept. A balance sheet may display organizational euphoria, and a series of income statements an enviable earnings performance, but no experienced investor, and certainly no accountant as an investor, will "buy, hold, or sell" purely on such a showing; he will need a great deal of additional information: something about the nature of the product or service constituting the organization's output, market conditions, competitive obstacles, pricing policies, rising costs, the likelihood that present outlets will be maintained, the management rating and the management outlook, the productivity of the organization's research-and-development activities, the current "price-earnings" ratio,[1] and so on. The impact of such factors on the organization's future is a matter for qualitative value judgment on the part of the investor, to which the undisputed outcome of past transactions can only contribute. Financial statements can never serve as controlling guides. The public accountant leaves general inferences to others.

This basically negative approach is reflected in both national and state securities laws, in SEC regulations and opinions, and in numerous court decisions. What the public accountant strives for is simply a "fair" presentation of financial data: a presentation that no one can call "misleading." Here no dichotomy is involved, for if a fi-

---

[1] The ratio of the current market price per share of common stock to the most recent annual net income per share. In this book we have not been concerned with these areas of investor interest.

nancial statement is regarded as *not* misleading, the two negatives do not make it a "leading" statement. "Fair" is the accountant's nearest approach to a positive asseveration. The British equivalent is "fair and true"; to the American accountant "fair" points to an underlying "opinion" concerning which differences might exist among persons of equal competence, while "true" suggests an adherence to some predetermined, universal standard that does not in fact exist, and is therefore a word to be avoided.

The public accountant's effort, then, is to prevent *misinterpretation* and rigorously to avoid pointing in any direction its opposite might suggest. Yet he must provide information for the interpretation of others. This he feels he accomplishes by presenting *conventional* statements: statements in conventional form containing conventional titles and sideheads that mean conventional things. He focuses his attention on the possible inferences that may be drawn from individual statement items. "Cash," for example, appearing on a balance sheet as a single word with no descriptive adjectives and with no qualifying footnote, means amounts on deposit in banks and possibly a minor amount of currency on hand, all unqualifiedly available for ordinary operating purposes; "receivables" standing alone means the portion of sales to customers that will be collected within a few weeks from the balance-sheet date; and so on. To him the conventional meanings associated with these terms are standards to which he must wherever possible conform. Where he is faced with a departure from any common standard he (1) endeavors to correct it by adjustment or elimination, but if for any reason this cannot be done, he (2) amplifies the item title by adding a descriptive phrase that acts as a bridge with convention, (3) provides a footnote having that effect, (4) qualifies his short-form report (or certificate) as we have already observed, (5) indicates in his report his disagreement with the item as presented, or (6) refuses to permit the association of his name with the statement.

Importance to management

As features of a business-management's report to investors and, in these days, to the world at large, financial statements are regarded as revealing the consequences of management's activities and responsibilities. The corporate image thus created has become a direct concern of corporate boards as well as corporate executives. A favorable financial showing stimulates public confidence and contributes to product acceptance. Again, reaching a top-level decision leading to new plant, new products, or a new field of activity is dependent in no small measure on the resulting modification in the appearance of the company's financial statements. Pressure for as favorable a showing as possible imposes on management an operational restraint that can and often does lead to better planning and the strengthening of delegated authority at points where it can be converted into controls—all of which will in turn narrow the gap between planning and action and hence between projected and actual operating results.

Dissecting financial statements

What does the reader of financial statements look for? How is his opinion of a business enterprise shaped, affirmed, or altered by a balance sheet or operating statement? Let us take the relatively simple situation portrayed by the financial statements on page 249 as an example. Here we have two balance sheets and two operating statements. We will compare the present position and the most recent operating statement with those of the preceding year, the latter representing our point of departure or standard of comparison. We will set forth some typical observations, assuming that these statements have been accompanied by an unqualified report of public accountants and hence that no question of "fairness" need be raised. This, however, will not bar comments on the scantiness of the information supplied.

Sales increased more than 6% over the preceding year [(412.7-389.4)/389.4] × 100 [we omit dollar signs and 00's here]; but for both years a net-worth turnover of 2 is indicated (389.4/184.1 and 412.7/192.4). [Before World War II the latter ratio was often less than 1.] Less realistic, however, is the inventory turnover; without a cost-of-sales figure, a physical turnover cannot be computed. If this figure (for 19-3) proved to be 280.0, the physical turnover would have been 4 (280.0/68.6).[2] The dollar turnover (usual with investment analysts) was nearly 6 (389.4/66.6 and 412.7/70.6). A ratio of more than 8 (389.4/47.9 and 412.7/51.5) defines the rela-

[2] Here 68.6 is the average; more common among analysts is the end-of-the-year figure—not as accurate but the results are comparable if the practice is consistently followed from one year to another.

tion between sales and receivables—which means that 45 days
(360/8) has been required for the collection of the average sale.

A net income of 17.1 has been earned on a net worth (at the
year end) of 192.4, a return of about 9%, and about 58% of it has
been paid out in dividends. [The ratios quoted in these comments
are approximations resulting from mental calculations—which for
most readers are accurate enough for their purposes.]

The dividend rate on paid-in capital has remained at 13%
(9.3/73.0 and 9.9/74.1) or a yield of 5% for both years on stockholders' equity (9.3/184.1 and 9.9/192.4). Also for both years the
net income has been approximately 4% of sales (16.6/389.4 and
17.1/412.7).

Current assets and current liabilities have increased proportionately by about 7% but the working-capital ratio has remained at 2.5.

Depreciation expense indicates a provision of 6% for both years
but the ratio of accumulated depreciation to fixed-asset costs has increased during the past year to nearly 51%. Because the accumulated
depreciation shows a net increase of but 9.0, new fixed-assets acquired must have been at least 17.8 (232.8 − 220.9 + 13.5 −
[117.7 − 110.1]), an 8% increase (17.8/220.9) in fixed assets since
the beginning of the year. [Any charge to operations of losses on the
disposal of old equipment would increase new acquisitions by the
same amounts.]

Cash funds of 30.6 (17.1 + 13.5) which were acquired during
the year from operations, along with additions to long-term obligations (2.9) and to paid-in capital (1.1), a total of 34.6, were invested in new fixed assets (17.8), additions of .8 to other assets
(24.8 − 24.0) and of 6.1 to working capital (162.7 − 66.2 −
151.8 + 61.4), while stockholders received dividends of 9.9.

At this point the reader of these statements would likely conclude that the enterprise had remained remarkably stable, and that
its financial structure had kept pace with the fairly substantial increase in sales; the basic reason for this will appear shortly. One
person to whom these statements were displayed deduced that the
increase in sales was attributable in part to price increases and in
part to physical volume, since inventories increased but 6%. Perhaps
so, but without further information (which was unavailable) this
conclusion could not be validated.

AN AVERAGE MANUFACTURING COMPANY

Comparative Balance Sheets—December 31, 19-3 and 19-2

Assets	19-3	19-2
Current Assets:		
Cash resources	$ 30,700	$ 29,300
Customers, net	51,500	47,900
Inventories, at cost or less	70,600	66,600
Prepaid expenses	9,900	8,000
Total current assets	$162,700	$151,800
Fixed assets:		
Land, buildings & equipment	$232,800	$220,900
Accumulated depreciation	117,700	110,100
Fixed assets, net	$115,100	$110,800
Other assets:	$ 24,800	$ 24,000
Total assets	$302,600	$286,600

Liabilities	19-3	19-2
Current liabilities:		
Bank loans	$ 7,900	$ 8,000
Income tax payable	11,700	10,000
Other	46,600	43,400
Total current liabilities	$ 66,200	$ 61,400
Long-term liabilities	$ 44,000	$ 41,100
Equity of stockholder:		
Paid-in capital	$ 74,100	$ 73,000
Retained earnings	118,300	111,100
Total net worth	$192,400	$184,100
Total liabilities	$302,600	$286,600

Comparative Income Statements
Years ended December 31

	19-3	19-2
Sales	$412,700	$389,400
Operating expense:		
Depreciation	$ 13,500	$ 12,800
Federal income tax	15,500	14,200
Other	366,600	345,800
Total expense	$395,600	$372,800
Net income	$ 17,100	$ 16,600
Dividends paid	9,900	9,300
Earnings retained	$ 7,200	$ 7,300

Standards of comparison

A balance sheet standing alone may create an *impression* of strength because it displays "adequate" working capital, a "safe" working-capital ratio, an "ample margin" for long-term investors, and a "satisfactory" build-up of retained earnings; but, in most cases, this can be regarded as little more than a first impression. Even a less number of good points could be extracted from any isolated income statement. A *standard of comparison* is required if one is to derive any significant amount of information from a financial statement. Two such standards are in common use: past balance sheets of the same organization (vertical standards)—which we have just illustrated—and contemporary balance sheets of similar organizations (horizontal standards). From the one we may expect to derive financial (positive or negative) growth or decline; from the other, relative strength, particularly in a competitive field where comparisons would be expected to have a more assured validity. Comparisons of income statements of both types yield conclusions as to an improved or declining earning ability and relative operating efficiency. Comparisons of the first type we have already noted.

Financial and operating ratios

Comparisons of the second type are often made in the form of percentage relationships within given financial statements and the corresponding percentage relationships derived from composite industry statements adopted as the standard of comparison. To illustrate let us first set forth (page 252) the financial picture of all

American manufacturing corporations as compiled by the Federal Trade Commission and the Securities and Exchange Commission.

We first note that the comparative statements on page 249 are actually not those of a single enterprise but composite statements (if we add six ciphers) of the nation's manufacturing enterprises. Viewed in their abbreviated status each of these statements as we have previously employed them may be regarded as a collection of arithmetic means (rather than the statement itself being an arithmetic mean), truly comparable, however.

Most financial analysts develop opinions of corporate enterprises partly by building up ratio data, with yearly or more frequent additions as annual, quarterly, or other reports make their appearance. On page 253 are twenty typical ratios, of which the first fourteen have been employed by Dun & Bradstreet for many years in developing industry statistics[3]; we have determined these ratios from the data provided on page 252. The results may seem somewhat surprising: over the past nine years there have been no more than minor fluctuations in fourteen ratios, slight upward trends in three (6, 7, 16), and slight downward trends in three (13, 19, 20).

Comments on these ratios follow:

1) Ratio 1 (the working-capital ratio) appears destined to remain at 2.5, a figure identical with a long-established rule-of-thumb "safety" margin. The slight upward bulge in 1958 was a natural consequence of the curtailed business of that year (lower sales, fewer purchases, reduced payables—note ratios 2 and 3 for 1958—and hence a more liquid position).

2) From ratios 2, 3, and 4, we might infer that 60% of net worth resides in fixed assets and that average operating conditions require borrowed capital equal to something more than 50% of net worth, two-fifths long-term and three-fifths short-term. The long-term ratio (ratio 4 − ratio 3) remained at a constant .20—.22 throughout the eight-year period.

3) Ratio 5, registering the working-capital investment in inventory, has decreased slightly, not because of recent more efficient minimization of inventory stock (ratio 14 indicates a fairly constant relationship of inventory to sales), but because of the larger portion of working capital required for unpaid customer accounts (ratio 13).

4) Ratio 6 indicates a somewhat decreased safety factor for long-term debt in that it has been offset in the overall financial picture by an increased ratio to working capital.

[3] *Key Business Ratios* (New York: Dun & Bradstreet, 1964). These ratios are averages of 70 industry groups based on approximately 6,000 samples, with composite high, median, and low ratios for each of the fourteen ratio classes. There is no consolidation of groups that would make the resulting ratios comparable with those on page 248.

AMERICAN MANUFACTURING CORPORATIONS
Composite Financial Statements
(in billions of dollars)

Income Statements	1950	1956	1957	1958	1959	1960	1961	1962	1963
Net sales	181.9	307.3	320.0	304.6	337.8	345.7	356.4	389.4	413.8
Depreciation	3.9	8.6	9.4	9.8	10.3	10.9	11.6	12.8	13.5
Federal income tax	10.3	13.6	12.7	10.0	13.4	12.3	12.2	14.2	15.4
Other expense	155.7	270.7	283.5	273.0	298.7	309.9	318.3	345.8	366.9
Net income	12.0	14.4	14.4	11.8	15.4	12.6	14.3	16.6	18.0
Dividends	5.7	7.4	7.6	7.4	7.9	8.3	8.6	9.3	9.9
Sampling tie-in	.3	1.4	.7	.8	.6	.3	.6	.4	.9
Retained earnings	6.0	5.6	6.1	3.6	6.9	4.0	5.1	6.9	7.2
Balance Sheets									
Cash & U.S. securities	24.6	27.7	26.7	27.8	29.7	27.6	28.1	29.3	30.8
Receivables	17.0	32.0	32.4	34.1	38.0	39.9	44.9	47.9	51.5
Inventories	31.2	54.8	56.3	52.9	57.9	60.4	62.8	66.6	70.5
Other current assets	1.4	3.2	3.9	4.1	5.3	5.9	6.8	8.0	9.9
Total current	74.2	117.7	119.3	118.9	130.9	133.8	142.6	151.8	162.7
Fixed assets	81.8	145.1	159.3	168.6	180.1	193.9	206.8	220.9	232.8
Accrued depreciation	−38.0	−65.9	−72.4	−78.8	−85.6	−93.4	−101.1	−110.1	−117.7
Other noncurrent assets	8.3	13.9	15.3	16.7	18.8	21.5	23.2	24.0	24.8
Assets = liabilities	126.3	210.8	221.5	225.4	244.2	255.8	271.5	286.6	302.6
Current liabilities	29.2	50.0	49.1	45.2	52.3	53.3	57.4	61.4	66.2
Long-term liabilities	11.2	26.1	28.2	30.4	31.7	34.9	38.2	41.1	44.0
Paid-in capital	37.3	56.2	59.6	61.6	65.1	68.5	71.7	73.0	74.1
Retained earnings	48.6	78.5	84.6	88.2	95.1	99.1	104.2	111.1	118.3

Notes: (1) Cost of sales is merged with "other expense" in FTC-SEC reports.

(2) Surplus charges and changes in reserves positioned above net worth in the FTC-SEC reports have been merged with "other expense"; the reserve balances have been added to retained earnings.

Source: Quarterly Financial Reports for Manufacturing Corporations 1950–1963. These reports are based on a sampling (10,607 in 1962) obtained by the Federal Trade Commission and the Securities and Exchange Commission; from this sampling the totals, reported above, are determined for all (165,863 filing tax returns in 1961) American manufacturing corporations. Although the sampling is but 7 per cent of the *total number,* it is estimated to account for about 87 per cent of the *total assets.* In terms of "receipts from all manufacturing activity in the United States . . . corporations account for more than 96% . . ." (in 1962).

AMERICAN MANUFACTURING CORPORATIONS

Comparisons of Financial & Operating Ratios
1950-1963

Description of ratios	1950	1956	1957	1958	1959	1960	1961	1962	1963
Balance-sheet elements only—									
1 current assets/current liabilities	2.5	2.4	2.4	2.6	2.5	2.5	2.5	2.5	2.5
2 fixed assets/net worth	.51	.59	.60	.60	.59	.60	.60	.60	.60
3 current liabilities/net worth	.34	.37	.34	.30	.33	.32	.33	.34	.35
4 all liabilities/net worth	.47	.57	.54	.50	.53	.53	.54	.55	.57
5 inventory/working capital	.70	.81	.80	.72	.73	.75	.74	.74	.73
6 long-term debt/working capital	.25	.39	.40	.41	.40	.43	.45	.46	.46
7 current liabilities/inventory	.93	.91	.87	.85	.90	.88	.91	.92	.94
Income-statement elements only—									
8 net income/sales	.07	.05	.05	.04	.05	.04	.04	.04	.04
Balance-sheet and income elements—									
9 net income/net worth	.14	.11	.10	.08	.09	.08	.08	.09	.09
10 net income/working capital	.27	.21	.21	.16	.19	.16	.17	.18	.19
11 sales/net worth	2.1	2.3	2.2	2.0	2.0	2.1	2.0	2.1	2.2
12 sales/working capital	4.0	4.5	4.6	4.1	4.3	4.3	4.2	4.3	4.3
13 sales/receivables	10.7	9.6	9.9	9.0	8.9	8.6	7.9	8.1	8.0
14 sales/inventory	5.8	5.6	5.7	5.8	5.8	5.7	5.7	5.8	5.9
Additional ratios:									
15 depreciation expense/fixed assets	.05	.06	.06	.06	.06	.06	.06	.06	.06
16 depreciation reserve/fixed assets	.46	.46	.46	.46	.47	.48	.49	.50	.51
17 net income/paid-in capital	.32	.26	.24	.18	.22	.19	.19	.22	.24
18 dividends/paid-in capital	.15	.13	.13	.12	.12	.12	.12	.13	.13
19 dividends/net income	.48	.51	.53	.63	.51	.66	.60	.56	.55
20 cash/retained earnings	.51	.29	.32	.32	.31	.28	.27	.26	.26

Note: These ratios are based on combined balance sheets and income statements shown above.

5) Ratio 7, showing a slight increase since 1957, appears to indicate that the payments of amounts owing suppliers has been extending over a longer period of time. This seems to be borne out by considering the opposite side of the picture (ratio 13).

6) Ratio 8 has hovered between .04 and .05 for 13 of the 15 years the FTC-SEC data have been available. For manufacturing industry as a whole the often-asserted "profit squeeze" has not been evident. The 1950 showing here and elsewhere among the ratios reflects the effects of a year of rapid recovery following the 1949 recession.

7) Ratios 9, 10, and 17 display a fairly unchanging relationship of earnings to the several elements of investment. As a constantly higher portion of invested capital is represented by retained earnings, an increase in ratio 17 might be considered a normal expectancy.

8) Ratios 11, 12, 13, and 14, displaying "turnovers," show no discernible trends except for ratio 13 which indicates, as we have already observed, the growing tendency of credit extension. Sales promotion, in the face of increasing competition, has carried with it the necessity of allowing the customer more time to pay.

9) Ratios 15 and 16 show that despite the increased business allowances for depreciation in tax returns, and a decrease from 49% in 1956 to 46% in 1963 in the ratio of income tax to net income before taxes, the recorded overall rate, 5.5% (rounded to .06 on page 253), has remained unchanged for book purposes. But accumulated depreciation has reached 51%, a normal expectancy as additions to fixed assets level off.

10) Ratio 18 for the 15-year period covered by the FTC-SEC statistics has fluctuated within narrow limits (.12—.15): an indication that the nation's manufacturers have paid out a consistently liberal return on invested capital. Some economists and a few accountants would discount these ratios by price-level changes during that period; but had industry's management as a whole been convinced that the shrinking dollar was increasing their costs, the inflationary trend would doubtless have been spurred.

11) Ratio 19 indicates that a somewhat declining proportion of annual net income has been paid out in dividends—which means that net income has been increasingly employed as a principal source of funds for the purchase of fixed assets. A funds statement covering the 15 years 1949-1963 has been prepared from the FTC-SEC as shown at the top of p. 255 (billions of dollars).

12) Over the 15-year period the ratio of cash to retained earnings has declined from a high of 51% (reflecting war gains) to 26%; the tendency, as we have just seen, has been to finance asset increases, including working capital, from reinvested earnings (ratio 20).

Disposal of funds			Sources of funds	
Operating costs less depreciation of $127.5	$3,893.8		Sales	$4,409.1
Federal income tax	183.6		Net increases in	
Surplus adjustments	22.3	$4,099.7	Long-term debt	32.8
Fixed assets, net	$ 201.2		Paid-in capital	39.6
Other assets	17.2			
Working capital (including cash of $12.7)	57.5	275.9		
Dividends		105.9		
		$4,481.5		$4,481.5

Because of the absence of any breakdown of "net sales" except on an industry basis and of "other expense" (the two largest and most complex items on both sets of statements), we are unable to make any worthwhile analysis of *trends* in income *sources* and in cost components. Within such large aggregates we would expect to find wide variations from year to year in such items as—

sales by product classes: a breakdown (the minimum: raw material, intermediate products, and consumer products) constituting at least 75% of the total

costs of sales capable of being matched against each such product class breakdowns of costs of sales by material, labor, and overhead, the last-named including depreciation

the principal elements of:
selling costs, including advertising
administrative costs, including compensation of officers
other costs and losses

fixed-asset additions and retirements

Although details of this sort are often supplied by individual companies upon request, their general unavailability in most annual reports to stockholders indicates that they are regarded by management as at least semiconfidential and that their release would presumably generate competitive hazards: the same reasons cited in opposition to the disclosure of a total sales figure in this country forty years ago and in England today. Actually, through data collected by trade associations, revealed in professional meetings of engineers and other technicians and in reports to the SEC, much of this information comes to light, is often pieced together by analysts, and could be and actually is currently available to competitors. It is likely that eventually these data will appear as a normal feature of all stockholders' reports, once management has overcome its reluctance to make them public. Experience does not bear out the contention that something will be lost by their publication.

National-income accounting

Numerous experiments were made by economists before World War II to establish a basis for giving dollar expression to the nation's economy as a whole, but it was not until the years immediately following the war that these ideas took their present form.[4] Since 1947 the Office of Business Economics of the U.S. Department of Commerce has been issuing an annual report on a "national accounting" in which estimates are made of the economic activities of business, government, and persons. Perhaps the leading feature of these estimates has been the determination of the dollar amount of *gross national product,* better known by the initials GNP: a figure much quoted in the press and by businessmen, congressmen, and others as indicating the present pinnacle, as well as the present trend of the economy. A summary of the 1962-1963 estimates appears on pages 258-9 where the GNP for the two years can be found: 554.9 and 583.9 billions of dollars, respectively. In reporting the more recent of these figures, one financial commentator has said that the nation's economy had risen 5% during 1963. The reader will have no difficulty determining the source of this statement, although the identification of GNP as a measure of the "total economy" might well be open to question.

Gross national product can be defined informally in terms of items *d, e, f,* and *g* on pages 258-9: sales to persons (consumers), sales to government (this includes state and local, as well as national), new assets created (buildings, machinery, increase in inventories, the last-named raising the whole to "production" or "value added" —presumably .8 of 1% in excess of "sales"), and net exports—all of

---

[4] See, for example, Carl S. Shoup, *National Income Analysis* (Boston: Houghton Mifflin Company, 1947) and Subcommittee on National Income Statistics, *Measurement of National Income and the Construction of Social Accounts* (Geneva: United Nations, 1947); the latter contains an appendix by Richard Stone providing 288 illustrative "journal entries" which are to be divided among the five sectors of a nation's economy.

which can be described as *the final business output* that has passed into the hands of "consumers" or ultimate users or that has been made available for their use. Items *a, b,* and *c,* added together, also yield the GNP total: the "gross receipts" of natural persons and government arising from business operations (excluding costs of sales to ultimate users arising from own production), and the "un-expended receipts" of business corporations. These three categories may be described as the disposition of the proceeds of the national output of final product, intermediate steps being omitted. The same elements on both sides are then distributed between the three sectors that follow: "persons," "government," and "savings." Items from *h* to *k,* are "transfers" between these groups. "Savings" is the nearest approach to a balance-sheet category: on the one hand new assets, including new foreign investments, and on the other, the three principal sources of new "surplus." But the commercial financial-statement analogy can be carried no further, for the suggestions that would lead to the determination of the economy's other assets and liabilities are as yet incomplete, if not unknown, provided we admit that the economy as a whole can be conceived as having—in the commercial sense—any assets or liabilities, for a "consolidated" balance sheet would cancel a good share of them.

We can fill in this picture of the national economy in somewhat greater detail by considering the cross-relations displayed on pages 258-9. If the reader will follow through on the eleven lettered "journal entries" (*a-k*), he will observe a family resemblance to the input-output breakdowns on pages 212-3. Each "debit" and each "credit" has been built up independently from numerous but different factual sources; many others have been estimated; and a few (imputed items) are wholly imaginary and without commercial parallels. Fortunately the last-named group is a small one, the principal items being noted below. Figures quoted relate to 1963.

a) Income of persons, 432.9: compensation of individuals from business operations, including not only salaries and wages but also profits of partnerships, proprietorships, real-estate holdings, farming operations, and dividends and interest received, not including interest on government bonds; the total, constituting more than nine-tenths of the 1963 receipts of individuals (i.e. $a + j + h$) had its origins in profit-making (or income-producing) operations.

b) Income of government, 94.6: taxes and social-insurance receipts, all paid out of business operations. The "negative income" of 1.0 rep-

U.S. NATIONAL INCOME
1963-1962
(billions of dollars)

	1963	1962
Payments to persons:		
Salaries & wages	325 2	309 1
Benefits from business	2 4	2 3*
Individuals' profits	37 6	36 5
Farming	13 0	13 3
Rents	12 3	12 0
Dividends	18 0	16 6
Interest	24 4	22 0
Personal earnings	a 432 9	411 8
Payments to government:		
Indirect taxes	55 9	53 0*
Corporate income taxes	24 6	22 2
Insurance contributions	15 1	13 7
Subsidies, net	-1 0	-1 7*
Government revenues	b 94 6	87 2
Retained by corporations:		
Depreciation provisions	50 8	49 4*
Undistributed profits	8 3	8 3
Statistical discrepancy	-2 7	-1 8*
New corporate funds	c 56 4	55 9
Disposition of GNP	583 9	551 9

Economic Activity of Business

	1963	1962
Sales to persons:		
Durables	52 1	48 2
Nondurables	167 5	161 4
Services	155 3	145 7
Consumer purchases	d 375 0	355 3
Sales to government:		
Durables	20 9	20 6
Nondurables	9 7	9 8
Services	73 3	68 9
New construction	18 7	17 7
Government purchases	e 122 6	117 0
Creation of new assets:		
Residential buildings	25 2	23 2
Other private construction	21 3	21 2
Producers' equipment	31 0	28 8
Inventory increase	4 4	5 6
New assets generated	f 82 0	78 8
Excess of exports	g 4 4	3 8
Gross national product	583 9	554 9

Economic Activity of Persons

				Personal earnings	a	432 9	411 8
Consumer purchases	d	375 0	355 3	Received from government	j	43 0	40 5
Taxes	h	61 6	57 7	Insurance contributions	h	−11 8	−10 2
Savings	i	27 5	29 1				
Consumption & savings		464 1	442 1	Personal income		464 1	442 1

Economic Activity of Government

				Collected from business	b	95 6	88 9
National defense	e	54 4	52 4	Collected from persons	h	73 4	67 9
Other expense	e	68 2	61 6				
Benefits paid to persons	j	31 3	32 5				
Interest	j	8 6	8 0				
Transactions abroad	g	1 6	1 5				
Subsidies, net	b	1 0	1 7				
Operating surplus	k	9	−3 9				
Consumption & savings		168 9	156 8	Government revenues		168 9	156 8

Savings

				Corporations	c	56 4	55 9
New assets	f	82 0	78 8	Persons	i	27 5	29 1
Foreign investments, net	g	2 8	2 3	Government	k	9	−3 9
Investment of savings		84 8	81 1	New capital		84 8	81 1

* Excluded in computing "national income."

Source: National Income Division of the U.S. Department of Commerce July 1964 and 1963.

resents the subsidies paid to business and the profits and losses from government business-type operations such as the post office and power projects.

c) Income retained by corporations, 56.4: depreciation provisions and undistributed earnings are alike in that they have remained in corporate working capital and represent what is left of business sales after payments of wages, taxes, and other expenses. The "statistical discrepancy" of −1.8 is a balancing figure arising from the methods of collecting the various amounts making up the two sides of this section. These methods involve sources of information that are "one-sided"; for example, the largest single item in this section—salaries and wages—is derived from social-security records, and there is no offsetting total from the same source that can be utilized here.

d) Sales to consumers, 375.0: compilations from many sources of consumer purchases, consisting of "durables" (*new* automobiles and parts, 22.7; household equipment, 17.1; radio and television equipment, 4.3; jewelry, 2.2; books and maps, 1.7; other, 4.1), "nondurables" (food, 65.8; purchased meals and beverages, 19.0; clothing, 30.6; gasoline and oil, 12.8; household supplies, 8.5; drugs, 4.3; recreational equipment, 8.3; toilet articles, 3.5; other, 14.7), and "services" (household utilities, 20.1; rent paid, 13.6; imputed rent of homeowners, 33.6; domestic service, 3.8; medical costs, 23.6; imputed services of financial institutions, 6.2; interest, 7.7; automobile repairs, rentals, and insurance, 7.6; purchased transportation, 3.7; theater admissions, 2.0; education, 5.7; foreign travel, 3.2; other, 24.5).

e) Sales to government, 122.6: breakdown by principal functions (military services, 49.5; other national defense, 6.1; health, education, and welfare [95% paid for by states and local government], 37.1; commerce and housing, 15.1; general government, 8.2; other, 6.6).

f) Creation of new assets, 82.0: the four items shown account only for the four largest classes of new assets that came into being during the year.

g) Excess of exports, 4.4: a net figure (exports, 30.7; imports, 26.3).

h) Collected from persons, 73.4: state and local government receipts are included (income taxes, 58.7; other taxes, 9.1; tax refunds, −5.7; social-insurance contributions, 11.3).

i) Savings by persons, 27.5: the excess of earnings and social-security receipts over consumer purchases and taxes.

j) Receipts of persons from government, 43.0: benefits and interest paid by government to persons (social insurance and retirement payments, 28.6; direct relief, 3.6; other, 2.2) and interest, net (interest received, 13.8; less interest paid, 5.2).

k) Government subsidies and operating losses, .9: agricultural and other subsidy costs (farm subsidies, 3.3; other, 1.0; state net income from public utilities and other operations, 3.4).

The author's intention in presenting this brief picture of national income has been twofold: to convey a rough idea of how a much-quoted figure, said to be related to accounting, is compiled, and to show the relation of the compilation to the accounting process. Those responsible for the annual production of national-income data are faced with two main difficulties:

1) Although dealing with the commercial output of consumer goods and services, the compilers have employed a number of noncommercial terms which give no little trouble to themselves as well as to those who endeavor to understand and make use of their reports. In putting together the summary on p. 258-9 the author has used terms more familiar to accountants and the commercial world, although minor inclusions under several of the headings, as noted in the descriptive matter above, go beyond the usual meaning of these terms.

2) A few noncommercial transactions ("imputed" income and costs) have been included which are thought to be of importance to the nation's "real" income; many other similar items could have been added. It might be better to include only actual transactions and "footnote" the noncommercial type; this would still permit comparisons as between years and with the national-income data of other nations. Rentals of owner-occupied homes is an example.

Accountants and management generally have taken little interest in computations of national income, largely because of the general feeling that the methods used and the results produced have not been closely enough tied in with commercial realities; and because, too, the relationship of the individual business unit to the whole economy has seemed remote and almost wholly incidental. However, participation by accountants and business management in further rationalizing the concept and in making the annual report more useful would doubtless be welcomed by the present compilers.

What is needed also is a broadening of the national-income coverage. Reporting, as they do, only sales of "final products" to ultimate consumers, the compilers omit all costs but labor, interest, and taxes, and all consideration of intermediate products. The FTC reports, on the other hand, attempt to account for one sector of the economy: all manufacturing corporations, regardless of the character of the product recipients—and there is no elimination of intermediate products. Consequently a reconciliation of the two sets of data is impossible. A better picture of the economic scene could be constructed if the efforts of the two compiling groups could be combined and the coverage could be extended to include all domestic industry. This would result in combined financial statements like the FTC's for retail operations, financial services, and other forms of business enterprise: in short, the whole economy. The national-income compilation would then be a reassembling of these data, using the accountant's consolidating techniques. Those who would regard such a project as an impossibly involved one should be reminded that much of the data is already available, that the filling-in of missing links would call for the application of recently developed and dependable sampling techniques, that modern devices are available for massive data processing, and that the two sides of the component "journal entries," coming from the same sources rather than having each half independently estimated, would yield industry pictures that would be more generally recognized as realistic sectors of the total economy. This extension of the accounting process—without the "inventory adjustments" of the FTC and the interpolation of "imputed" income and expense now embodied in the determination of GNP—would yield data of great importance to both business and government.

Pressures for revaluation

Accounting is often described as dynamic: it is being said at present, as it has often been said in the past, that its principles are undergoing revision. It is more accurate to say that as the economic picture changes, the forms of compilation and the emphasis required in accounting reports change; but no evidence has appeared that *basic* accounting principles, as we have explained them in this book, have been altered during the past half-century. The present drive of business to expand has led to the demand for lower income taxes that without downward price adjustments would increase liquid assets (and retained earnings) for that purpose. The business community, although accustomed to sharing half its earnings since World War II with the Federal government, has suddenly become critical of this arrangement; its demands, already acceded to in some measure, at least, by the Congress, included greater allowances for depreciation and, finally, lowered rates of tax. But stepped-up depreciation allowances, including the "investment credit," proved to be of limited benefit. A number of accountants were induced to revive the idea of fixed-asset revaluation in order to provide a higher base for depreciation rates. This led to "research" efforts on the part of revaluation enthusiasts which have resulted in price-level and revaluation proposals, principally for fixed assets.

During the inflationary period of the 1920's, many accountants were persuaded to accept reproduction costs or index-number recastings of cost as bases for fixed-asset values. Appraisal companies, aided by members of the academic world, issued bulletins and published articles urging the adoption of replacement costs. Their recommendations were widely accepted, and there can be little doubt that an added impetus was thus given to the inflationary movement of that period. It was found that in these pre-SEC days new capital could be raised by writing up assets and issuing new securities against them. Little attention was given to the possibility of using any basis other than cost for depreciation expense in income-tax returns.

The ephemeral character of this movement became clear when the long depression of the 1930's led to reversals of asset writeups. The primacy of historical cost was again proclaimed despite in many cases substantially higher replacement costs and the changing value of the dollar. Only a handful of business firms emerged from that era with the writeups still appearing in their balance sheets.

At the close of 1963 the AICPA issued a report of its research staff recommending, with some serious reservations, that where revaluation is deemed of sufficient importance, price-level-adjusted balance sheets and income statements supplementing the conventional statements be added to the accountant's reports.[5] Only a few professional accountants have developed any enthusiasm over this report.

The problem illustrated

> . . . if management is to adopt the *right forward policy* for a manufacturing investment, the *valuation* of fixed assets *must* be on the basis of current cost, that is to say, *on the assumption* that the assets were replaced today. If this is not done, management *can delude itself* as to the *effectiveness* of the *earning power* of its investment in fixed assets . . . (italics supplied)

[5] *Reporting the Price Effects of Price-Level Adjustments* (New York: AICPA, Research Report No. 3, 1963).

We have quoted here from the paper of a prominent English accountant presented to the second European Congress of Accountants at Edinburgh and reported in *The Accountant* of January 11, 1964. The italicized words and phrases are not unlike those employed by a number of accountants in the United States. What do they mean? A *right* forward policy suggests that there may be a *wrong* forward policy adopted or unwittingly followed by management; but policy for what? Could this refer to a desire for a *balance-sheet display* of a greater asset total, "a more favorable" *ratio of fixed assets* to present or prospective long-term obligations, the *budgeting* of forthcoming asset replacements, or the *pricing* of products? One would have to envisage a management so naïve as to be *misled* ("delude itself") in any of these ways by continuing with historical cost. The speaker then states that he is referring to the *effectiveness* of the fixed-asset *earning power;* it may be he is merely implying that management may be surprised to learn that the fixed-asset earning-power ratio (fixed assets/net income?) is high when based on historical cost and low when based on "current cost"; it may be, therefore, that this discovery will lead management to remedy the situation by adopting any of several alternatives: sell the undervalued fixed assets and buy less costly ones, switch to a new product line where profit margins would be greater, add to the depreciation allowance and report less earnings, or increase the price of the organization's output. Before the adoption of any of these alternatives, however, many other considerations would be involved in comparison with which "undervalued" assets would be of minor if not negligible importance. It is doubtful if in these days any management decision would ever turn on the "earning power of the investment in fixed assets," however this phrase may be interpreted. The worth of the services supplied by fixed assets to any operation is but one of the value contributions made by the various factors of production. Factor costs are jointly, not severally, contributed; and any attempt to determine the worth of any one factor by somehow splitting "value added" (including profit) brings us back to the same imponderables we encountered in assaying the allocation of any group of joint or common costs.

Selling prices, to the extent they are capable of being influenced by management judgments, belong to the realm of forward accounting; they are compounded of market potentials, hoped-for profit, and probable outlays including allocated historical costs of fixed assets and anticipated costs of their replacements as yet unrecorded. And, finally, can one be expected to believe that management, in a free economy, would deliberately discard the competitive advantage accruing from a low-cost investment in fixed assets?

Summary

Our examination of the fundamentals of the accounting process has now been completed. Though basically a compilation for a single economic unit of its exchanges of goods and services, accounting has accommodated itself to the customs of the commercial world in which *credit*, both received and granted, and the acquisition of goods and services before their purposes have been served have been the chief complicating factors. Periodic pauses in the compilatory activity permit the abstraction of summations that provide pictures designed to inform both management and outsiders of an organization's financial status and to set forth the most recent sector of the continuum of its operating performance. These pictures can be subjected to varied forms of comparison and analysis out of which are developed conclusions and opinions of investors and others as to the organization's character and prospects. Moreover, these financial pictures of individual organizations lend themselves well to combinations and consolidations yielding status and trends within any given industry, collection of industries, and the whole of the national economy. These possibilities show much promise for the future.

In Quest of Principles

In this book we have dealt with present-day accounting, and, in particular, with its employment in the individual business firm where management plays an important role in shaping and enforcing the firm's accounting policies. We have been concerned with accounting *as it is*, not as some would like it to be. We have noted that the basic framework of accounting, though remaining unaltered, can nevertheless be readily adapted to changing business patterns and to developing areas of management interests. We have observed modern management leaning heavily on *accounting* as a principal aid in establishing and maintaining operating objectives, and on *accountants* in providing from time to time revealing pictures of the corporate image that may be viewed and interpreted by outsiders. We have commented on the ever-increasing participation by accountants, both public and private, in the making of management decisions. In our approach to the essentials of accounting, we have been guided by the following assumptions which have served us in lieu of "principles":

267

Substance of accounting

1. *Unit.* Business enterprises, nonprofit institutions, government agencies, and frequently persons, are commonly regarded as centers of economic activity; by accountants they are conceived as economic units, each having an independent existence. The incoming-and-outgoing elements of their transactions with outsiders are the assets, liabilities, expenses, and revenues of accountants.

2. *Function.* Interpreting, recording, and reporting the transactions of individual economic units have been and continue to be the primary functions of accounting.

3. *Medium.* Double-entry bookkeeping, known and practiced for centuries, is the universal medium for classifying and accumulating the external (i.e. exchange) transactions of the economic unit, the purpose of its debit-and-credit complex being to register things acquired and their sources.

4. *Goal.* External transactions, conformed by internal transactions (reclassifications of external transactions) to the operating pattern of the economic unit, provide the detail of financial statements and other periodic summaries.

Meaning of financial statements

5. A *balance sheet,* made up of investments in assets carried at cost or depreciated cost, liabilities to outsiders at amounts to be paid, and net worth or owners' contributions at amounts paid in plus retained profits—all at a given point of time—is essentially a report of external transactions the disposition of which rests with the future.

6. An *income statement,* complementing a balance sheet, reports external transactions disposed of in whole or in part during the reporting period.

7. A *funds-flow statement* is the summation of a period's external transactions identified with balance-sheet and income-statement items at the period end.

8. A *cost-flow statement* is a summation of a period's internal transactions in which operating costs over a given period are

followed from their original classifications to their end-of-the-period balance-sheet and income-statement positions.

Comparability

Although the lack of comparability of financial statements has often been asserted, one who looks for similarities as well as differences in corporate reports will be struck by the great preponderance of the former. Financial statements of American corporations (a few exceptions could be cited) are directly comparable, item by item, and in total. Types of differences are relatively few, and are mostly limited to the costing of inventories (including the continued recognition of *lifo*), the accumulation of depreciation at accelerated rates and the often related deferment of income tax, the capitalization of leases, the disposition of research-and-development outlays, and the accrual of prospective pension costs; there are a few other problem areas of lesser importance. But even in these situations, with the help of disclosures normally provided, one arrives at a comparability that serves most purposes. The common difficulty running through these differences is that of allocation; its resolution in each case does *not* require the introduction of new or revised "principles" or a search for legal guidance, but agreements on answers to the recurrent question: when are costs and consequent benefits or losses to be recognized?

Our notes on fixed-asset revaluations in Chapter 16 needs no supplement here. With minor divergencies, modifications of depreciated historical costs have been regarded as lying outside the pale of the transaction-recording processes of accounting, and comparability has not been affected. Accounting does not "measure" values.

Uses of financial statements

As we have followed accounting through its varied involvements, we have deliberately avoided references to most of the notions recently associated with postulates and principles, especially those in which AICPA researchers became so unhappily and inextricably enmeshed in 1961-1962. These notions, perhaps inspired at least in part by the failure of AICPA committees to give some degree of recognition to upward revaluations of fixed assets, have found no acceptance among professional accountants, and a new start is in the making.

In Chapter 16 we touched on current uses of financial statements, our purpose being to gain some idea of the outsider's uses of the accountant's conventional endproducts. Those who are now about to expatiate once more on postulates and principles, and possibly on modified practices based on them, will certainly be obligated to give detailed consideration to a field of inquiry hitherto bypassed, lest their efforts be as unproductive as those of their predecessors. Who reads financial statements other than the now almost mythological *investor* with his alleged buy-hold-sell preoccupation? Who is misled or is likely to be misled by financial statements that have adhered to historical costs? And precisely how are they misled? Do the terms "misleading" and "not misleading" have any real meaning beyond their use as slogans? How are statements read, anyway? What sections of financial statements are of most interest and which are of little interest to readers? To what extent are financial statements being relied on by anyone as a basis for hypothesis, belief, or action of any kind?

Instead of providing answers to such basic questions, or without denying that such questions can be answered, our researchers in this field have proposed reforms with only the vaguest references to their possible utility; even more unfortunate, their proposals at critical points have been almost stultified and rendered incomprehensible by an abundance of pointless adjectives (perhaps intended to be disarming but more likely unintended symbols of distasteful or even unperceived areas of research), such as *acceptable, adequate, preferable, sound, proper, appropriate, meaningful, realistic*—to name but a few—none of them referring to a standard of comparison or supplying any clue as to intended financial-statement purposes. Perhaps there would be room for the emergence of purposes if our researchers, in further pursuits of refractory principles, can be persuaded to forswear the employment of adjectives altogether.

In any event, it seems clear at the moment that an extended inquiry into financial-statement applications now deserve priority over the search for "principles"; such an inquiry could provide a wholly different outlook on the significance of accountants' reports and on the meaning and character of "principles." It might even point the way to a dramatic simplification of financial statements.

Index